D0655217

1988.

To Ian,

With grateful thanks from the
Committee and Members of
Strathclyde Police Motor Club.

BIRDS
of the
TIDELINE

BIRDS
of the
TIDELINE

SHOREBIRDS OF THE
NORTHERN HEMISPHERE

ALAN RICHARDS

DRAGON'S WORLD

I dedicate this book to my dear cousin Marcia
and her husband Peter Fox, whose wonderful hospitality
and great kindness made my birding visit to California even
more enjoyable and memorable

TITLE PAGE PICTURE
Birds gather to roost on an industrialised estuary

KEY TO THE MAPS
Yellow areas indicate birds' breeding ranges.
Blue areas indicate winter ranges.
Green areas indicate where breeding and
winter ranges overlap.

Dragon's World Ltd
Limpsfield
Surrey RH8 0DY
Great Britain

First published by Dragon's World 1988
© Dragon's World 1988
© Text and selection of photographs Alan Richards 1988
Copyright in the photographs remains the property of the individual photographers

All rights reserved

No part of this book may be reproduced or transmitted in
any form or by any means, electronic or mechanical, including
photocopy, recording, or any information storage and retrieval
system, without permission in writing from Dragon's World Ltd,
except by a reviewer who may quote brief passages in a review.

British Library Cataloguing in Publication Data
Richards, Alan, *1933–*
Birds of the tideline.
1. Northern hemisphere. Shorebirds
I. Title
598′.33

ISBN 1 85028 060 6

Typeset by Florencetype Typesetters, Weston-Super-Mare

Printed in Spain by SIRVEN GRAFIC, S.A.
D.L. B.-38.972-88

CONTENTS

PREFACE

My interest in wild birds began whilst I was a pupil at Bablake School in Coventry, the city where I was born. I cannot say for sure what triggered this enthusiasm for wildlife and birds in particular. In recent years I have searched my mind on many occasions in an attempt to ascertain the moment of truth, but to no avail – as far as I can recall it just happened!

One thing is for certain: my enthusiasm for birds never developed as a follow-on from egg collecting, and I never pursued this course – though it must be said that finding nests was a major ingredient of the interest. In the late 1940s 'egging' was still an 'accepted schoolboy activity' and I recollect that you could buy birds' eggs through the post from catalogue lists (just as you could buy foreign stamps), though happily this has long been prohibited.

Neither my father nor my mother had any knowledge of birds, for both were townspeople. But we lived on the outskirts of the then rapidly expanding city of Coventry and access to the countryside was within easy walking distance. At that time there were still green fields between Coundon (home territory) and the nearby village of Allesley (now within the city boundary). It was over the 'Allesley fields', and sometimes beyond them, that the foundations of my birdwatching experiences were laid. I shared some of my earliest birdwatching thrills with a life-long school friend, Ken Roberts, and on occasions also with another school friend, Brian Dudley.

For a time Ken and I avidly pursued our interest together and after only a few months had the audacity to start to write a book on the subject! Certainly in those far off days there wasn't the choice of bird literature that there is today. Such well thumbed works as *Birds of the Wayside and Woodland* edited by Enid Blyton (a condensation of T.A. Coward's three-volume *Birds of the British Isles and their Eggs*), Eric

Fitch Dagleish's *What's that Bird?*, *The Observer's Book of Birds*, and the Rev. C.A. Johns', *British Birds in their Haunts*, taught us all there was to know! Though the birds typical of the fields and hedgerows near to home were always keenly sought and observed, one very soon yearned to see the more unusual species one read of, and names like Little Stint, Curlew Sandpiper, Black-tailed Godwit and many others equally tantalising and seemingly unviewable, were dreamed about.

These dreams began to be a reality in 1948 with the discovery of Baginton sewage farm, which lay just outside the city boundary on the south-east side, where the river Avon ran its meandering course. Formerly much more extensive, in 1948 it comprised just 18 acres of land across which sewage effluent ran via various drains and channels. One big advantage of this place was that it remained unfrozen even in the severest frosts and was an all-year-round source of food for many birds including waders. It was here that Ken Roberts and I got to know two experienced senior birdwatchers of the day who helped and encouraged us greatly; they were Ron Lee and Bill Wright. Both were regular watchers at this amazing place. Ron Lee particularly was a great source of inspiration, and it was he who introduced us both and enrolled us as members of the West Midland Bird Club, which proved to be the most important step I ever took in my 'ornithological career'. Ron worked at the nearby factory of Armstrong-Whitworth and spent each lunch hour birdwatching especially in spring and autumn. He didn't miss much and was turning up all sorts of incredible records for the time, such as the first Sanderling ever recorded in Warwickshire. In those far off days, very few waders, or coastal species at all, had been observed in this inland county – about as far from the sea as you could get! In those days the status of wading birds in Warwickshire was being rapidly changed and the Annual Reports of the West Midland Bird Club, which detailed the observations of its members, carried the initials of the author among others, for such occurrences as the first Bar-tailed Godwit and the fifth Wood Sandpiper for the county. Also at this time I was an enthusiastic member of the then RSPB Junior Bird Recorders Club (now YOC) and my well documented reports of birds seen at Baginton earned me the Saltzman prize, which was presented to members who submitted material on a regular basis. Waders and wildfowl were now those species most keenly observed and most eagerly sought after, all other species paled into insignificance! To pursue this interest further I decided the time had come to visit the true haunt of all wading birds, the coast. In September 1950 I arranged a two week holiday at St. Annes-on-Sea, Lancashire at the mouth of the Ribble estuary. It was an unforgettable fortnight of Dunlins, Sanderlings, Turnstones, Grey Plovers, Ringed Plovers, Oystercatchers, Redshanks, Curlews, godwits, gulls and terns, which only whetted my appetite for more.

This was the first of many memorable visits to coastal locations in search of shorebirds in Britain and beyond, which still goes on today. This book is testimony to my enthusiasm for this group of birds. I hope readers will also enjoy finding out about them and looking at the marvellous photographs. But there is, of course, no substitute for the real thing: go out and look at the birds for yourself!

ALAN RICHARDS
1 MAY 1988

INTRODUCTION

Amongst the world's approximately 8,500 species of birds there are some 202 that are generally called 'waders' by European birdwatchers or 'shorebirds' by American birders. Most of these birds are placed in two families, namely the Sandpipers (Scolopacidae, 85 species) and the Plovers (Charadriidae, 62 species). Additionally the Oystercatchers (Haematopodidae, 6 species), Avocets and Stilts (Recurvirostridae, 6 species), and Stone Curlews (Burhinidae, 9 species) are also readily recognised as belonging within this group. The terminology also includes the Lilytrotters (Jacanidae, 7 species), Painted Snipe (Rostratulidae, 2 species), Coursers and Pratincoles (Glareolidae, 17 species), the Crab Plover (Dromididae, 1 species), the Ibisbill (Ibidorhynchidae, 1 species), Seed Snipes (Thincoridae, 4 species) and the Sheathbills (Chionidae, 2 species). The majority of these latter families are not ostensibly shorebirds nor do they spend much of their lives wading. Nevertheless all these 12 families belong to the sub-order Charadrii of the order Charadriiformes (which additionally embraces the gulls, the terns and the auks).

This book, however, does not set out to cover all the Charadrii worldwide but concentrates only on those species in the first five mentioned families above that breed in North America (Neararctic) and in Northern Europe (Western Palearctic). In all, 75 species are dealt with in detail and most are illustrated with several photographs, showing the birds in their different plumages wherever this is possible.

Waders or shorebirds are undoubtedly some of the most interesting of the world's birds and also some of the greatest avian travellers, their migrations spanning the globe. In addition they have wide diversity of plumage, many showing complete changes of appearance from summer to winter. Their manner of feeding has great variety, while their displays and courtship

▽ *A welter of wings over the Dee estuary, England*

rituals include some of the most amazing demonstrations of flight and vocalization to be found within any group of birds.

Though we call these birds 'waders' or 'shorebirds' it is only for part of their lives that they actually live up to either of these terms. In the breeding season many species nest miles from the sea, some on barren tundras, others in muskeg swamps, others on prairie lands, and a few in dry arid situations. If any generality of habitat can be ascribed to them for all times of the year, it is as birds of open spaces (although the woodcock and American Woodcock are exceptions to this). It is during the winter months that they really live up to their name of shorebirds for it is then that they wade most and are mainly to be found on the coast, haunting mud flats, estuaries, and marshes. In such locations they often form huge concentrations, their daily routine dictated by the rise and fall of the tides. It is in such a setting that most observers are familiar with these birds, and we probably know more about their lives during this part of the year. Even today we have scant knowledge of the breeding biology of a number of species and only in recent times have the nests of some of them actually been discovered.

It is perhaps due to these birds' association with wetlands that the European expression 'wader' has come about (although in USA this term is applied to birds such as herons, storks, and ibises). In recent years the growing concern for the environment and the wildlife it contains has certainly led to a greater interest and study of wading birds, particularly because much of the wetland habitat that these birds use has been lost to development with many other areas under threat.

In Britain the various proposed barrages across major estuaries have brought conservationists into conflict with developers, and never before have waders been such a matter of national and indeed international concern. In Britain our knowledge of these birds has been greatly added to in recent times through the establishment of the Wader Study Group, the Birds and Estuaries enquiry initiated by the British Trust for Ornithology, and through the work of many others, particularly ringing groups such as the 'Wash Wader Ringing Group'.

Equally, concern and interest in shorebirds has never been more evident in North

▽ *An estuary with saltmarsh, a haven for many birds*

America. It is only in relatively recent times that many of these birds have begun to come back in anything like their former numbers, since hunting restrictions were introduced and since the setting up of many wildlife reserves throughout the continent where they can exist in safety and be viewed by the growing army of birders.

Europe and North America share many of the same species of shorebirds, either as breeding species or as visitors. Particularly in Britain and Europe the increase in the numbers of birdwatchers in recent years, along with improved optical equipment and acquired field identification skills, has shown the extent of these occurrences of North American waders, and it is hoped that this book will provide birders on both sides of the Atlantic with a wider view of this amazing group of birds.

NOTE: Classification
The names used in this book generally follow those in common use in Britain and North America. The sequence of the species dealt with is based on the 'List of Recent Holarctic Bird Species (non-passerines)' by K.H. Voous which appeared in *The Ibis* No. 4 October 1973, volume 115. The only exception to this listing is that the American Oystercatcher (*Haematopus palliatis*) has been given the prominence and treatment of a full species whereas Voous only refers to is as 'sometimes treated as specifically distinct'. The Voous order does show some variation to that normally used by North American ornithologists where the AOU checklist prevails, but we trust this will not detract from any value this book might provide for readers in the Americas.

◁ *A blizzard of Knot whirl above the Cheshire Dee*

▽ *Golden Plover and Lapwings feeding at low tide*

A GUIDE TO THE SPECIES

Oystercatcher
Haematopus ostralegus

OTHER NAMES: Eurasian Oystercatcher,
European Oystercatcher
LENGTH: 400-460 mm (16-18 in)

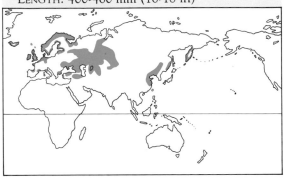

Of all the wading birds that haunt the shore-line, this is one of the most obvious and one of the easiest to identify – even from a great distance. The clear-cut black and white of the body plumage, the long red bill, the pink legs, and the red quizzical eye quickly add up to the Oystercatcher. In addition, the broad white wing bar and white rump heighten the effect of its black and whiteness when the bird is seen in flight. This bold combination of colours has earned it the country name of 'seapie'. This is perhaps more appropriate, for I doubt that there are many observers who have witnessed this bird actually catching an oyster around European shores in recent times. In years gone by, when oysters were naturally more abundant, they may well have been a major food source, but today cockles, mussels and limpets are the more usual fare. These molluscs are either opened by hammering or by a swift stab through the shell-closing muscle as the bivalve lies open in a pool. Individual oystercatchers will use one method or another, not both, and appear to be conditioned to adopt the technique used by their parents.

There are two main groups of oystercatcher: the black and white and the black, of which the former is more widespread. The family Haematopodidae, which embraces both groups, occurs throughout the world. Most authorities recognize eleven species within the family, of which Meade-Waldo's Black Oyster-catcher of the Canary Islands is now probably extinct. Of the others, only the western or American Black Oystercatcher (*Haematopus bachmani*) and the American Oystercatcher (*Haematopus palliatus*) are indigenous to the area covered by this book, and they are dealt with separately.

In Britain, the Oystercatcher is a widespread breeding bird with probably 40,000 to 50,000 pairs nesting around much of the coast, particularly in northern and western Scotland. Many also breed well away from the sea, not only along sea lochs, but also near fresh water. This move inland has been noted in Scotland since the last century, but has only become evident in northern Britain since the early part of this one. In even more recent times, however, there have been a number of cases of this bird nesting at sand and gravel workings and reservoirs in the English midlands, about as far from the sea as one can get. There is, of course, an inland breeding population of this bird in central Asia, where birds nest in an area which was probably the site of the ancient Sarmatic sea. Nevertheless, it is along the coast that the species is best known, where it mainly nests on dune or shingle.

Most Oystercatchers return to their breeding grounds in February and early March, but they continue to flock together to roost before nesting begins in earnest. The main territorial display comprises lengthy piping rituals, during which displaying birds adopt a characteristic posture with head and bill pointing downwards. The birds round their shoulders and curve their necks, looking as if they are trying to bring up their last meal. To start with only two or three birds may be involved, but very soon others join in, all moving around and calling shrilly in 'clockwise chaos'.

By the end of March, territory has usually been staked out; many nest scrapes are made weeks before laying commences, usually towards the end of April or in early May. The nest is generally no more than a depression

▷An adult Oystercatcher in full breeding plumage (with bright orange bill tipped with yellow, red eye ring and pink legs)|

▽ A fully grown Oystercatcher chick crouches in the grass. Remnants of its downy plumage still show, particularly around the head. As yet the bill is still only half its full length.

scratched out in the sand or shingle. At times it might be decorated with pieces of shell or other debris such as fragments of plants or rabbit droppings. The usual clutch is three to four eggs which hatch out in around 28 days if the bird is not overly disturbed. As soon as the young are hatched and dry out, they leave the nest. Unlike most other waders, however, they are fed by the adults during the early days of their life. The young can fly after about a month, but stay with their parents for some considerable time afterwards. It is during this time that they gain their dietary preferences and learn how to open mussels and to prise limpets from rocks as they watch the adult birds go about their business. This skill at opening cockles and mussels has at times brought them into conflict with fishermen who allege that their livelihood is threatened by the Oystercatcher, although study has disproved this claim.

During the winter, most British breeding birds move south. Few leave the country completely, although some do move to Spain and Portugal. Birds from Iceland and the Faeroes winter along the western seaboard of Britain, while birds from Norway are to be found along the British east coast.

At all times of the year the Oystercatcher is a noisy bird and its loud incessant 'kleepering' forms a major backdrop to the sounds of estuary, mud flat, and sand flat wherever they congregate. In winter especially, flocks of Oystercatchers can run into thousands at favoured sites. In Britain for example, six estuaries hold about half the wintering population which in total may well exceed 300,000 birds.

◁Concentrations of Oystercatchers occur on suitable mud flats and estuaries throughout the winter months. Large roosts numbering several thousands congregate at favoured locations such as Hilbre Island in the Dee Estuary. This photograph of part of such a roost was taken in September.

▷The American Oystercatcher is very like its European counterpart and some authorities do not even give it full species status. However, its legs are usually much paler at all times, as can be clearly seen in this photograph.

American Oystercatcher
Haematopus palliatus

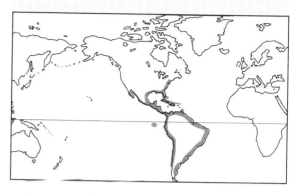

Mainly found along the Atlantic coastal strip from Long Island south to New Jersey, this bird is currently expanding northwards. It is re-colonizing areas from which it was driven by excessive shooting, formerly occurring as far north as Labrador. On the western seaboard however, its distribution has always been fairly static, being found only sparingly in California.

Like its European counterpart, this species needs an area with large expanses of relatively undisturbed shore and flats. But it rarely collects together in such large concentrations as the Oystercatcher and is only normally seen in scattered pairs or small groups or flocks. Its usual daily routine, as with most other waders, is determined by the cycle of tides – it roosts at high water and feeds between half tide and ebb. Exposed sandbanks are particularly favoured, where the birds will rest, preen or doze, often quite near to roosting groups of gulls, terns or other shorebirds, but always keeping their distance. As the tide recedes and oyster beds are uncovered, the American Oystercatcher starts to wade or swim from clump to clump of coon oysters, feeding on this favoured food. While the molluscs'

LENGTH: 400 mm (16 in)

valves are still open it can insert its bill with great force. This no doubt paralyses the oyster's nerve, preventing closure, thus enabling the bird to extract the succulent flesh. Other intertidal invertebrates are readily taken, for oysters are by no means a dietary mainstay.

In appearance the American Oystercatcher is like the Oystercatcher, but is browner on the upperparts with a yellow eye and red eye ring, and has paler legs (nearly white in the adult bird). It has a shorter wing bar, and darker tail, back, and wings, but otherwise it exhibits the typical black and white look of the Oystercatcher. It is also similar in its voice, which is loud and distinctive, the usual alarm call being the characteristic 'kleep, kleep, kleep' while the piping display performed by these birds is also identical to *H. ostralegus*.

Mainly sedentary, the American Oystercatcher breeds only in coastal situations, never moving great distances from the sea. It settles down into its territory around March or April when it lays 2 to 3 stone-coloured eggs which are blotched with black. The nest is a scrape hollowed out on sand or shingle. There are five races of this bird and as well as the nominate race described above, namely: *frazari*, found in West Mexico; *galapagensis*, confined to the Galapagos Islands; *pitanay*, occurring from West Panama to Chile; and *durnfordi*, found in Argentina.

American Black Oystercatcher

Haematopus bachmani

OTHER NAME: Black Oystercatcher
LENGTH: 430-450 mm (17-18 in)

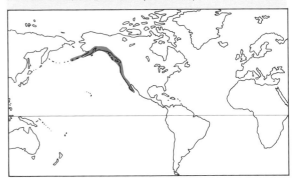

There are six species of black oystercatcher, the American Black, African Black, Canarian Black, Blackish, Sooty, and the black form of Variable, and they are distributed along the coasts of the Americas, Africa, Australia, and New Zealand. Several are rare (the Canary Island species is probably extinct) and all are confined to rocky or sandy shores. The American Black Oystercatcher occurs on the Pacific coast from the Aleutians south to Baja California.

This species is patchily distributed, occurring along the rockier sections of the coast, and becoming a little more widespread in the fall and winter. It does not occur inland. Feeding singly or in small groups on rocky reefs and islets, it may sometimes also be found on adjacent beaches, and is often seen alongside other rock-loving species such as the Surfbird, Black Turnstone and Rock Sandpiper. Its food and feeding methods are similar to those of the other species of oystercatcher.

In all except the southernmost part of its range, where it overlaps and has even been known to hybridize with the American Oystercatcher, the American Black is the only species of oystercatcher. In any event, it is easy to identify, being a large, heavily-built all-black shorebird. Both sexes are black with a brown tinge to the back, wings, and tail. This colour scheme can make it surprisingly difficult to pick out against the dark rocks. Adults have an orange-red bill, a yellow eye with a red eyering, and dull grey-flesh feet. On young birds the bare parts are duller, with a darker tip to the bill, and juveniles also have fine brown fringes to the feathers of their upperparts. Its vocabulary is similar to other oystercatchers, and includes a shrill piping 'peep-peep-peep' and a 'pee-up'. The American Black is almost identical in appearance to the Blackish Oystercatcher, and cannot be separated in the field. Fortunately, the Blackish Oystercatcher is restricted to the coast of South America from Peru southwards, so confusion is unlikely.

The American Black Oystercatcher nests on open rocks and shell beds, both on the mainland and on small islets, and will sometimes use the top of an isolated rock pinnacle. Indeed, the breeding territory often contains a prominent rock or some other elevated position, from which the bird can keep a sharp lookout. The birds are watching for intruding rivals, which are vigorously seen off, as much as for approaching danger. The nest itself is a simple shallow scrape, both sexes helping in its construction.

The courtship display is similar to that of other oystercatchers. Male and female run alongside each other with their heads forward and bills pointing downward, calling vociferously. A similar display is used in the defence of the pairs' territory. The sexes are quite faithful to each other, a large percentage breeding together for several years running. The normal clutch is two eggs, though one to three may be laid, and these are incubated by both the male and the female for 24 to 29 days. The eggs are similar in size and colour to those of the American Oystercatcher. On hatching, the chicks, like those of all waders, can walk and feed themselves, and they are tended by the parents until they fledge after about 40 days. Although immatures are identical to the adults after the first winter, they have a prolonged period of sexual immaturity and females probably do not breed until they are four years old.

◁Like the nests of other Oystercatcher species, that of the Black Oystercatcher is a mere scrape to begin with. It is only when the full clutch is completed and during incubation that material is added.

▽On dark seaweed-covered rocks the Black Oystercatcher is much more difficult to see than its pied relations. However, the orange-red bill and pink legs combine with the black plumage to produce a striking-looking bird.

Black-winged Stilt

Himantopus himantopus

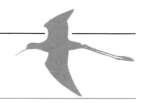

This is one of the most graceful of all waders. It can be readily identified by its extremely long, pink legs, needle-like black bill, and simple black and white body colour. It is a slender bird, and most of its length is accounted for by the legs and bill. The body itself is approximately the same size as most *Tringa* waders but it has a somewhat diminutive head in addition to a long slim neck.

Throughout its widespread global range, the Black-winged Stilt shows several plumage types. These are all variations on the basic themes of black upperparts and wings, and white below, with greater or lesser amounts of black or grey

OTHER NAMES: Black-necked Stilt, Pied Stilt
LENGTH: 350-400 mm (14-16 in)

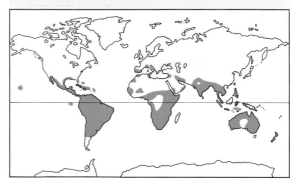

on the head and neck. In North America the adults have more extensive black areas on the head and neck, while in Europe the male bird can be completely white-headed.

Generally preferring warmer climes, the Black-winged Stilt occurs throughout all the continents except Antarctica. It can be found in a variety of habitats including coastal marshes, lagoons, salt pans, sewage farms, inland lakes, and both fresh- and salt-water marshes. It is an active bird, wading easily with deliberate strides through shallow water as it seeks such food items as the larval forms of insects, molluscs, worms, and some small fish. Feeding techniques include picking food from the surface and from within water. The birds will also peck food from plants and from the ground, when they have to flex their long legs.

Stilts are gregarious outside the breeding season and are usually colonial when nesting. Breeding behaviour and display involves an elaborate and complicated series of in-flight and on-the-ground manoeuvres and postures. These can involve single pairs or groups of birds from the colony. The nest, which can vary from a shallow scrape to a substantial structure made of vegetation, may be sited on dry land or in shallow water. The usual clutch of four eggs can be laid throughout the spring period, the exact time depending on climate and geographical situation. The eggs are stone-coloured, and evenly spotted, and blotched with dark brown. Both sexes share the incubation, which normally takes about 23 days. The young hatch out simultaneously and can feed themselves straight away. While the young are

◁ The nominate race of the Black-winged Stilt is mainly white headed, a condition that applies more generally to the male bird. This photograph shows a female approaching her nest, which contains five eggs.

△ The long pink legs of the Black-winged Stilt allow it to feed in much deeper water than most other wading birds. Here we see a bird in a Kenyan setting, its image mirrored in the waters of Lake Naivasha.

△*This newly hatched chick shows well the characteristic long legs and the needle-like bill of the Black-winged Stilt even at this early age.*

small, the adults continue to brood them, especially at night. Fledging usually takes place after about four weeks and the young birds become quite independent a couple of weeks later. In their first year the young stilts are usually browner on the mantle and wings and fuzzy grey on the head and neck.

While nesting, the parents are highly territorial and very protective. They will readily fly up to meet and mob predators such as Marsh Harriers. Very often several birds will join forces, their high pitched 'kik-kik-kik' calls forming a continual and monotonous barrage, which only ceases as the threat is driven away. The adults have a softer single-note 'kek', which they utter as a contact call. In general, stilts have a fairly wide vocabulary and their noisy behaviour draws attention to their presence, making nesting locations easily detectable by the birdwatcher.

Black-winged Stilts are easily disturbed and readily take to the air, although they soon settle back at a preferred feeding area. (However, at places like salt pans birds will quickly accept the presence of workers and become quite approachable.) The flight is strong and direct with the almost triangular black wings contrasting markedly with the white rump and tail. The conspicuous pink legs and feet protrude beyond the tail to a length comparable with the bird's body.

In the northern parts of their range, stilts are migratory, leaving Eurasia and North America in the autumn for tropical quarters. In March and April they return, often migrating in pairs or small groups. In Great Britain the species bred successfully in 1987 after a gap of forty-two years. The recent increase in the number of birds occurring in spring and summer may well lead to regular breeding of this species if the trend persists. With such a wide world distribution and the ability to use a wide range of habitats, the Black-winged Stilt is likely to have a promising future.

Avocet

Recurvirostra avosetta

This bird belongs to the family Recurvirostridae, which includes two distinct groups, the very similar long-legged straight-billed stilts and three other species of avocets that are patchily distributed throughout the world. These are: the American Avocet, the red-necked Avocet, and the andean avocet.

This species more than any other symbolizes the bird protection movement in England. It is used as the emblem of the Royal Society for the Protection of Birds and represents one of their most successful protection enterprises.

Avocets formerly bred regularly in Britain, along the eastern coastline from the river Humber south to Sussex, but were never common. However, during the 18th and 19th centuries numbers declined until the last breeding colony was recorded in 1825.

Nearly 100 years were to elapse before Avocets bred again in the British Isles, when two pairs nested in County Wexford, Ireland in

OTHER NAME: Pied Avocet
LENGTH: 420-450 mm (16½-18 in)

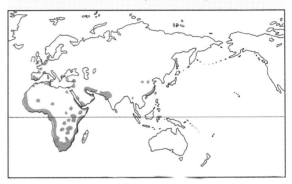

▽ *An adult Avocet approaches its nest containing four eggs at a site in southern France. The location of the nest in this instance is dry, in which case little nest material is used. If the nest had been near water, considerably more nest material might have been incorporated.*

◁ *This photograph shows another dry nest site of an Avocet, at which two newly hatched young share the location with an unhatched egg.*

▷ *The elegant Avocet, with its striking black and white plumage and characteristic upward-curved bill is easily identified. This incubating bird surveys its grassy setting.*

1938, although re-colonization of the English east coast did not begin until the early 1940s. Because of wartime restrictions the complete story is not fully known, but breeding was confirmed during 1941–46 in both Essex and Norfolk. It was the discovery in 1947 of 4 pairs nesting at Minsmere and 4 or 5 pairs nesting on Havergate Island, both in Suffolk, that led to the major revival of this bird's status as a regular breeder in Britain. Credit for the subsequent and continued breeding success of the avocet in Britain surely belongs to the R.S.P.B., who established reserves at both these places. The return of the Avocet, however, would have been less likely had it not been for the increase in numbers of this bird in other parts of Europe, particularly the Netherlands, where the population quadrupled between the 1920s and late 1960s.

The Avocet's contrasting black and white plumage, long lead-blue legs and distinctive slender up-curved bill (which gives rise to the local Norfolk name of 'awl bird') are unmistakeable. These features combine to form one of our most attractive wading birds, making it a great favourite with all who know it. When feeding, the side to side sweeping action of the Avocet's bill is particularly distinctive as it sieves the watery ooze for food. It finds its prey more by touch than by sight and eats mainly small molluscs, crustaceans and worms. Favourite hunting grounds are shallow brackish or saline estuaries, lakes, marshes, and pools, where the water is around 2–5 cm (1–2 in) deep. This bird also quite frequently wades deeply to feed, with the water touching its belly. At times it will even up-end like a duck. On dry ground it will peck at insects with the tip of its bill, or peck them from plants. The young birds, whose beaks are initially short and straight, feed from birth by pecking for food in this way.

The Avocet is probably even more attractive when seen flying. It looks mainly white if viewed from below, while the black wing tips look less pointed than those of most other wading birds. The upper parts with the narrow black chevron give a good clue to identification,

even if you do not notice the upturned bill or trailing legs. When they are on their wintering grounds, the movements of these birds *en masse* as they progress from one feeding area to another make a memorable sight. At this time, their fluty 'kluit' call adds a further unforgettable dimension to the grace and beauty of these birds.

Avocets are colonial, and many will nest close together in suitable locations, often on sandy or muddy islands, with scrapes no more than a metre (3–4 ft) apart. The amount of material used to line the scrape varies considerably. In some instances there is none at all, but at times during the course of incubation, quite sizeable structures of grass stems and debris are created, especially if the nest is sited near water and there is a possibility of flooding. The 3 or 4 eggs are pale buff, spotted irregularly with black and underlying ashy marks. These are usually laid early in May, there being only one brood. The eggs are incubated for 22 to 24 days, the young leaving the nest within hours of hatching. The parent shepherds them to the nearest

water where they are soon feeding for themselves and swimming.

A very aggressive species in defence of its territory, the Avocet will run with lowered head and spread wings to drive off intruders. At other times it will 'edge' towards a rival, lifting and fluttering its wings. These displays are usually sufficient to see off other birds, but the species often shows considerable aggression and will knock down rivals and trample them.

The Avocet is mainly migratory throughout its range, which extends in western Europe from the British Isles and the Netherlands south to Spain and eastwards, spasmodically, through Europe to Asia. It is present all the year in much of its African habitat and also in parts of Western Europe. In Britain the eastern breeding localities are mainly deserted in winter. By October the winter distribution of avocets is to be found on estuaries along the English channel and southern North Sea coasts, with concentrations in Devon, Cornwall and Suffolk. There are a few winter records from elsewhere around the coast, including Ireland.

American Avocet

Recurvirostra americana

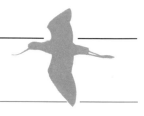

The American Avocet differs from all the other avocets, in that it has a seasonal plumage transformation. It is also the largest and longest-legged of the four and some would say the most handsome and elegant of all the American shore birds.

During the breeding season this large, shy, unconfiding bird has a bright brownish-orange head and neck, replacing the dull grey and white of its winter plumage, and contrasting markedly with the black and white striped upperparts. With its needle-thin upturned black bill, long blue-grey legs, and white underparts, this species is almost impossible to misidentify.

The breeding range stretches from west to central U.S.A., to central southern Canada, including the states of Saskatchewan, Minnesota, Utah, and Colorado. There are also sporadic occurrences in Texas, New Mexico, and the west coast of California. Nesting takes place between April and June at the edge of saline and alkaline pools and lakes on the prairie lands. The nest is a shallow depression in gravel or sun-baked ground, made amongst sparsely vegetated terrain. It is scraped out by the female who lowers her body, breast first, and, with tail elevated, uses her long legs to shape the nest. The four eggs are laid on a lining of weed stems and grass. They are cryptically coloured pale-ashy-yellow to green-brown and evenly spotted with dark brown. The incubation period lasts for 24 days, during which time the parents vigorously protect the nest and also the feeding area, which will be utilized by the young at a later stage.

Breeding density can vary from colonies, usually of 15 to 20 pairs, to small loose gatherings of just a few pairs. Whatever the situation, the gentle appearance of the adults is deceiving. Intruders are chased off in a mass show of aggression, as the nesting avocets instinctively take to the air, fearlessly pursuing airborne predators in endless sorties. They occasionally connect with their delicate but effectively used spear-like bills, incessantly emitting a sharp

LENGTH: 435-470 mm (17-18½ in)

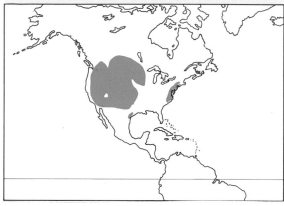

penetrating 'pleet' note, until the foe has been banished. Land predators are similarly dealt with, being dive-bombed until they vacate the area. This parental protection continues well after the five-week fledging period.

The young quickly learn to feed in the characteristic sweeping manner of the adults, involving a side to side scything action through muddy water and soft mud. They scoop up a variety of foodstuffs including dragonfly nymphs, water boatman, beetles, insects and their larvae, and also aquatic seeds if these are present. This method is the most usual feeding technique of the American Avocet, but these birds also occasionally probe in mud or snatch insects from the surface. At other times, large numbers gather into feeding 'packs', line up abreast, and systematically forage, their heads submerged beneath the ever-deepening water. When the water gets too deep, they resort to swimming and upending, duck fashion, with wings held up, using their webbed feet effectively as they do so.

After nesting, the young and adults collect together on the breeding grounds, at which point there is a general drift to the coasts of

▷ *The adult male American Avocet in its breeding plumage with rusty-coloured head and neck is one of the most delightful shorebirds there is.*

△ *The American Avocet incubates its eggs.*

California and the Gulf of Mexico. Here flocks of up to 300 or more American Avocets can be encountered in a variety of habitats including fresh-water lakes, coastal lagoons, tidal beaches and estuaries, forming a spectacular mass of black and white feathers as they feed in tight sweeping groups.

Although most gregarious during this period, groups and even solitary birds associate with smaller waders and ducks, dwarfing them along the shoreline. Although some birds stay at these fall 'staging posts', the numbers diminish as a southerly dispersal occurs, when most birds fly off to central America or the West Indies for the winter. In flight their shape is distinctive, with their neck and legs fully extended, the fast direct wing beats giving an almost dart-like appearance as the American Avocets dash low along the coastline.

Unlike many other American waders, whose numbers have diminished this century, the American Avocet's plight seems more secure for the moment. The saline and semi-saline lakes and pools that are its preferred habitat have not yet been exploited by man, ensuring that we have an ever-present supply of elegance along our shores and lake-sides for years to come.

Stone-curlew

Burhinus oedicnemus

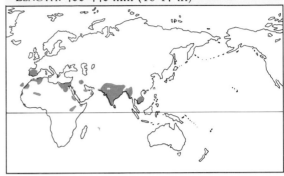

The Stone-curlew belongs to the family Burhinidae, of which there are 9 members, this species being the only representative covered in this book. Its breeding range worldwide is rather fragmented, stretching from western to eastern Europe, the Middle East, southern Asia, India, Sri-Lanka, and also North Africa. Throughout this area there are different races due to climatic variation and the isolation of certain populations. In its southern range, the Stone-curlew's breeding takes place mainly in desert regions.

Over most of Europe, apart from Spain and France where the populations are static, the species is on the decline due to drastic changes in agriculture and possibly colder summers. Britain is at the north-western limit of the Stone-curlew's range.

Though Stone-curlews may winter in southern England, this bird is mainly a summer visitor, arriving quite early in March or April. Particularly active at dusk it can be heard calling with its plaintive wailing note well into the night. During the breeding season, the establishment of territory is a highly vocal

OTHER NAMES: Thickknee, European Stone-Curlew
LENGTH: 400-440 mm (16-17 in)

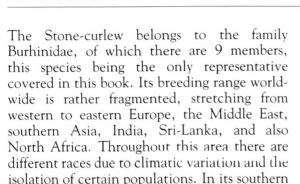

affair. There are long periods of bubbling notes, during which the birds involved frequently take wing and circle the area. Its strong pattern of light and dark bands can be seen when the bird is in flight. In defence of its breeding site the male is especially aggressive, not only to other males, but to other species of bird as well. Should any be unwise enough to enter his domain he adopts a most intimidating pose. With head and neck lowered and

◁ *Sitting immobile on its nest, the female Stone-curlew relies on its cryptic plumage to avoid detection, but its large unblinking yellow eye usually betrays its presence. To the rear the male approaches stealthily to affect the changeover, which becomes more frequent as the time for hatching approaches.*

thrust forward, wings held slightly open, he runs at the intruder on bent legs. This is usually sufficient to see off any transgressor. When disturbed by a more fearsome foe, the bird will sometimes run before sinking to the ground and 'freezing'. The Stone-curlew's twilight activity limits its likelihood of being observed during the day, and its streaked, sandy-brown plumage makes it extremely diffi-

cult to see on the stony, sandy soil it favours. When located, however, the first thing you notice is its large disproportionate piercing yellow eye. The bird's upper body is light brown with darker and paler streaking, creating a cryptic pattern. An obvious feature in its plumage, however, is a broad light-grey patch on its wings. Its rear end is long and protruding, formed by a broad, long tail and folded

◁ *An adult Stone-curlew fluffs up her feathers prior to settling down to incubate the heavily marked eggs. Two is the usual number for a complete clutch of this species.*

▷ *The speckled downy plumage of a recently hatched Stone-curlew chick is well camouflaged on the dry sandy sparsely vegetated terrain it inhabits.*

wings. The bill is yellow, short and sharply tipped black. The legs are also yellow and bulbous at the knee, hence the popular name 'thickknee'. Below, the bird is heavily streaked on the breast, while the rest of the body is whitish in colour. When the Stone-curlew takes flight the long wings reveal a conspicuous double white wing bar. At the same time it invariably calls 'coor-lee' – a similar cry to that of a curlew, but shriller.

Most British birdwatchers who wish to make certain of seeing this bird visit the Weeting Heath reserve in the east of England. Here an open grassy area, with sandy soil closely cropped by hundreds of rabbits, provides an ideal setting where nesting Stone-curlews can be viewed from hides with no danger of disturbing this strange and now rare breeding bird. When it moves it does so stealthily, taking short pattering steps, or runs rapidly forward in a horizontal attitude, with tail and head held on the same plane. Suddenly it will freeze, stretching its neck up and tail downwards, slowly rotating its head, and arrogantly surveying its surroundings. This pattern may be continued over a hundred yards or more. The bird will occasionally peck the ground, but this action appears to be a gesture, rather than a genuine attempt to find food.

In Britain the population has declined from 2,000 pairs in the 1930s to a current total of about 200 pairs. These are now mainly confined to a few counties in the south and east with Suffolk and Norfolk the bird's particular stronghold. In Britain its preferred habitat includes heaths, dry cultivated land, downlands and forest rides. The nest is a shallow scrape in the sand or soil about 2.5 cm (1in) deep. This is lined with a varying array of materials including small stones, flints, shells, and rabbit droppings. The two pale buffish eggs are rounded, heavily streaked and blotched dark brown. Incubation is carried out by both parents though change-over is infrequent until just before hatching, at around 26 days, when both birds exchange duties every 10 to 15 minutes or so. After hatching, the young soon dry out and are running about in a matter of hours. They are then usually led to moister ground where feeding is easier. In 5 to 6 weeks they are fully fledged, at which time family groups join together and form small autumnal flocks.

The diet preferences of Stone-curlews vary enormously – beetles, wood lice, grasshoppers, worms, and many insects are caught on the surface by a pecking motion. At times this bird will stalk, heron-like when, with a quick chase and a stab, mice and voles are caught and swallowed whole. Other food includes lizards, frogs, tadpoles, and plant seeds. On the breeding grounds the eggs and chicks of its neighbours are sometimes eaten.

Little Ringed Plover
Charadrius dubius

This bird is a smaller, freshwater version of the Ringed Plover. Its plumage is, at first glance, very similar to the larger bird and inexperienced observers may confuse the two. The Little Ringed Plover always looks small-headed and has a generally nimbler manner and slimmer appearance compared to the larger-headed and rounder-bodied Ringed Plover. In both birds, the upperparts are mid-brown and the underparts white, but the Little Ringed Plover's black breast is less extensive and it has a less intense black facial mark. When it is at rest, however, it is the yellow orbital eye ring that immediately identifies this bird and additionally its flesh-coloured legs help put a name to it. When seen in flight, the lack of any wing bar plus its shrill piping 'pew pew' call are sufficient features to proclaim the Little Ringed Plover's identity.

Its feeding techniques are characteristic of the plover family. Food is snatched from the surface on drier ground, while in soft muddy situations the bird often rapidly patters the ooze with its feet to bring invertebrates to the surface. By either means it secures a variety of prey that includes worms, mosquito larvae, insect pupae, snails, beetles and at times the seeds of aquatic plants.

This species has no close equivalent in North America. Its breeding range stretches from Britain and continental Europe, embracing central Scandinavia to the Mediterranean and North Africa, hence eastwards through Asia to Japan, Borneo, and Papua New Guinea. Its wide distribution through north-western Europe, however, is of recent origin, beginning early this century. The course of its spread is not known for certain, but it is undoubtedly linked to man-made changes to the environment, which have provided suitable nesting sites in areas where they were previously non-existent.

Before 1938, the Little Ringed Plover was unknown as a breeding bird in Britain and was in fact an extreme rarity even as a migrant, which it still is in Ireland. In that year, a pair

LENGTH: 140-170 mm (5½-6½ in)

nested on the dried out bed of a reservoir at Tring, Hertfordshire. In 1944, two pairs bred at the same location and another pair bred in Middlesex. Since that time colonization has continued, and by the early 1970s the breeding population was about 400 pairs. At the beginning of the 1980s this total had probably doubled, but with nesting birds still concentrated in south-east England through to the east, west and north-east Midlands, Cheshire, South Lancashire, and parts of Yorkshire. Western extremities of the country and Scotland have yet to be colonized.

This increase of the British breeding population is certainly due in part to such activities as sand and gravel extractions, open-cast mining and reservoir and motorway construction, which provide sandy gravelly areas and small islands with muddy margins to fresh or brackish pools of water. Additionally, sewage works and also more natural situations such as small freshwater lakes and rivers with stony and shingly stretches have been utilized.

Towards the end of March, or even earlier in the month if the weather is kind, this little wading bird arrives back at its breeding ground, often along with, or before, those other accepted heralds of spring, the Sand Martins and Wheatears.

By April the male has established his territory. He circles the area in a 'butterfly' display flight with deep arched downward strokes of his wings. They almost touch at the tips in a rather jerky manner, tilting from side to side as he goes. During this performance the bird calls continuously.

◁*Against a background of sand and gravel extraction a Little Ringed Plover incubates its eggs. Such industry has greatly aided the colonization of this species in Britain over the last 30 years.*

▷*A Little Ringed Plover cautiously approaches its nest, which contains four speckled eggs.*

On the ground a series of elaborate displays takes place. These include one in which the male fluffs up his breast feathers while marching 'goose-step' fashion around his mate. Several scrapes are made by the male in sandy or dry ground, and the female chooses one in which to lay her four or sometimes three eggs. These are anything from buff to grey-green in colour, speckled with small purple-brown spots. Incubation lasts up to 23 days and is carried out by both parents. During this time the male defends the area against all intruders. If disturbed by human or animal, the sitting bird will feign injury by dragging its wing along the ground, or will run in circles around the

△ An immature Little Ringed Plover. Though the yellow orbital ring can be seen in this photograph the bird's other features are less distinctive and confusion with the Ringed Plover, or possibly the Kentish Plover, is more likely at this stage of plumage.

nest area to lure the intruder away from the eggs or young. The young fledge after 23 days and by the end of July, along with the parents, move to suitable gathering areas such as large reservoirs, especially in central England. At such places small flocks of up to twenty or more birds may come together and stay until late August or early September, before they move south for their long migratory journey to east and west Africa.

Ringed Plover
Charadrius hiaticula

My first experience of this species was at an inland sewage marsh in the English midlands back in the late 1940s. In spring and autumn a sprinkling of these birds occurred here annually. Later on its occurrences were even more extensively documented by midland bird-watchers. This was because with the addition of other man-made habitats over the next couple of decades, particularly sand and gravel workings and new reservoirs, the numbers of the Ringed Plover increased considerably. In some years totals of 100 or more were recorded together at some sites, particularly in the fall. There were even isolated records of the bird's nesting at one or two locations about as far from its more typical coastal habitat as one could get. Some of these passage birds were no doubt from the British resident population, estimated to be in the region of 30,000 breeding pairs, making their relatively short movements from winter quarters to breeding locations. However, others were certainly from farther afield. This was shown very vividly one day in August 1972 when at Draycote Water, a recently constructed large reservoir near Coventry, a wader with bright yellow underparts turned out to be one of five birds colour-marked only that summer in Greenland. It is interesting and statistically amazing that another of the five turned up on the English east coast around the same time. These birds from Greenland belong to the race *Charadrius h. hiaticula*, which, as well as breeding in that country, also nests in Britain, east Baffin Island, Iceland, and parts of western Europe, north to Scandinavia. The slightly smaller *Charadrius h. tundra* breeds on the tundras of northern Scandinavia through Russia to Siberia. So the Ringed Plover is actually at the extreme south-western edge of its breeding range in Europe. This may account for its scarcity in south-west Wales and south-west England, though a few pairs do nest farther west in Brittany, France.

In its usual coastal environment, this small rotund and lively shore bird is a common sight,

OTHER NAMES: Common Ringed Plover, Greater Ringed Plover
LENGTH: 180-200 mm (7-8 in)

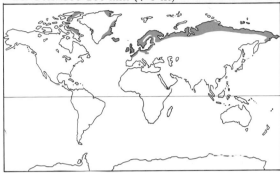

getting its name from the complete black and white rings around its neck with the black broadening at the front of the upper breast to form a broad collar. Young birds, however, lack this feature and inexperienced observers might mistake them for Kentish Plovers. Additionally, however, the Ringed Plover has a brown back and crown, orange-yellow legs (flesh coloured in juveniles) and a short orange bill with a black tip. The relatively short bill is used to pick up its food in typical plover manner, taking one or two steps, or running quickly forward to secure a mollusc, worm or insect which it locates by sight. Sometimes the birds tap their feet to make their prey come to the surface.

This species does not usually occur in large concentrations. The birds tend to be more scattered across sand flats, maintaining loose contact with others of their kind. Only at high tide, when roosting birds gather, are they to be found together in any number. But even then they do not huddle together in the same density as Dunlin or Knot. In flight, however, they will bunch into compact groups.

The normal direct flight of the Ringed Plover is rapid and generally low over the shore or sea. It is in this type of flight that the conspicuous white wing bar is evident, which precludes confusion with the similar but slightly smaller Little Ringed Plover.

◁This Ringed Plover chick is seven days old but like the parent bird shows a white collar, a distruptive plumage feature which helps to camouflage both young and adult birds against a background of shingle.

▷This lively rotund shorebird does not show the distinct winter/summer change of plumage exhibited by some other wading birds, but in this autumn shot of a non-breeding Ringed Plover the less colourful legs, the ill defined supercilium and the more diffused breast band are evident.

▷Dune or shingle provides a favourite nesting site for the Ringed Plover and this photograph shows a parent bird incubating its full clutch of four heavily speckled eggs.

The liquid 'toolee' note of this bird is also quite distinctive. Additionally there is a piping 'kluup' call, while the song is a long trilling 'tooli – tooli – tooli' delivered in nuptial flight, at which time the bird flies round the nesting territory with slow wingbeats, on fully extended wings in butterfly fashion. The birds return to the nesting areas from February onwards, but such displays might be witnessed well into June or even later. The male makes several scrapes in the sand, shingle, or turf when the nest, such as it is, might be decorated with small fragments of shell, or even rabbit droppings. Usually the nest is in an open situation, but quite often it is located in the shelter of plants or marram grass. The clutch consists of 3 or 4 eggs. These are pear-shaped, buff-coloured, and covered with blackish brown speckles or blotches, which are often concentrated at the large end. Sometimes two broods are raised. In more northerly latitudes as many as 6 or 7 eggs might be laid in one brood.

While it is on the nest, the disruptive pattern of the bird's feathers makes it extremely difficult to see even in an open situation. The young hatch out after 24 to 25 days and are tended by the parents, at which time the adults often feign injury in their attempts to lure predators, human or animal, away.

Around most of Britain this shore bird nests in all suitable coastal areas, with a stronghold in the Outer Hebrides and high-density breeding in the Orkneys, Shetlands, and Norfolk. In Scotland and north-east England particularly, there has been increased nesting at inland sites notably on the shingle banks of rivers and natural lakes. The well known 'Breckland' colony (in Suffolk, England) has declined considerably in recent years, but numbers overall do not seem to have changed that much over the last 100 years. There is a total breeding British and Irish population of possibly upwards of 10,000 pairs. The winter population of major estuaries is supplemented by European visitors to up to around 25,000 individuals.

Many Ringed Plovers, however, winter in south-west Europe, especially in Portugal. Others move to Africa where they constitute a high proportion of the shore bird community. The species is virtually unknown in the U.S.A., although a pair bred in Alaska in 1970. The very similar Semipalmated Plover is the counterpart of this species in the U.S.A., and is dealt with on the following pages.

Semipalmated Plover

Charadrius semipalmatus

This, the North American counterpart of the Ringed Plover, is similar in many ways and some authorities have considered it to belong to the same species. But although the differences between the two species are quite subtle, the populations of each are almost entirely isolated and currently both are classified as full species.

Slightly smaller than the Ringed Plover, the Semipalmated Plover looks more compact and rounded in the field, with the body and wings less attenuated at the rear and the bill slightly stubbier. Adults in breeding plumage have a white forehead, above which is a black forecrown that meets the lower black facial line

LENGTH: 170-190 mm (6½-7½ in)

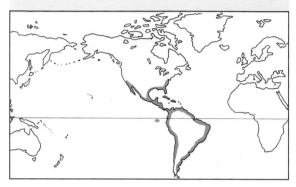

around the eye. The dark eye has a slim yellow orbital ring, slightly stronger than that of the Ringed Plover. Behind the eye the black ear coverts soon fade to light brown, which meets with the light brown of the crown and nape. Like the Ringed Plover, the Semipalmated Plover has a full white neck collar in all seasons. Above and behind the eye a diffuse and somewhat restricted rear white eyebrow can be observed at close range. Below the bright white collar and throat, a full black breast band is slightly thinner than that of the Ringed Plover. The upperparts and rump are the same light brown as the smaller coverts. The slim white wing bar is again slightly less conspicuous than that on the Ringed Plover. The sides to the upper tail coverts are narrowly white while the tail itself is grey brown with fine white outer feathers. The lower underparts are clear white. At this stage the bill is orange with a black tip and the legs and feet are yellowish-orange. The feet of all ages of Semipalmated Plovers have a greater amount of webbing between the three toes than that on Ringed Plovers, giving rise to the common name. Ringed Plovers do have a small amount of webbing, but this is virtually impossible to discern in the field.

One of the best distinguishing features of these two plovers is the contact call. Semi-palmateds give a sharp 'chuwit' quite different from the melodic 'toolee' of the Ringed Plover.

Outside the breeding season the habitat choice of Semipalmated Plovers is often wide sandy or muddy beaches and coastal lagoons, all of which attract fair numbers. Inland, birds can also be found on gravel pits, open freshwater pools and along wide rivers. Birds travel to the tropics to spend the winter on vast undisturbed coastal wetlands like those on the Caribbean coastline of Venezuela. Here they mingle with smaller sandpipers and other *Charadrius* plovers, showing their strong social nature. In typical plover style they run rapidly about in different directions with heads up, often pausing before dabbling quickly.

The breeding range of the Semipalmated Plover extends from Alaska across the whole of northern Canada to Newfoundland. During the high summer months the birds favour undisturbed open and flat areas of tundra and gravel plains to raise their young. The nesting requirements, feeding, and reproductive behaviour are very similar to those described for the tundra race of Ringed Plover. Where the ranges of these two birds meet on Baffin Island, a small amount of mixed-pair breeding takes place. However, there is no area of integration between the two and these pairings are likely to be only casual.

◁A Semipalmated Plover sits tight on its tundra nest site.

▷The nest and eggs of a Semipalmated Plover.

△ In this photograph of a Semipalmated Plover, taken in Manitoba, Canada, the more extensive webbing between the toes can be seen.

Adults commence the journey south from the breeding grounds as early as July, but the young follow later. Passage birds reach their highest numbers in the U.S.A., in August and September when migrants often travel overland through the continental interior of North America.

In winter plumage the black areas of the adults' heads are replaced by olive-brown or white; an indistinct slim pale supercilium joins the white forehead just in front and above the eye. The breast band too becomes greyish-brown and may be almost broken in the centre. Juveniles are like winter adults with the features of the upperparts being fringed with pale buff. In both juveniles and adults, in winter, the legs may be dull yellowish, while the bill is predominantly dark grey.

Many birds spend the winter along the coasts of the more southerly states in the U.S.A. Large numbers move farther south to Central and South America. There is a single accepted occurrence of the Semipalmated Plover in the British Isles: a juvenile on St Agnes, Isles of Scilly, from October 9 to at least November 9, 1978. As a common coastal migrant in the U.S.A., it could be expected to occur in Britain more frequently. However, its similarity to its close relative the Ringed Plover is such that individuals could very easily be overlooked among the flocks of the commoner species that frequent coastal estuaries and mud flats. The few rather subtle differences (foot-webbing apart) are discernible only at relatively close range. It was the distinctive call that first drew attention to the St Agnes individual.

Wilson's Plover
Charadrius wilsonia

Outside the breeding season this engaging little bird is usually to be found in groups or small flocks often in association with Semipalmated Plovers and other shoreline feeders. Unlike these, however, Wilson's Plover seems less dependent upon the state of the tide for its life support. The large thick bill, which gives rise to its alternative name, is used to snatch its food, especially fiddler crabs, from the sand. These are usually caught with precise and deliberate moves, as this bird lunges forward to secure its prey. At other times it will dash rapidly across the mud in pursuit of whatever has caught its eye. As well as crabs, various other seashore invertebrates are taken.

The longish thick bill is a feature of the juvenile birds as well as the adult. On the young, it looks so disproportionate it could well belong to a bird twice its size. Otherwise the species has the general appearance of a small pale plover, the adult male in breeding plumage having a broad neck band (which is brown in the female) while the rest of the plumage comprises darkish grey-brown back and wings, and a distinct white collar and forehead, with the rest of the head grey, showing a thin white supercilium. Sometimes there is a cinnamon-coloured ear patch. The pink legs are also useful for identification. However, there can be times when confusion as to this bird's identity might arise, especially if a juvenile Kildeer turns up alongside Wilson's Plovers in their dune world. At such times, the Kildeer's larger size might not be obvious and when distance diffuses the double breast band into one, this bird's largish bill could lead to an identification error being made. However, Wilson's Plovers are always much more approachable, and close views of this bird can usually be obtained, when plumage differences should be discernible. On the other hand, your first introduction to the species might well be in its duneland breeding territory, when you are suddenly confronted with this sturdy looking bird. It will stand before you, erect and motionless, its bill raised in a challenging

OTHER NAME: Thick-billed plover
LENGTH: 180-205 mm (7-8 in)

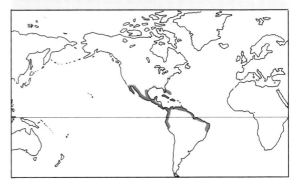

△ *An immature Wilson's Plover photographed in Florida in the autumn. The scaly patterning of its juvenile plumage is evident, while its disproportionately large black bill is also very noticeable.*

manner. As you approach, it will momentarily bob its head and body, give a weak subdued 'whit' note and then beat a hasty retreat with short rapid steps. After a few yards it pauses, turns, and awaits your further advance. It will continue like this until finally taking flight reluctantly, returning to its starting point in a wide arc with slow wingbeats.

Most Wilson's Plovers breed between the Equator and the Tropic of Cancer but in the east they breed from Maryland, almost continuously south through the West Indies to north-east Brazil. The birds also winter largely within the limits of this breeding range. On the Pacific coast it is to be found from southern California through central America to Peru. In these areas, four distinct races occur which show colour variations from black and dark brown to chestnut on the chest band, as well as differing amounts of orange on the nape and variations in cheek colour.

Those birds that return from winter quarters to the more northerly limits of their range, choose a variety of nesting locations. These range from shingle beaches to dunes or the dry sandy edges of coastal pools. In such settings the species is colonial, although the nests are well spaced. Little is known of their display routine and birds may well be pair-bonded to begin with. The male makes numerous scrapes before the female finally chooses one. This is usually lined with small pebbles and shell fragments. The eggs, three or sometimes only two in number, are buff-coloured, evenly spotted and blotched with brown. Egg laying is usually completed by the first week in May. Both parents share incubation which takes 24-25 days. After a further 21 days, during which time they are closely guarded with all the usual 'plover type' ploys such as injury feigning, the young can fly. From then on family parties join up and feed among the dunes and on the foreshore, at which time the juveniles, with their scaly-looking upperparts, are easily recognised.

▽ *An adult Wilson's Plover stands over its eggs in a typical duneland nesting location.*

Killdeer

Charadrius vociferus

This, the largest of the 'ringed' plovers, is probably the most familiar of the Neararctic shorebirds to American birdwatchers. It is encountered widely across the North American continent in a variety of habitats. Its striking plumage and vociferous habits single it out from its close relatives and make it a favourite species for many people.

The Killdeer is a distinctive bird because it is the only wader within its range with a broad double black breast band. This pattern contrasts with the remainder of the underparts, which are clean white. The head is quite large, set on a fairly short and thick neck, and shows a black and white face pattern with a brownish hind crown. The upperparts are a dark earth brown colour, but as the bird takes to the air, a bright rufous-orange rump and upper tail are revealed. The remainder of the tail is again dark brown, but it is narrowly edged with white and appears rather long. In flight a conspicuous white wing bar is revealed, extending along the greater coverts and across the primaries. At rest, the legs can be seen to be a dull yellowish grey colour and the bill fine and dark. A bright orange-red eye ring gives the bird a deceptively gentle appearance.

Most observers have found this species to be fairly wary, often being the first to be alert to danger. The call, as the bird's name suggests, is a rather loud and penetrating 'kill-dee' or 'kill-deeah' and is frequently heard in response to even the smallest disturbance. If flushed, the bird will often fly quite low, using easy and graceful wing beats, before landing some distance away.

Not especially gregarious, the Killdeer is generally found singly or in pairs in many habitats from the seashore up to land about 2,500 metres (8,200 ft) above sea-level. It displays a preference for open spaces, however, and avoids densely vegetated marsh and wooded areas. The bird feeds on short grassy areas and bare ground such as meadows and arable fields. It can often also be found close to human habitation on gravel tracks, lawns, and

Length: 230-260 mm (9-10 in)

golf courses. These areas provide ample insect food, which comprises the majority of this species' diet, along with the few supplementary worms and invertebrates that are also taken. Individuals can be seen feeding in typical plover fashion, first running a few paces then stopping to scan for prey before dipping down to gather the chosen item. It is also not uncommon to see birds following the plough in search of freshly unearthed larvae and worms.

This species is fairly catholic in its choice of breeding habitat and may excavate a shallow scrape in areas of gravel, short vegetation or bare ground. The Killdeer is in fact so trusting in its siting of its nest that eggs have even been laid on gravelled house roofs and between railway tracks! The male lays claim to a territory by means of a spectacular song flight which entails circling a restricted area, often to some height, while calling loudly. During the breeding season this song may be heard at any time of day or night. Meanwhile, the female lays four buff-coloured eggs with darker blotches. She incubates these for twenty-four days. The young, like the eggs before them, are well camouflaged. They fledge after about twenty-five days. During this period of greatest vulnerability, both parents employ an extravagant distraction display. This can be directed towards any potential enemy – from a dog to a tractor – which approaches too close to the nesting territory. The birds feign a broken wing, limp, and display their orangey rumps while making their noisy alarm call.

The timing of the breeding season varies with latitude. Some populations in the south of the species' range are mainly sedentary, while others nesting to the north migrate from lower latitudes as spring approaches. The whole population is generally found wintering south of a line from California to New York, and there is a slightly smaller, resident subspecies in Peru. Migrating Killdeers are some of the first waders to be seen in the northern U.S.A. and Canada in Spring, with passage commencing as early as February. By May nesting will be taking place as far north as southern Alaska, the Hudson Bay, and Newfoundland. The return south begins in July, with late breeders not reaching their winter quarters until November. Possibly as a result of this protracted passage, some birds each year are carried northwards up

△ This picture shows a typical Killdeer nest and clutch comprising four buff-coloured eggs, blotched with dark brown.

▷ The Killdeer favours a great variety of nest sites; here a bird photographed in Edmonton, Canada has selected a grassy setting.

◁ The ever-alert adult Killdeer stands poised to take flight. At this time its penetrating 'kill-dee' call will be uttered until danger or intruder has passed.

the Atlantic seaboard with late Autumn storms, and it may be individuals from this reverse migration that have been recorded in western Europe during the winter months.

The Killdeer is a bird of character and one of the more interesting members of the Charadriinae family. Previously persecuted by hunters in the U.S.A., its numbers have now recovered and this species has now regained its former status as the common plover of the Nearctic region.

Of 43 Killdeers noted in Britain and Ireland, 34 have been recorded since 1958. Prior to the mid 1970s, records averaged less than one per year. The bird has appeared slightly more regularly since then, occurring annually between 1978 and 1985 and amassing a total of 18 individuals in this period. There was a peak

of five in 1979 but this included an influx of four into the Isles of Scilly in November and December. Thus, this very numerous American species has not shown such an upsurge in observations as some of its compatriots, and its occurrences remain rather unpredictable. This may well be related to its tendency to occur during the winter months (rather than in the autumn as with the majority of American visitors). Of the 18 records referred to above, 14 arrived between November and March, with five in January. This has been attributed to a unique trait of the Killdeer to be carried northwards along the Atlantic coast of America during winter storms. Records were widely scattered, with four in Scotland, two in Wales, and three in inland English counties.

Piping Plover
Charadrius melodus

The similarity of this species to both the Semi-palmated Plover and the smaller Snowy Plover can cause identification problems, especially when only distant views are obtained. With patience though, the tight flocks of small plovers that dash to and fro across the sands should eventually come close enough for their visual differences to be appreciated. You can then see that the upperparts of the Piping Plover are light sandy grey, whereas those of the Semipalmated Plover are brown and those of the smaller Snowy Plover are midway between the two. In its breeding plumage the Piping Plover has a black bar across its forehead and a black breast-band, which is sometimes incomplete especially on females. The legs are orange and so is the base of the short, black-tipped bill. All the black on the bird's forehead and breast is lost in its winter plumage, at which time the bill becomes completely black, similar to that of the Snowy Plover, but shorter and stubbier. Juveniles are like winter adults, but with slightly scaly upperparts and duller legs. In all plumages the dark eye stands out from the pale face.

When disturbed, Piping Plovers run across the sand in short bursts, stopping to bob nervously. They take flight reluctantly, but when they do so they are fast and erratic fliers, twisting and tilting from side to side and uttering a plaintive 'peep-lo' whistle as they disappear along the shoreline. In flight the white wing bars and conspicuous white rump contrast with the dark grey-black flight feathers and pale grey wing coverts and body.

In North America the Piping Plover has two distinct breeding areas, giving rise to the possibility of racial differences. Indeed some authorities maintain that two races exist. The first population is referred to as the Interior Piping Plover. This small population breeds from southern Canada through the Dakotas to the southern shores of the Great Lakes. Here it nests on the open shorelines of shallow pools and lakes, making its scrape in gravel or stony mud. The second population, called the

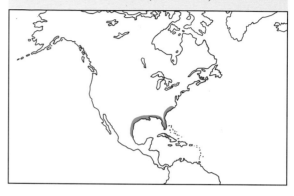

Length: 170-190 mm (6¾-7½ in)

eastern Piping Plover, is purely a coast-dweller, breeding among sand dunes and pebbly sandy beaches along the Atlantic coast from Newfoundland to Virginia.

Adult eastern Piping Plovers arrive on their breeding grounds at the end of March, while those that nest in the interior arrive somewhat later. To establish territory and secure a mate, male Piping Plovers in both locations indulge in a slow butterfly-like flight, circling above the site and uttering a series of rapid 'kuk' notes. The nest is a mere scrape in a dry or sandy situation, liberally lined with small pebbles and shells. The eggs, usually four in number, are light grey-brown with fine spots. These are laid in May or June. Both adults share the incubation until hatching takes place after about 30 days.

The young quickly learn to feed like their parents. This process, as with most small plovers, involves short dashes across the sand, with brief stops to stretch the neck and move the head sideways to watch and listen before suddenly rushing forward to snatch prey from the surface. Periodically, a slow, deliberate pecking motion is also used. The Piping Plover's food incudes worms, crustaceans, beetles, fly larvae, molluscs, and insects.

Should you approach too close to the nest, a sharp 'piping' call alerts you to the fact you are intruding on to the bird's territory. This

△ A Piping Plover settles down to incubate its four grey-brown finely spotted eggs.

▽ In this photograph the orange legs and orange, black-tipped bill of the summer-plumaged Piping Plover are evident. These features help to distinguish this bird from the Snowy Plover or the Semipalmated Plover.

perfectly camouflaged bird is almost invisible against the sand, but the orange legs invariably draw your attention to its location. At such times it will resort to injury feigning, dragging its wings through the sand to entice you to follow it away from its nest. The bird performs this act to all intruders, human or not, until the young fledge after 30 to 35 days.

As the fall approaches, adult and young birds gather on the north Atlantic coast, mainly during the first part of August, and start to drift southwards for the winter. On passage they visit tidal beaches, mud flats and, to a lesser extent, coastal lagoons and pools. Both interior and eastern birds winter together along the shores of the Atlantic and the Gulf of Mexico, from South Carolina to Mexico and on the northern coast of Cuba. The Piping Plover has occurred as a rare vagrant in California. Sadly this species is rapidly declining throughout its range, due to an increase in leisure activity along the coast and at inland waters during its breeding season.

Kentish Plover
Charadrius alexandrinus

The Kentish Plover is not only one of smallest 'sand plovers', but also the most cosmopolitan. Its general plumage tones vary throughout the world with the American Snowy Plover showing the palest form. These variations can be attributed partly to racial differences and perhaps more locally to habitat preference. The species' simple colour-scheme makes it one of the more visually cryptic among waders among dunes, beaches, and saline pools.

Places such as the Camargue in southern France contain the exact requirements for this bird's year-round success. Here Kentish Plovers can be seen among the étangs and marismas in typical alert and upright stance looking like a diminutive 'sentinel of the saltpans' and very much a characteristic bird of the area.

Smaller than the familiar Ringed Plover the Kentish has proportionally longer legs and a characteristically prominent 'head and shoulders' body form. The upperparts are pale-sandy in colour, with the breeding male displaying a small white forehead, black fore-crown band, and rufous tinged hindcrown. Below the slim white brow, the black eye band completes the head pattern. There is also a characteristic black shoulder patch, which never forms a complete breast band. The complete white collar is a useful feature for

OTHER NAME: Snowy Plover
LENGTH: 150-170 mm (6-6½ in)

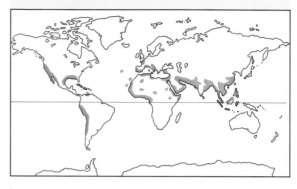

identification in the field at all times of the year. The underparts are wholly white at every season. The female Kentish Plover has the same pattern as the male, but the black areas are replaced by brown. The winter plumage of both sexes is similar to the breeding female in European birds. The legs are dark grey along with a shortish slender black bill and conspicuous large black eye. In North America the Snowy Plover has the same general pattern as the Kentish, but the upperparts are a pale sandy grey colour and breeding males have a pale fawn hindcrown and sometimes all-white lores. The legs of the Snowy Plover are often a much paler colour than the Kentish Plover. In flight the bird shows quite a slim outline with the narrow white wing bar and white sides to the tail evident in all races. Calls, however, differ on either side of the Atlantic. In Europe birds give a soft 'twit', while in North America a softer disyllabic 'ku-whet' is the usual note.

Equally at home on dune systems and saline coastal lagoons, the Kentish Plover can also be found on inland steppe and sand desert, also large sandy rivers and lakes where vegetation is at a minimum. Birds generally avoid muddy and rocky shorelines. Food items include small insects, molluscs, crustaceans, and worms. These are obtained in the usual plover manner, by running, stopping, and pecking in a fairly random fashion.

The bird's breeding range forms a virtually continuous band throughout the warmer zones of the Northern Hemisphere. The continental interior populations are migratory, whereas coastal breeding birds are more likely to be sedentary. Many of the northern birds winter along the sandy shores of the tropics.

The breeding season starts early at southern latitudes with pairs sometimes mating in January. Bigamy is rare and pairs have been recorded as being loyal for six seasons in succession. The preferred breeding habitat is relatively undisturbed dry or sandy ground near to water. Here the male makes several scrapes in flat, rather even ground and one of these is chosen by the female. This is lined with small pebbles and shell fragments. The clutch, usually of three eggs, is laid in early May. The eggs are pale buff with a sprinkling of black spots and streaks, sometimes zoned. Incubation takes about 26 days. During this time the female sits in the daytime, with the male taking over at night. The young are usually well able to feed themselves, although still tended by both parents. When disturbed, the chicks scatter and lie prostrate in the sand, becoming very difficult to see for any would-be predator. The fledging period of about four weeks also marks the time the young birds become independent. Juveniles of all races resemble the female, being even less well defined around the head and having more noticeable pale fringes to the features of the upperparts.

Outside the breeding season Kentish Plovers may form scattered groups rather than large flocks, often associating with other *Charadrius* plovers. In Europe the breeding population is generally declining and in Great Britain the bird is becoming rarer even as a casual visitor. Up to 40 pairs used to breed in the area of south-east of England from which its common name was derived. In North America it is fairly well represented on the west coast, in the midwest and round the Gulf of Mexico. However, it remains rare on the east coast except in Florida where Cuban birds spend the winter.

▷ *In this instance a Kentish Plover has chosen a more vegetated site for its nest and eggs.*

◁ *A Kentish Plover over its eggs in a typical dried-mud nesting location.*

Mountain Plover

Charadrius montanus

Contrary to its English name, the Mountain Plover is not an inhabitant of mountains. It breeds on arid upland grasslands and winters in semi-desert areas. Often tame, it prefers to run rather than fly when disturbed, and when it does fly it frequently stays close to the ground and will crouch on landing.

When breeding, the Mountain Plover requires grazed short-grass prairies. Numbers have greatly declined in the twentieth century as a consequence of the disappearance of the buffalo and the ploughing-up of the wildlands. Even the ungrazed areas that remain and the land that has been cultivated and subsequently allowed to go fallow are usually unsuitable for this bird because the vegetation is too tall and rank. Breeding Mountain Plovers are to be found from southern Alberta and Saskatchewan south to Montana, and also from central Wyoming south to New Mexico and northwest Texas. But the species' range is declining – it once extended into the Dakotas, for example.

Mountain Plovers arrive on their breeding grounds in small flocks from late March onwards, and courtship and mating both take place within these flocks. The sexual display involves the construction of a ritual nest-scrape, and is very similar to that of many other species of plover. Once the pair-bond has been sealed, the birds disperse and begin to stake-out their territories. Several displays are used to establish and defend these: the birds give a clear 'wee-wee-wee', both from the ground and in flight, and may indulge in a 'falling-leaf display', in which the bird drops from a height of up to 10 m (30 ft) with its wings held in a V-shape. As they do this they rock back and forth. They also have a 'butterfly flight', in which the birds fly around with slow, deep wingbeats.

Several nest scrapes are constructed before the female chooses one in which to lay the clutch of three eggs. Incubation lasts for 29 days, and is usually performed by the male alone. In some cases the female may go on to

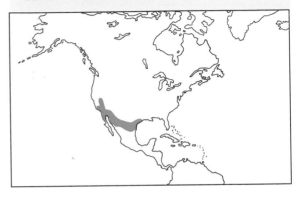

LENGTH: 210-235 mm (8-9 in)

lay a second clutch about two weeks after the first, and will tend to this clutch alone. This ingenious technique allows the birds to produce two broods concurrently. The young fledge after about 33 days, and from mid-June onwards adults and young begin to gather in flocks, which are sometimes quite large.

Although those that leave the breeding grounds earliest are back in the winter quarters by mid-July, most birds remain until September. The Mountain Plover winters from California and south-west Arizona in a band across northern Mexico to southern Texas. Cactus desert and dry dirt fields, often well away from water, are favoured, and flocks of Mountain Plovers will sometimes join other species of waders and gulls behind the plough. Their major source of food is insects, especially grasshoppers, from which they get much of the water that they need. Away from their regular wintering areas, Mountain Plovers are vagrants to Washington, Oregon, Alabama, Florida, Virginia and Massachusetts. Sightings have also been recorded in Nebraska and Kansas.

Between the Semipalmated Plover and the Killdeer in size, the Mountain Plover looks and behaves like a typical small plover. The species is notable for being un-noteworthy – it is rather plain. The upperparts are pale brown and the underparts whitish, washed buff on the breast and flanks. In breeding plumage the

△A rather plain-looking bird, the Mountain Plover has no outstanding field marks or plumage colouration that quickly identifies the species. But for its smaller size and yellow-ochre coloured legs it looks like an American Golden Plover in winter dress.

males and females are similar, with a white forehead and short supercilium extending back to just behind the eye, neatly set-off by a narrow black line from the eye to the bill, and a black forecrown. Birds in winter and juvenile plumage lack these prominent head markings, but often have a good buffish breast-band. Adults can look very plain-faced, the black markings on the head being replaced by a dull pale brown. Juveniles have a buffish eyebrow, rather than white. They are also darker and more prominently scaled over the entire upper-

parts. In flight the species is long-winged, with a variable narrow white wingbar and white fringe to the tail, which is dark-centred. The underwing is conspicuously white. The yellowish-brown legs are quite long and the bill is black. Calls include a variety of whistles as well as a shrill 'kip'.

The Mountain Plover can be distinguished from most similar plovers by its larger size, dull ochre legs, and overall paleness. In the breeding season, its lack of dark breast bands is another useful clue to its identity. It is closer in appearance to a non-breeding American Golden Plover, but that species is slightly larger than the Mountain Plover, and has spangled upperparts, dark legs, and a smoky-grey, rather than white, underwing.

Dotterel

Charadrius morinellus

Among the Palearctic plovers, the Dotterel has evolved to become best adapted to the lifestyle on barren mountain plateaux, sometimes as high as 2800 metres (9000 ft). However, its colourful summer plumage and individual tameness have in the past been its downfall. Due to persecution by man, this beautiful species is a comparative rarity in Britain. Although now given full protection, the Dotterel still only maintains a small breeding population.

Smaller than the adult Golden Plover, the Dotterel is quite distinctive. The sexes are similar, although the female is brighter. The crown is dark and a conspicuous broad white supercilium meets at the nape. The white cheeks and throat are bordered by a medium-grey hind neck and upper chest. A slim but prominent white breast band forms the upper demarcation line to a rather rufous lower breast and black belly. The under tail coverts are white. The upperparts are mainly dark with narrow buff and golden fringes to the feathers, giving a very spangled appearance. The bill is short and dark, while the legs are a dull yellowish colour. The large black eye is bright and prominent. In flight, dotterels look fairly plain

OTHER NAME: Eurasian Dotterel
LENGTH: 200-220 mm (8½ in)

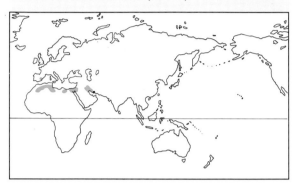

at all times of the year, the rump and tail both being mainly grey. Winter adults lose the rich coloration of the underparts, becoming rather pale, but with the breast band remaining fairly evident. The scaly upperparts are more enhanced and the supercilium takes on a creamy buff hue. Juveniles look like even paler versions of the adult winter plumage. At all times Dotterels look compact and stocky, especially on the ground.

The species has a wide distribution across Eurasia with the mountains of Scandinavia and

◁ *A juvenile Dotterel at a coastal site rests awhile before continuing its migration.*

▷ *An adult Dotterel broods recently hatched chicks on its Norwegian nesting grounds.*

northern Siberia holding the majority of breeding birds. More isolated smaller populations occur in the Alps, Scotland, and central Asia. The winter range is confined to the drier semi-desert zones of North Africa and the Middle East, where the species' habits have been little studied by ornithologists.

Dotterels prefer open sparsely vegetated upland habitats like those on raised tundra plateaux and 'whaleback' mountain ridges. On migration they regularly occur at traditional upland stopover sites as well as on large open agricultural fields especially in Cambridgeshire and in the east-coast English counties. Here they spend a few days resting and feeding before heading off on the second stage of their northern-bound spring migration. There is no specific preference for water or wetlands, either on migration or when breeding, and whatever the situation, the bird will seek out insects, worms, some molluscs, and plant material if it is available. However, insects make up the largest percentage of food items, especially on the breeding grounds. The feeding action of the Dotterel is similar to that adopted by most other plovers with the 'probe and push' method of surface foraging being the most common in the species.

The winter quarters of the Dotterel are vacated in April when small groups or 'trips' move north to areas such as the Pyrenees, the Caucasus, the Netherlands, and Britain. It was during the last century at such half-way resting stages that large numbers of birds were shot both for food and as a valuable source of feathers for fly-fishing.

△ A Dotterel over its nest. The broad white supercilium which meets at the nape is very clear in this photograph.

As they arrive on their breeding grounds in May, Dotterels gather in loose flocks, waiting for the snows to melt. Amidst much aggressive behaviour involving mainly females, the breeding pairs form and take up territory. Where the required habitat is extensive, scattered breeding groups can exist. The nest site is on the ground, often half-concealed by a boulder or vegetation. The nest consists of a shallow scrape lined by the male, in which the clutch of three eggs is laid. Because of the short breeding season at high altitude, the females may take on a second mate and lay two clutches one after the other. In these cases she shares the incubating with the second male while the first continues on his own. In the straightforward monogamous relationship it is the male who completes most of the parental duties. The eggs hatch after 26 days and the young can feed themselves at once. The fledging period is about four weeks, during which time both young and adults group together in flocks which remain on the breeding ground for a few more weeks.

In autumn only small numbers of Dotterels are evident in western Europe. The majority of the birds probably reach their winter homes in one hop. They can migrate for long distances over land due to the high fat reserves put on in the late summer premigratory feeding. Straying individuals have less of a habitat preference at this time and sometimes turn up on beaches and offshore islands.

Dotterels are fairly quiet, but do utter a small trill as they take to flight. The birds are more vocal on their nesting grounds especially in the immediate vicinity of the nest. An estimated eighty pairs breed in Great Britain, a number which is slowly increasing at present. An impressive 28,000 pairs are estimated to nest in Norway, and this is the main hub of the western population.

American Golden Plover

Pluvialis dominica

This, the North American counterpart of the Golden Plover, differs from that species in many ways. Another species, the Pacific Golden Plover, is very similar, and these two have only recently been appointed to full taxonomic status.

The American Golden Plover is slightly smaller than the *Pluvialis apricaria* and also has longer wings and legs. It appears slimmer in the neck and around the belly. The bill is typically plover-like, being quite chunky and black. The lustrous dark eye and pale eyebrow give the rather bulbous head a distinctive facial expression. In summer plumage the adults are very smart, even more so than their European counterparts. The jet-black face, throat, centre of the chest, belly and undertail coverts form a continuous and solidly dark underside. The extreme rear undertail coverts can have a few small white bars. The black face extends just over the bill and above this the prominent white forehead extends into a thick eyebrow. This white blaze envelops the rear ear coverts and then continues to broaden at the sides of the neck to form an oval patch flanking the black of the chest. Unlike the other two golden plover species, this white area stops abruptly just below the shoulder. All of the upperparts are a mixture of small black, golden and white feathers giving an even greater spangled effect than the European bird. In flight, the wings look long, while the upperparts are generally dark with a golden tinge. Although still rather uniform, winter adults can be distinguished from European Golden Plovers at the same stage by their slimmer appearance, generally much greyer body plumage, and a more prominent pale eyebrow. In flight the dusky grey underwing and axillaries are further useful field marks. As in all 'black-bellied' plover species the legs are dark grey. Plumage differences with Pacific Golden Plover are slightly more subtle.

American Golden Plovers are very gregarious and can be seen in sizeable flocks in the Mississippi Valley on spring migration. Birds also often halt on the northern prairies to feed

OTHER NAME: American Lesser Golden Plover
LENGTH: 230-260 mm (9-10 in)

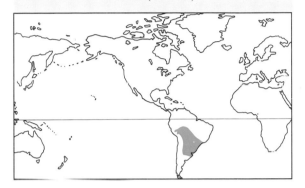

△ An American Golden Plover in winter plumage looks a very undistinguished bird, but its slim neck, round-bellied appearance and smaller size are aids to identification when distinguishing the species from its European counterpart.

up before continuing on to their breeding grounds. These extend from western Alaska to Baffin Island, where they arrive in late May. In the summer the American Golden Plover is a true tundra species preferring dry gentle slopes with short vegetation for nesting. The reproductive cycle and behaviour is very similar to that of the Golden Plover.

When the young birds fledge, usually in late July, they remain in the nesting zone, but move to wetter areas such as moss swamps to feed. These juveniles are fairly distinctive. The crown and mantle can be lightly spangled with gold and white, while the bold silver-white eyebrow is more noticeable behind the eye. The ear coverts, underparts and smaller wing coverts tend to be very grey, especially when compared to juveniles of both Golden and Pacific Golden Plovers. At this stage the juveniles can be confused with non-breeding Grey Plovers. But their size, bill structure and lack of black axillaries rule out that identification.

Both American and Pacific Golden Plovers have a wide range of contact calls. The two most familiar, 'chu-wit' and 'tu-ee' are shared by both species and differ only from that of the Golden Plover.

Food choice is governed by the changing seasons. On its breeding grounds invertebrates (consisting mainly of adult and larval insects) form the American Golden Plover's basic diet, but berries and other vegetable matter are also taken. On migration and in the winter quarters worms and insects such as crickets are a major food source.

The migration of the American Golden Plover is particularly interesting. Many birds, especially the adults, at first head eastwards from the arctic breeding zones. The route then takes them well out into mid north Atlantic before they fly due south to central South America. This journey, typical of long winged Nearctic waders, involves thousands of miles of non-stop flight. The Atlantic loop, as the flight path is often known, does make this and other American waders susceptible to bad-weather displacement. Following hurricane-force westerly winds in the north Atlantic, it is not

◁An American Golden Plover in summer plumage on its breeding grounds in Manitoba, Canada.

▷An American Golden Plover stands over its eggs at a typical tundra nesting location.

unusual for the American Golden Plover to be found in the British Isles.

Although records of its visits to Britain are confused by the fact that the American Golden Plover was until recently classified jointly with the Pacific Golden Plover, it seems that the Pacific is a very rare vagrant to Britain. The vast majority of records involve American Golden Plover. It appears that 116 records in Britain and Ireland up to 1986 can be ascribed to this species compared with only four as yet officially accepted occurrences of the Pacific Golden Plover (one or two recent claims are still being adjudicated). The American Golden Plover has been recorded annually since 1966 and during the past ten years there has been an average of eight per year. This represents a significant increase compared with an average of less than two per year during the previous twenty years. The increase is no doubt due partly to greater observer awareness of the field character of the species (including its separation from the Golden Plover), which has encouraged more diligent examination of

Golden Plover flocks.

In the five years 1982-1986, no less than 33 of the 45 records (73 per cent) were in western Britain or Ireland, a pattern conforming to expectation for a transatlantic visitor. It is notable, however, that seven of the remaining occurrences were in the north-east of England between Tyne and Wear and Lincolnshire, six in the catchment area of the River Humber.

Once on the wintering grounds, birds can be found on short grassland and tilled agricultural fields like those in Argentina. Further north in Venezuela, coastal lagoons, mud flats and inland shallow ponds are favoured.

The species is still recovering from massive persecution in the earlier part of this century when vast numbers of the birds were slaughtered and put in barrels for the food market, a fate shared with the extinct Passenger Pigeon. But when time seemed to be running out for the American Golden Plover, changes in human food requirements and a generally increased conservation awareness saved the day and the species.

Pacific Golden Plover

Pluvialis fulva

Until recently the Pacific Golden Plover and the American Golden Plover were treated as a single species, named the Lesser Golden Plover. However, research has shown that the two birds breed alongside each other in an area 1,300 km (800 miles) across in Alaska without hybridizing, and this fact, together with their rather different patterns of moult and migration, has led to the decision to classify them as two species.

The three species of Golden Plover are similar in all plumages, and their general characteristics have already been described. Both American and Pacific can be distinguished from *apricaria* at all times by their smoky grey, rather than white, axillaries and underwing coverts. Both are also smaller, longer-winged and longer-legged, but this can only be readily appreciated in direct comparison. Distinguishing the Pacific from the American Golden Plover is not, however, quite so straightforward.

In breeding plumage, both Pacific and American Golden Plovers have predominantly black underparts, but the Pacific has a narrow white line all the way along its flanks from the eyebrow to the undertail, usually broken by black bars on the flanks. Importantly, the Pacific also has largely white undertail coverts. The American Golden Plover has largely black undertail coverts and flanks. The white 'shoulder patch' at the side of the breast of the American, though shared with the Pacific, is larger and rather more prominent. (Birds in moult, however, may closely resemble the Pacific). The tone of the upperparts is also usually different, the Pacific being distinctly more golden-spangled, but this is a very variable feature.

Differences between the two species are more apparent in winter and juvenile plumage, when the Pacific is essentially yellowish-buff and the American brownish-grey. More specifically, the Pacific has a yellowish eyebrow, bright yellow spangles on the upperparts, and the breast is brownish-buff in adults and buffish

OTHER NAMES: Asian Golden Plover, Eastern Golden Plover, Asiatic Lesser Golden Plover
LENGTH: 230-260 mm (9-10 in)

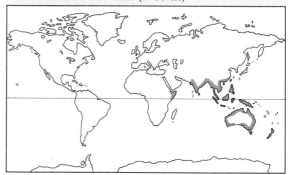

in juveniles, mottled bright yellow in both. In the American Golden Plover the eyebrow is whitish, the upperparts are spangled pale yellow or whitish and the breast is greyish, mottled white. Both species can often be distinguished from the Golden Plover by their call, which includes a 'chewit', reminiscent of a subdued Spotted Redshank or a loud Semipalmated Plover, and a plaintive 'ki-wee'. Unhelpfully, there are as yet no clearly worked-out differences between the calls of the two smaller species of Golden Plover.

The Pacific Golden Plover breeds in Arctic Siberia from the Yamal Peninsula eastwards, and also in western Alaska and the Bering Sea islands. The nesting habitat is well-drained tundra beyond the tree-line, with a short sward of moss and lichen. The birds arrive in early June but comparatively little information is available concerning their courtship and breeding biology, mainly because of their long confusion with American Golden Plover. The nest is a shallow depression in the ground, sparsely lined with grass and the leaves of dwarf birch. It is often placed near a small bush. Four, occasionally five, eggs are laid; these are a variable cinnamon-buff in colour, with many irregularly scattered dark spots. Both sexes incubate, and the eggs hatch in about 27 days, after which the young are escorted by their parents down into valley mires to feed. Food comprises a variety of small invertebrates throughout the year and this diet is supplemented by berries in the autumn.

The Pacific Golden Plover is a prodigious migrant, often travelling enormous distances non-stop, for example 4,500 km (2,800 miles)

from the Pribilof Islands in the Bering Sea to Hawaii. Adults leave the breeding grounds from late July onwards, several weeks before the juveniles. The species winters in an area that extends from north-east Africa, around the shores of the Indian Ocean to south-east Asia, and south to Australia and New Zealand. Birds also reach many Pacific islands and a few can be found in southern California. Not surprisingly, there are far-flung records of vagrants from Cape Town, New England, Chile, the Galapagos Islands, and Western Europe, but only four have been recorded in Britain, all since 1976.

In winter, unlike the other two Golden Plover species, Pacifics are largely coastal, where they can be found in a variety of habitats – intertidal mud, beaches, prawn-ponds, and reefs – but especially areas of short grass such as golf courses, playing fields, and coastal saltmarshes. They are often rather tame and approachable. Birds begin to depart for the breeding areas as early as March, but many first-years do not make the journey, preferring to spend the summer in the winter quarters, which constitutes another difference from American Golden Plover.

△ *This Pacific Golden Plover in winter plumage was photographed in Oman.*

▷ *The more distinct golden spangled upperparts of a winter-plumaged Pacific Golden Plover are evident on this bird, which was photographed in Hong Kong during October.*

Golden Plover

Pluvialis apricaria

The plaintive 'tlu-i' call of the Golden Plover is a distinctive sound both on its upland moorland breeding grounds and its lowland pasture wintering areas. This highly gregarious species forms large flocks, often alongside the Lapwing, with which it shares common ground for much of the year.

Smaller than the Lapwing, the Golden Plover has an oval body shape, shortish, dull grey legs, and a small dark plover bill. It is a predominently brown bird for most of the year, yet in summer the adults become black on the face, and down the centre of the chest to the lower breast and belly. This black area is neatly bordered down the sides of the neck and breast by white, giving the underparts a smart pied appearance. On the head, a dull pale eyebrow is present, while the upper parts are a dark base colour heavily spangled with gold on the crown, nape, mantle and wings. The under tail coverts are white, sometimes flecked with grey. The amount of black on the face varies within the species; birds breeding in the northern part of the range are the darkest, while some southern individuals remain much paler. In flight the upper wing is a uniform light brown, with darker wing tips, and on some birds a thin pale wing bar is evident. The under wing and axillaries are bright silvery white, an identification feature which distinguishes this bird from the American and Pacific Golden Plovers. The rump and tail are almost the same colour as the upperparts at all seasons

Flocks of Golden Plovers have a typical fast whirling flight and sometimes take a while to resettle after they have been disturbed before they finally come in to land quickly.

The breeding range of the species extends from Greenland and Iceland in the west across far northern Europe to central Siberia. Dartmoor in south-west England is the southernmost nesting outpost. The winter range is much more concentrated with the British Isles, France, and the Low Countries holding perhaps 80 per cent of the total world population. Other scattered winter sites are located around

OTHER NAMES: Eurasian Golden Plover, Greater Golden Plover
LENGTH: 260-290 mm (10-11½ in)

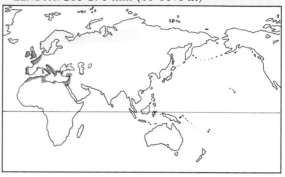

the fringe of the Mediterranean, south to the Nile Delta.

The preferred summer habitat is open unrestricted moorland, particularly short heather-covered slopes with the occasional hummock which can be used as a lookout post. Golden Plovers do not particularly favour wet areas. The birds arrive here in April and May and take part in small communal courtship displays with the male's continuous trilling song adding a further dimension to the wild desolate moorland that is the bird's home throughout the summer.

Once the pairs are established in their territories, the male makes several shallow scrapes on the ground among low vegetation, one of which is chosen by the female as the nest. After lining the nest with heather, stems, twigs and lichens, the usual clutch of four eggs is laid. These are more oval than Lapwings' eggs and usually creamy buff, occasionally pale green, with bold blotches and spots of dark brown. Incubation is usually performed by both parents, but sometimes the male takes the greater share. While one bird is sitting, its partner will keep open a watchful eye for predators from a nearby vantage point. Golden Plovers often share their territory with a pair of Dunlin. Both off-duty partners from each species may associate closely both on the ground and in flight. This has given rise to the

▷ This Golden Plover chick is only a day or two old, but it can already fend for itself.

▽ A Golden Plover on its nest in Norway, where birds are much darker on the face than more southerly breeding birds

◁A Golden Plover on its Scottish nesting territory. The bird in this photograph shows a smaller area of black summer plumage typical of the southern form of this species.

Dunlin's country English name of 'plover's page'. The eggs hatch after about four weeks and the young can feed themselves at once, being tended by both parents. The fledging period is also about four weeks, after which the juveniles are left by the adults, who migrate south. The young birds are very like the winter adults at this stage, with additional sparsely barred belly and flanks. They head south a few weeks after the adults to join up at the winter quarters.

In winter, Golden Plovers can be found on low-elevation permanent short grasslands, open agricultural fields and flat ground adjacent to estuaries. Here the food consists mainly of earthworms and beetles which are taken in typical plover feeding fashion. On the breeding grounds the diet is more extensive with vegetable matter, such as seeds and berries, supplementing adult and larval invertebrate items. Feeding birds tend to work a particular zone of a field, methodically pecking and probing, rather like a Song Thrush.

Some British Golden Plovers migrate south to France and Iberia for the winter while ringing studies have shown that others only move about 100 kilometres (60 miles) or so. Out of the three distinct species of Golden Plover, it is the Golden Plover which has evolved the shortest migration. Both the American and Pacific Golden Plovers make much longer winter trips, penetrating the tropics to a far greater degree. This may be due largely to the comparatively warmer latitudes of the maritime climate of western Europe, conditions that keep the fields and pastures from freezing, unlike those in the continental interiors of Asia and North America.

Grey Plover
Pluvialis squatarola

This bird has one of the most mournful-sounding calls there is, a far carrying 'tlee-oo-ee' (the second syllable being lower pitched). For me it encapsulates the ethereal world of sand, sea, and sky which comprises this bird's winter home. As a breeding species it is distributed almost all the way around the North Pole, except for an unusual gap in its range that misses out Greenland, Iceland, and Scandinavia. Otherwise it nests almost continuously throughout the entire arctic regions of mainland Russia, Siberia, and North America. Within this vast area its usual nesting habitat is lowland tundra north of the tree limit, generally excluding coastal locations and avoiding most of the smaller Arctic islands. It is in such a setting that the male sets up territory and courts his mate with a series of high-flying zig-zag and butterfly-like display flights not dissimilar to those of the Golden Plover. The nest is a scrape on the mossy lichen-covered ground, generally on a raised ridge or hillock to give a commanding view of the chosen area. The eggs, normally four in number, are buffish grey with darker spotting, providing the more-than-adequate camouflage that is so necessary for ground-nesting birds. The eggs are laid around the last week of May, to late June in its more northerly limit, and the sexes share incubation throughout the 23 days it takes for the young to hatch out. Both birds continue to share parental duties after this time.

In its summer plumage this species is one of the most strikingly beautiful of all shore birds, the intense black of its underparts reaching down to the belly, (hence its North American name of Black-bellied Plover). This black area is separated from the silvery spangled grey and black upperparts by a broad band of pure white feathers. The bill and legs are black. The female has less white in the upperparts than the male, while her underparts are more brown than black. The birds are seen in their breeding plumage from March onwards, before they start to move to their nesting areas. However, some birds are found to be migrating northwards

OTHER NAMES: Black-bellied Plover, Silver Plover
LENGTH: 270-310 mm (10½-12 in)

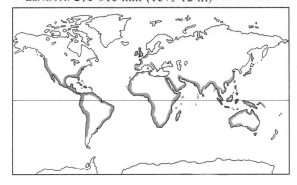

before the moult is complete, at which times some strange mixtures of winter and summer plumage may be encountered. Equally, on the return passage in the autumn, similar, sometimes puzzling combinations of dress might occasionally be seen.

Though the Grey Plover closely resembles the Golden Plover in its winter colours, it is a somewhat larger and stouter bird with silver grey spangling instead of gold on the upperparts, and so is generally distinct. However, the young birds of the year do have a yellowish tinge to their upperparts and when at rest this may cause some problems of identification. But in flight, any doubts as to which species the bird might be are quickly dispelled, for the Grey Plover shows a conspicuous black 'arm pit'. Both adult and immature birds display this field mark, not to be found in any other species. Additionally, there is a prominent wing bar, and a noticeably white rump and tail.

Generally shy and wary, the Grey Plover is usually only found in smallish flocks or groups scattered about mud flats and estuaries, sometimes in association with other shore birds, particularly curlews, Golden Plovers, and, in North America, Willets. Grey Plovers eat a variety of inter-tidal invertebrates, but will frequently resort to coastal grassland. Here they will join with Golden Plovers to feed on creatures such as worms and leather jackets.

◁A Grey Plover in winter plumage. This species is more a bird of mudflats and estuaries than the similar looking Golden Plover, which shows a preference for short grassland and agricultural fields.

▽ In summer plumage the Grey Plover is a strikingly beautiful bird with the intense black of the underparts reaching down to its belly.

This bird's global distribution produces a complicated pattern of migratory movements, but there is no evidence that Grey Plovers from North America cross the Atlantic. On the other hand, ringing recoveries show that Grey Plovers visiting Britain and Ireland come from the Russian and Siberian breeding populations. Though few in number, recoveries of ringed birds indicate birds coming through Britain migrate along the Baltic down the west European coast to west Africa. Some even end up as far south as the south African coasts. Though most movements of migrating birds are coastal, there are regular occurences inland with small numbers noted at reservoir margins and other watery habitats.

In Britain, recent counts suggest a midwinter total of 20,000 birds, which probably represents more than a third of Europe's population of this bird. Large numbers also occur on the Wadden Sea in autumn and spring with concentrations also in western France, Iberia and west Africa.

In North America, spring passage extends from mid-April to beyond mid-May, generally peaking towards the end of April. In the east, birds arrive via the West Indies to points along the Atlantic coast as far as New England and thence generally fly overland. In the west, the tendency is to follow the Pacific coast. The return migration in the fall is probably made by following the birds' spring movement in reverse, although there may perhaps be a more easterly bias.

Lapwing

Vanellus vanellus

A common and familiar bird throughout much of the Western Paleartic, the Lapwing is well known enough to be afforded many country names (over 40 in Britain alone) which either relate to its appearance or to its call. This is a bird that is hard to overlook in the areas where it congregates in large numbers during the winter or where it breeds during the spring and summer. The nuptial display of the Lapwing is in fact one of the first signs of spring over most of lowland Britain, for it is typically a bird of agricultural areas, especially favouring permanent pasture and ploughed land where the nest is often sited amongst growing corn. In some parts, however, the Lapwing might equally be associated with marginal areas such as sand and gravel workings, sewage farms, the borders of reservoirs, and even refuse tips. On the other hand it is equally at home in more elevated places and in upland Britain is found in all but the most exposed situations, where its cry mingles with other moorland species such as Curlew and Snipe.

In such settings, the distinctive aerial performances of the Lapwing take place as the male stakes out its territory, attracting a mate and defending the nest site against other males. Depending upon the weather, this display may well be done in early March or even before, if conditions are particularly benign. It is usually the 'pee-a-weet a weet weet' call of this bird that draws one's attention to its black and white form as it tumbles about the sky. This spring flight is an incredible display. Rising from the ground, the Lapwing gains height with slow deliberate wing beats; then, increasing speed, it will plunge earthwards, rolling and twisting in a series of manoeuvres that leaves the senses reeling. The performance is usually accompanied by the bird's cries, but on occasions it is silent, though it will make a strange buzzing sound with its wings. A low, corkscrewing flight over the ground also takes place and is sometimes accompanied by calls, but at other times only by the Lapwing's characteristic wing buzzing.

OTHER NAMES: Northern Lapwing, Peewit, Green Plover
LENGTH: 280-310 mm (11-12 in)

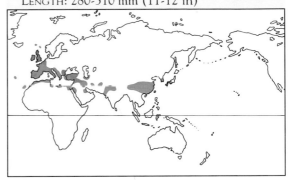

On the ground, the Lapwing's courtship entails a great deal of bowing when the orange-brown under-tail is revealed. It is at this point that the bird utters a variety of wheezing calls. The nest is a simple scrape created by the male and quite frequently several will be scratched out before the female selects one in which to lay the eggs. These are pyriform in shape, and there is usually a clutch of four although sometimes three and occasionally five are laid. The background colour of these is generally stone to brown and covered with spots and blotches of black. As the eggs are incubated, pieces of straw and grass are added to the scrape and by

△ *A newly hatched Lapwing chick in its speckled 'salt- and-pepper' downy plumage.*

67

the time the eggs hatch in approximately 28 days, quite a collection of nest material may have accrued.

Within a very short time of hatching the young are capable of locomotion, but if undisturbed they stay in the nest for most of the first day or even overnight. During the first hours, if conditions are stormy, they may be recalled to the nest for protection. Indeed, the parents will brood the chicks as required in the first two weeks of life away from the nest.

In these early vulnerable days after hatching the speckled 'salt and pepper' coloration of the chick's downy plumage renders them virtually invisible. This is especially effective when they freeze and crouch, alerted by their parent's warning cry and avoiding detection when danger approaches.

When eggs are in the nest, or there are young to protect, the adult lapwing will often use injury feigning – dragging an apparently broken wing to lure away an intruder. Such

behaviour is not confined to this species, and other wading birds use it as required, generally to good effect against animals.

Following the decline in the numbers of the Lapwing during the latter half of the last century and the early part of this one, the bird is currently enjoying a revival of its fortunes, not only in Britain, but also in Europe as a whole. The expansion of its breeding range is most surely linked to climatic change and since the 1930s the bird has bred in northern Scotland and the Scottish Islands. Since 1935 it has regularly bred in the Faeroes. Its spread northwards into Scandinavia has been marked and in Finland its range has moved northwards almost 1000 km since 1970. Its status in Belgium, Luxembourg, and northern Italy has also improved in recent times. Whereas the breeding population of Britain is possibly in the region of 250,000 pairs, the wintering total may well be over a million, many of which will be migrants of Scandinavian, Danish, Dutch

◁*This young Lapwing has buff tips to the edges of its feathers, giving it a scaly appearance. At this age the bird's general colouring is much duller and the crest has not developed to its full length.*

▷*A Lapwing approaches its nest in a strawberry field. There is a full clutch of four heavily marked eggs. The green and purplish gloss on the wings of this species is very evident in this photograph.*

and north German origin, since Britain (along with France and the Iberian peninsula) forms the major wintering region for this bird. Bad weather, however, does greatly influence the Lapwing's distribution within the region, for these birds are most susceptible to freezing conditions when 'cold-weather' movements take place. Large numbers of Lapwings move west prior to the onset of snow and ice.

The Lapwing is not usually known for its long migrations, but many do move to escape bad weather. Such westward movements have sometimes caused exceptional Atlantic crossings. The most notable on record was in December 1927, when birds moving westwards out of England were caught up in strong easterly winds sweeping them past Ireland, some hundreds ultimately reaching Newfoundland. Most American sightings of the Lapwing pertain to this single event, but there have been other scattered occurrences of Lapwings reaching the American eastern seaboard south to the

Carolinas and even Bermuda, the Bahamas and Barbados. Whether viewed as a straggler on the American continent, or on its more usual European home ground, the Lapwing is easily identified by its long crest, dark glossy green upperparts, white underparts and orange brown under-tail coverts. At a distance, however, it looks black and white, but when in flight the deep flapping of its broad rounded wings give a distinctive flickering appearance that can identify it even at considerable range.

Gregarious during the winter, the Lapwing favours particular areas, even returning annually to feed in specific fields where worms and leather jackets are taken in typical plover fashion. The bird is sometimes known as the friend of the farmer, because of the soil insects it eats. Marshy situations are often visited – the presence of nearby water is often the attraction when noisy bathing parties can be observed. Saltings and muddy estuarine conditions are more favoured during freezing weather.

Surfbird

Aphriza virgata

Confined in the breeding season to Alaska and north-west Canada, and in the winter to the Pacific coast of the Americas, the Surfbird is an enigmatic shorebird. It has a plover's bill, looks like the Siberian Great Knot in its breeding dress, resembles a Black Turnstone in winter plumage, and in behaviour is also similar to a Turnstone. It is probably closely related to the Great Knot, but this issue is not yet settled and the Surfbird may yet find a place with the turnstones. It only lives up to its name in winter, feeding on the edge of the breakers.

The Surfbird is an infrequent breeder in Alaska and the Yukon, with proven records of nesting from the southern coastal ranges and the Tanana-Yukon highlands. Its breeding habitat is in the alpine zone above the timber-line, often in the more precipitous areas and near scree-slopes, with dwarf vegetation.

In the summer Surfbirds feed on flies and beetles, which they pursue on the sun-warmed slopes. Surfbirds are generally scarce in the breeding areas, and this, coupled with their shyness at this time of year, has resulted in a dearth of information concerning the species' breeding biology. Few nests have ever been found, the first as recently as 1926.

LENGTH: 235-255 mm (9¼–10 in)

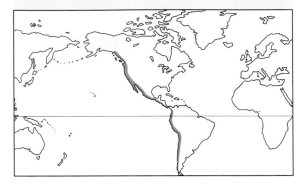

Three or four eggs are laid in a shallow natural depression lined with lichen and reindeer moss. They are buff, boldly marked with brown. The bird sits very tight on its eggs if approached by grazing animals, flying off in the animal's face at the last moment to scare it away. The chicks appear in late June or early July, and have left the breeding grounds by late July. Surfbirds are probably monogamous, with both sexes incubating the eggs.

Surfbirds winter along the Pacific coast of the Americas south to Tierra del Fuego. They

◁ *The Surfbird in summer plumage is heavily flecked with dark grey and has dark bold chevrons along its flanks. But the bright rusty-buff scapulars with black tips probably form its most conspicuous feature.*

▷ *A group of Turnstones and Surfbirds on spring migration during May, photographed in Peru. Even at this time the Surfbirds, whose yellow legs show clearly, show little sign of the summer plumage yet to come.*

are very rare away from the coast, though the species is a rare spring migrant in Texas and a vagrant to Pennsylvania. It feeds along the water's edge on rocks or pebble beaches, either alone or in groups of up to several hundred birds, often in company with Black Turnstones and Rock Sandpipers. It will sometimes also use sandy beaches, but is rarely found on mud. In the winter the Surfbird eats mussels, barnacles, and periwinkles. Non-breeding birds may spend summer in the winter quarters.

A chunky short-legged medium-sized wader, the Surfbird is often tame and lethargic. It has a short, stout, plover-like bill with a yellow-ochre base to the lower mandible. The legs are yellowish. In summer plumage the head, neck, and breast are white, very heavily flecked with dark grey to give a greyish impression at any distance. The rest of the underparts are white, with large and bold black chevrons along the flanks. The upper back is finely variegated in black and buff, but most prominent are the scapulars, which are a bright rusty-buff with black tips, forming a conspicuous patch of colour on an otherwise drab bird. The coverts and wings are dull brown.

In winter the Surfbird is superficially similar to a large, pale Black Turnstone. The head, neck, breast, and upperparts are a dull grey, with a small white patch on the chin and a few small chevrons remaining on the flanks. The juvenile Surfbird resembles the winter adult, though slightly browner, but each upperpart feather has a dark subterminal line and fine buff fringe (reminiscent of a juvenile Red Knot), and the breast is heavily marked with brown.

In flight the species shows a prominent white wingbar and wide white rump, but it lacks the white lower back and patches at the base of the wing shown by the Black Turnstone, so is easily distinguished from the species. The underwing is white, as in a Turnstone, with a little grey at the base of the primaries and on the leading edge of the wing. The species is often silent, but does give a whistled 'kee-wee-ah'.

Knot

Calidris canutus

If ever a bird typifies the large expanses of mud in tidal basins and estuaries in winter, then it is the Knot. A stout rotund medium-sized wader with short greenish-grey legs and black bill, it is well known in western Europe for its large communal gatherings and impressive collective aerial flights. It is on such occasions that most people get to know this bird. However when seen at close quarters, the Knot is less impressive. It is mainly a plain medium-grey above, with an indistinct pale supercilium, while the underparts are dull white, suffused with pale grey on the breast. In flight the bird shows an indistinct pale grey rump and a pencil-

OTHER NAMES: Red Knot, Lesser Knot
LENGTH: 230-250 mm (9–9¾ in)

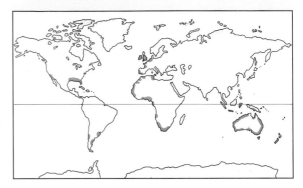

▷ *A juvenile Knot in early autumn, showing the buffish wash over its underparts.*

◁ *A winter-plumaged Knot in the foreground stands with a group of Redshanks on the Red Rocks of the Dee estuary waiting for the tide to turn.*

thin wing bar along its length; the tail and wings are a uniform grey. The seasonal change from this very drab winter dress to the rich reddish summer plumage is one of the more dramatic transformations among 'Calidrid' waders. At this time the breeding adults acquire rich orange-chestnut underparts from face to belly, with a small amount of brown spotting, especially on the paler undertail coverts. The upperparts become a mixture of black, white, chestnut, and gold. The wings, however, retain the plain grey effect throughout, giving the bird good contrast at this stage.

Knots have a fast direct flight on longish wings. As they fly they give a characteristic call which is best described as 'puk' or 'knut', hence the bird's name. On migration and at the winter quarters large numbers of birds perform amazing synchronized aerial displays on the way to and from the roost. Huge clouds of birds spiral this way and that giving the body of the flock an ever-changing form. My introduction to this species was on the west coast of Britain where appropriately, at a place called Knott-End-on-Sea, I first witnessed the distant smoke-like form of thousands of these birds as they demonstrated their aerial manoeuvrability. These flights can last for up to an hour before the birds descend and pack close together in tight roosting groups that can number many thousands of individuals. Roosts can be

several miles away from the feeding grounds. A good example is the one at Titchwell, Norfolk, to which the birds come from the Wash, one of the species' most important wintering areas. At such times these flocks are very vocal, the birds producing a continual chatter.

The preferred winter habitat of the Knot consists of large open mud flats backed by salt marsh and fields. Here, as one would expect from a predominantly inter-tidal species, the Knot feeds mainly on invertebrates, chiefly molluscs, with crustaceans, worms, and insects augmenting the diet. These are taken by a variety of methods involving the bill being inserted into the mud or sand to different depths. On the tundra breeding grounds both adult and larval insects and some plant material make up the main food items for parents and young alike.

The islands and peninsulas of the high Arctic tundra are the summer home of the species, where the breeding range is wide, but fragmented throughout the Holarctic region, with the Canadian islands, Greenland, and Siberia holding the main populations. Birds heading north in the spring tend to set off quite late in May and often make the flight in one go. During early June pairs are established on their territories, which are usually near the coast on flat, rather barren terrain. Here the male demonstrates his availability and territory by a flight display. The bird rises steeply to 30 metres (100 ft) or more on rapidly beating wings; then with wings set and tail spread, the male circles downwards, calling continuously.

The nest is usually sited on dry rocky ground among dwarf willow or other well vegetated locations. Three or four eggs are laid. They are slightly glossy, and pale olive green in colour with small brown markings. These are incubated by both parents for about 21 days. The young feed themselves but are tended by both parents at the early family stage. The female, however, leaves the group before fledging takes place at 20 days old. The male then also leaves the young to fend for themselves.

Young birds in their first autumn plumage are not unlike winter adults, but the breast is often washed with a dull pale buffish colour and the features of the upperparts are neatly fringed with silver and buff, giving a more scaly appearance.

Like other high Arctic breeding waders, the Knot's return journey south begins in late July and August. The winter dispersal from the breeding grounds takes place in four general directions. Those birds from the Canadian Arctic south of 75 degrees north, move to South America (mainly Argentina). Those from the Canadian high Arctic islands and northern Greenland migrate to western Europe. Breeding birds from north central Siberia, and possibly some from farther east, pass through western Europe to spend the winter in West Africa. Those migrating from north-east Siberia and northern Alaska find their way mainly to Australia and New Zealand. Some are also to be found in the East Indies and small numbers reach the pacific coast of South America.

In Britain a winter population of 200,000 to 300,000 birds is concentrated at all the major estuaries; many of these have earlier completed their post-migratory moult in the area of the Dutch Wadden Sea. Smaller numbers can be found in Europe and North Africa, but the other major winter concentration is the Banc d'Arguin, Mauretania, on the West African coast. Here upwards of 350,000 birds have been counted in recent years. Migrating Knots tend to be almost exclusively maritime, often taking a longer route over the sea in preference to crossing land. In Britain, very small numbers occur on passage at reservoirs and gravel pits, while inland in central Europe the species is rare.

In North America the spring migration of the Knot takes place along the eastern and western seaboards in late April and early May. The species is particularly numerous at this time of the year in the Florida peninsula, from where some birds may go inland through the prairie provinces; most undoubtedly keep to the Atlantic coast route northwards, however. Likewise autumn passage birds are to be found on both the east and west coasts as the more protracted southward movement takes place.

As with many other North American shore birds the Knot suffered at the hands of gunners and numbers were brought to an all time low in the early 1930s. Happily, since legal protection was introduced, this bird's status has greatly improved.

△ A bird photographed in Florida in spring is beginning to show the rich red colouring of its breeding plumage. This justly earns it the name of Red Knot in North America.

Sanderling
Calidris alba

Perhaps one of the most delightful of birds that feeds along the tideline, the Sanderling has a plumage and manner that make it distinctive among the small sandpipers. About the same size as the Dunlin, it is rather more thickset, with black legs (but no hind toe) and a short straight dark bill. In the winter it is one of the palest of waders, with brilliant white underparts, bright silver back, and a prominent blackish patch on the inner wing at the shoulder. The dark eye shows up well on the bird's almost white head. By May Sanderlings are moulting into their summer plumage. This comprises bright chestnut on the head, upper breast, and upperparts. The lower breast and belly remain bright white, while on the mantle and scapulars grey and white flecking is mixed in with the chestnut colour. It is only in late spring when the Sanderling could be confused with another species, but its size and behaviour should eliminate any doubt.

The Sanderling's flight is fast and sometimes erratic. When it flies it shows a conspicuous broad white bar along the wing, and bright white sides to the upper tail coverts in both summer and winter dress. When on the wing it often utters the quiet, distinctive 'twick' call.

The species prefers long sandy beaches with rough wave action on which to spend the winter. At this time the Sanderlings are very active, feeding with quick probing actions. These are interspersed with short fast runs and occasional pauses that make the bird look like a clockwork toy. Individuals often chase receding waves to pick up items that are briefly exposed before returning quickly a metre of so up the beach as the next wave crashes in. Food items consist mainly of adult and larval dipteran flies, small beetles, sandhoppers, spiders, and burrowing amphipods. On the breeding grounds the bird's animal food is supplemented by plant buds, seeds, algae, and mosses.

The breeding range of the Sanderling covers three major areas, Arctic Canada, Greenland, and Siberia. In these regions it is a bird of the flat tundra, preferring some vegetation and

LENGTH: 200-210 mm (7¾-8¼ in)

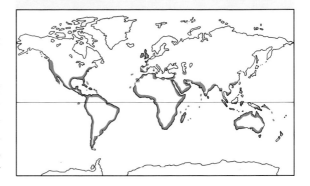

close proximity to fresh water. Arriving in June the birds remain together in small flocks until the snows have melted and nesting commences. The male's display comprises a steeply ascending flight on vibrating wings; the male calls either while circling upwards to 20 metres (over 60 ft) above the ground, or during the downward flight. On the ground the feathers are puffed out and the wings drooped. The nest is sited on the ground and consists of a small scrape sometimes partly filled with small willow leaves or other dry vegetation. The four eggs are usually greenish olive, but sometimes brownish with sparse darker spotting. Usually laid in late June, the eggs take about four weeks to hatch. Females often lay a second clutch, which is incubated solely by the male while she tends the first. All the young hatch together and feed themselves, although they are still tended by their parents. Fledging takes about 17 days, shortly after which the juveniles become independent. Before the juvenile birds moult between September and December, they have darker grey marks on the back than winter adults, giving them a rather chequered appearance. Also the cap of the juvenile has blackish streaks and some birds have a diffused yellowish-buff wash on the breast.

Sanderlings begin to leave their breeding grounds in late July through to mid-August with juveniles moving in the latter half of that

month. The bird's migrations are long-distant with the wintering range spanning the major continents from North to South America, and Europe, Africa, and Australiasia. This is a bird likely to be found on virtually any suitable beach throughout the world – it is indeed a cosmopolitan species.

When the Sanderlings pass through Britain in spring and autumn, small numbers occur at inland locations, particularly during spring. They sometimes accompany Dunlins and Ringed Plovers, pausing briefly on gravel pits or reservoirs. Not as numerous as some other shore birds, the Sanderling's winter population in Great Britain and Ireland is probably around 8,000 individuals; this represents about 80 per cent of the European wintering population. In North America this species is to be found on both east and west coasts where suitable conditions exist. Formerly shot in considerable numbers for food, it was considered an excellent table bird.

This is a very individual and interesting species and its sometimes comical behaviour gives the Sanderling great appeal to bird watchers across the globe.

△ *A group of Sanderlings in non-breeding plumage on a Florida shoreline in early spring.*

▽ *The Sanderling is a familiar shorebird on sandy beaches. This one is in its summer plumage.*

Semipalmated Sandpiper

Calidris pusilla

One of a group of seven small shorebirds known as 'peeps' in North America and 'stints' in Britain, the Semipalmated Sandpiper shares a special feature with the Western Sandpiper – partial webbing between its toes.

The Semipalmated Sandpiper breeds from the mouth of the River Yukon on the west coast of Alaska east to Victoria Island, around Hudson Bay and on to Baffin Island and Labrador. The preferred habitat is wet coastal and low inland tundra. Semipalmated Sandpipers arrive on their breeding grounds in small, quarrelsome flocks. There may be 90 per cent snow cover on arrival, but the flocks soon break up and the males quickly establish territories. They attract females in an aerial display, flying at low level and often hovering, all the time giving a monotonous trilling 'ree-ree-ree' or 'di-jip-di-jip-di-jip'. Pairing soon takes place and nesting is quickly underway.

The nest is in a depression located on a hummock or knoll, often by water or on damp ground, or sometimes hidden among willows near a pond or river. It is lined with grass and willow leaves. Four eggs are laid. These are dull white to olive-buff, and there are reddish brown speckles that often coalesce into bigger

Length: 130-150mm (5-6 in)

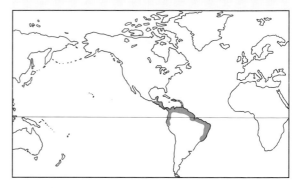

△ A Semipalmated Sandpiper at its nest on the Canadian tundra.

◁ A Semipalmated Sandpiper on its nesting ground calls to its mate.

blotches at the larger end of the egg. Both male and female incubate, for 19 or 20 days, and both attend the young, although the female may leave the breeding area shortly after hatching. The chicks fledge after 16 days and gather into flocks prior to departure.

As is often the case, birds from different areas use different routes south across North America. Alaskan birds migrate through the Great Plains, but may occur further east, especially in the fall. The central Canadian population moves south-east to hit the Atlantic coast between the Gulf of St Lawrence and Virginia, where there is a concentration of up to 100,000 birds in the upper Bay of Fundy in early August. They then head out across the western Atlantic. Eastern Canadian birds also move via the Gulf of St Lawrence across the Atlantic direct to the Caribbean. The species is rare in the west and very rare north of California; in California itself, Semipalmated Sandpipers are seen on the coast in the fall, but in spring they tend to be encountered inland.

Semipalmated Sandpipers winter on the Pacific coast of Central America north to Guatemala, in the West Indies, and in coastal South America south to Peru and Uruguay. A very few winter in southern Florida. The species is coastal in winter, and often occurs in large flocks on estuary mudflats.

In the spring, the central Canadian population joins Alaskan birds on migration through the Great Plains, while east Canadian birds follow the Atlantic coast northwards. The species is a vagrant to Chile, Argentina, Paraguay, and the Falkland Islands, as well as to western Europe.

The Semipalmated Sandpiper is a typical peep, noticeably smaller than a Dunlin, vivacious, and often tame. It can be distinguished from the Least Sandpiper by its blackish, rather than pale legs. Distinguishing it from the Western Sandpiper requires more care because both birds have black legs and partial webbing between the toes. One of the most useful features for identification in all plumages is the bill. The Semipalmated Sandpiper's bill is usually short and straight with a deep base. It is blunt-tipped in profile and in good head-on

views usually shows an expansion of the tip.

In breeding plumage the Semipalmated Sandpiper is the dullest of the dark-legged peeps, the upperparts a mixture of black, buff and grey, never showing the prominent rusty scapulars typical of the Western Sandpiper. It has an extensive streaked breast band, but lacks the Western's heavy chevrons on the flanks. In winter, it is grey above with a lightly streaked breast band, and is practically identical to the Western and only really distinguishable by bill-shape and call. Juveniles are variable in appearance, but are usually a neat, scaly, dull-brown above and may resemble Baird's Sandpiper. Compared to the Western Sandpiper the scapulars have duller and less rusty fringes and the supercilium is better defined, giving a more capped appearance with a dark line through the eye. Compared to the Little Stint, the Semipalmated Sandpiper is duller, the lower scapulars have dark anchor-shaped centres, and it lacks white Vs on the upperparts or a split supercilium.

In flight, like all peeps, the Semipalmated Sandpiper shows a narrow whitish wingbar and white sides to the rump and tail. The calls are generally harsher and lower-pitched than the Western Sandpiper's. They are usually described as a 'churk' or 'chrup'. Sometimes there is also a 'chirrup', reminiscent of a Pectoral Sandpiper.

The identification of Semipalmated Sandpipers and Western Sandpipers can still prove extremely difficult. However, viewed at close range using one of the newer, high-quality telescopes, a typical Semipalmated Sandpiper can be identified with much greater confidence than seemed likely a few years ago. The pattern of records almost certainly reflects this improved knowledge rather than a real change in the species' status: before 1980 only ten reports from Great Britain were officially accepted yet between 1980 and 1986 a further 38 individuals were successfully identified, with as many as ten in 1984. Thus, from being an apparently very rare visitor, the Semipalmated Sandpiper is currently the tenth most regular of the Nearctic waders reaching Britain and Ireland. Of the 38 individuals since 1980, 24 were seen in Ireland, nine in south-west England.

Western Sandpiper

Calidris mauri

This is the largest of the group of birds known as the peeps. It resembles the Dunlin, but can be distinguished by size as well as by many plumage features. It shares with the Semi-palmated Sandpiper a special feature in this group, partial webbing between the toes.

The Western Sandpiper has a restricted breeding range, confined to northern and western Alaska and the east coast of the Chukotskiy peninsula in extreme eastern Siberia. It nests on better-drained tundra, from sea level to the lower slopes of the mountains. It prefers ridges and hummocks of heath interspersed with low-lying marshes, small pools, and lakes. Suitable areas support a remarkably high population of this bird, with pairs holding tiny territories at close quarters to their neighbours. They feed in both the wet and the drier heath areas, mostly on insects, especially flies.

The species arrives on its breeding grounds in mid-May, and at first the birds gather in small flocks. Disputes between rival males quickly break up these flocks, and the birds often return to the previous year's territory. The male advertises his presence by singing and calling. The song is a series of ascending notes followed by a buzzing trill ('. . . tweer-tweer-tweer . . .'), performed during an aerial display. He either patrols the area slowly or uses a fast, low-level flight interrupted by a stall and a steep glide to the ground.

The females generally arrive on the breeding grounds a few days later than the males, and courtship consists of neck preening, nest-scraping and a pose in which the tail is held vertically. Once the pair bond has been formed it will persist throughout the breeding season. The pair is monogamous and both sexes take an active part in family life. The nest is usually well-hidden under a small bush. Four eggs are incubated for 21 days and the chicks develop rapidly and fledge after about 19 days.

On passage the whole population, including the birds from Siberia, moves south through the Pacific states and provinces. The birds appear from early July, but the peak is not

LENGTH: 140-170 mm (5½–6¾ in)

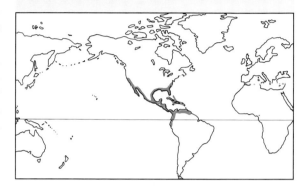

reached until September. Most follow the coast, but some move inland in the coastal states, stopping off at any suitable wetland. Small numbers also move south-east across the U.S.A., and occur on the Atlantic coast from Massachusetts southwards. Spring passage through the States spans early April to June.

Western Sandpipers winter on the Pacific coast from California south to Peru, on the

△ *A Western Sandpiper in summer plumage.*

Gulf of Mexico, on the Atlantic coast north to New England, in the Caribbean, and on the Atlantic coast of South America east to Surinam. They occur in large flocks out on the open flats, often in company with other small waders. Many of the birds spend the summer in their winter quarters. The Western Sandpiper is a vagrant to Japan, Australia, and Western Europe, but there have only been six records in Britain and Ireland.

The Western Sandpiper is difficult to distinguish from the Semipalmated Sandpiper. (The Least Sandpiper, the third American peep, can be distinguished from the web-footed pair by its pale yellowish or greenish legs, as well as its smaller size, and short, fine bill.) The appearance of the Western Sandpiper often recalls the Dunlin, as it is relatively longer-legged and longer-billed than a Semipalmated Sandpiper with an angular head, thick neck and heavy 'shoulders'. It is more prone to wade in shallow water, probing with its bill.

In breeding plumage the important points to look for are the rusty-orange centres to the upper scapulars, and the rufous patch on the crown and ear-coverts, contrasting with the grey coverts, nape, and mantle. The breast is heavily marked with dark streaks, often extending as a distinctive line of chevrons along the flanks.

Juveniles are also relatively distinct from the Semipalmated Sandpiper, being less scaly and less uniform, with bright chestnut fringes to the upper scapulars and greyish lower scapulars, a contrast which Semipalmated Sandpipers always lack. Westerns are also pale-faced, with a beady eye, less well-defined supercilium, and dark eyestripe. Any rufous colouring on the crown is duller than the scapulars (the reverse of the bright Semipalmateds). In winter plumage the two species are nearly identical, except for size, bill-shape and call.

As well as being longer than that of other peeps; the Western Sandpiper's bill usually has a slightly decurved, drooped tip. The shape recalls a Dunlin's bill rather than the typically stubby bill of the Semipalmated Sandpiper, but on the east coast, female Semipalmateds tend

△A Western Sandpiper in non-breeding plumage requires careful scrutiny to distinguish it from the very similar Semipalmated Sandpiper. This bird has a typically longer, heavy, decurved bill which aids identification.

to have long, even slightly drooped bills, rendering the distinction less useful. The typical call is a thin, squeaky 'jeet' or 'cheep', recalling the White-rumped Sandpiper, but shorter and less sibilant.

The history of this species in the British Isles has proved more problematical than possibly any other American wader. Of the seven officially accepted records, the first (on Fair Isle between May 28 and June 3, 1956) was trapped yet initially identified as a Semipalmated Sandpiper, while the fourth (in the Isles of Scilly in August 1969) was originally claimed – but rejected – as a Semipalmated and only officially accepted in 1984 after a re-examination of photographs revealed it to be a moulting adult Western. Problems still persist, and a small sandpiper which wintered in Suffolk in 1982–83, and which was regarded by many observers as a Western, has been accepted by the British Bird Rarities Committee as a long-billed Semipalmated Sandpiper.

In addition to the Fair Isle and Scilly records, Western Sandpipers have appeared in County Wicklow in 1960, County Kerry in 1961, Essex and Devon in 1973, and Cheshire in 1975. With no acceptable occurrence during the past decade, the next unequivocal individual is eagerly awaited.

Little Stint

Calidris minuta

This compact, active little sandpiper is plentiful in the western and central Palearctic, where it breeds on the arctic tundra of Scandinavia and northern Russia. Outside the breeding season it is found mostly around the coast, though a few individuals do occur regularly inland. Most winter in Africa, around the Mediterranean, or in India.

Little Stints are noticeably smaller than the far commoner Dunlin and they have shorter, finer bills. Often they are tame and easily approached. The breeding birds have rufous heads, necks, and breasts, with brown streaks. Their black back feathers also have bright rufous edges, which add to their smart appearance, and there is often a creamy edge to the mantle. Their underparts are white, except for a buff wash and slight streaking on the upper breast. In winter, the adult birds are basically a brownish-grey above, but the intensity of colour varies with abrasion, as the feathers have dark centres and pale edges. Their streaked heads show white supercilia, while the underparts are again white, except for some light grey streaking on the breast. Juveniles have dark rufous crowns, which are accentuated by lateral white stripes and bold, white

LENGTH: 120-140 mm (4¾–5½ in)

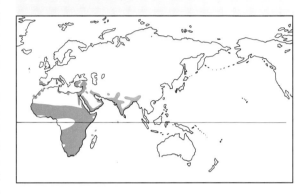

supercilia. Their napes are grey and their dark upper feathers are fringed rufous and white, with very distinctive white edges to the mantle which form a V on their backs. The underparts are again white, except for buff breasts which are streaked at the sides. In all plumages the legs are black. In flight the little stint recalls a small Dunlin, with clear white wing bars and white sides to the rump and upper tail. They are fluent, agile fliers, with flocks twisting and turning in unison. Their usual call is a short, low-pitched 'tit' or 'chit'.

▷ A juvenile Little Stint photographed in Britain during September.

In western Europe confusion is most likely with the similarly sized Temminck's Stint, but the latter looks even smaller in the field, has paler legs and longer wings, and shows a different tail pattern in flight. Three very rare vagrants to Europe, namely the Red-necked Stint and the Semipalmated and Western Sandpipers, are also very similar. Indeed it requires great care and skill to tell these three species from the Little Stint or from one another. Little Stints, however, are equally rare as vagrants to North America.

The Little Stints move northwards to their breeding grounds between April and early June, but few pass through Britain at this time. The birds are neither faithful to particular sites nor territorial, but both sexes indulge in display flights and song. Most nest on drier ground at low altitude. Their breeding cycle, evolved to suit the short tundra summer, sees males and females simultaneously incubating separate clutches. The nest is a shallow cup lined with leaves and pieces of grass, and it is sited on open ground near water. The four pale green eggs boldly blotched with brown are laid in late June or early July, and incubation lasts for three weeks. The males incubate the first clutch and the females the second.

By July the adults are already returning south, and they are followed in late August by the juveniles. The birds' passage is protracted and often continues until the end of October. It also follows a more westerly route than that in spring and this brings many more birds through Britain. Most of these are juveniles. A few birds over-winter in Britain.

On migration Little Stints are gregarious and often form noisy flocks in association with Dunlins and Curlew Sandpipers. Despite their sociable nature, they will sometimes defend a good feeding territory from other small waders. Migrating birds often stop over in sheltered creeks, at inland waters and along river banks to feed and rest. Some winter inland in Africa, but most resort to the coast, frequenting soft, muddy backwaters and secluded inlets.

Little Stints prefer to feed on exposed mud rather than in shallow water, though they will wade, as well as creeping, walking, and running. Their fast feeding action is due to their taking food from, or just beneath, the surface rather than probing. Their diet mainly comprises invertebrates such as insects, beetles, worms, and small molluscs and crustaceans.

◁ *This Little Stint in non-breeding plumage is wintering in Africa.*

Temminck's Stint
Calidris temminckii

At all seasons this tiny, mouse-like wader is readily distinguished from all the other small sandpipers and stints by its plain, dull appearance and distinctive call. Because of the overlap in their ranges, confusion is most likely with a Little Stint. However, Temminck's Stint, although fractionally the larger, is the slimmer and more attenuated of the two birds. Its tail projects beyond its closed wings, its bill is shorter and finer, and its legs are shorter too. In the field this combination of features can easily create the illusion that Temminck's Stint is the smaller of the two birds. Unlike the Little Stint, Temminck's Stint never shows a strong supercilium and never has pale Vs on its back. Furthermore its legs are pale rather than black, dull green or yellow being the usual colours. In flight Temminck's Stint shows a shorter, narrower white wing-bar. It also has white sides to the rump and distinctive white, rather than grey, outer tail feathers, which are most obvious on take-off and landing. This combination makes the tail appear long and narrow in flight.

At no time is Temminck's Stint a brightly coloured or distinctively patterned bird. Indeed, the plain head and upperparts and clouded breast at times recall a dull, miniature Common Sandpiper. In breeding plumage the mantle and scapular feathers have black centres and buff edges, which give a darker, drabber appearance than the Little Stint. At this time of the year, the head and breast are mottled and streaked brown on a grey background, the chin and belly are white, and there is an indistinct pale supercilium. Non-breeding birds are more uniform, being dark grey-brown above with dusky grey-brown streaking to the head and breast and a more extensive pale chin. As with the Common Sandpiper, the breast streaking is palest in the centre and most extensive on the sides. Temminck's Stint has the darkest breast of any small sandpiper or stint in winter plumage. At a distance the juveniles also look uniform. However, dark sub-terminal edges and buff fringes to the

LENGTH: 130-150 mm (5-6 in)

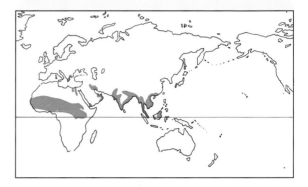

feathers give them a warmer brown appearance and at close quarters these feathers give a slightly scaly look to the upperparts. Juveniles also have very fine, pale buff streaking on the head and breast, a white chin and belly, and an indistinct, pale supercilium.

When flushed, Temminck's Stint frequently 'towers' like a Common Snipe. Though fast, the bird's flight is fluttering and erratic. The call is a quick, dry 'tirirririri' rattle, reminiscent of the 'reel' of a Grasshopper Warbler.

The bird's main breeding range stretches across the arctic tundra from Norway to north-

△ *A four- or five-day-old Temminck's Stint chick.*

eastern Siberia, but a few individuals nest farther south in southern Scandinavia. There is also a small population, averaging three or four pairs a year, which maintains a tenuous foothold in Scotland. Birds returning to their breeding territories pass northwards through Europe between mid-April and mid-May. By the end of May the males are displaying over their breeding grounds. They circle and hover with a moth-like flight while delivering their trilling song. Most territories are on the short tundra turf or the sandy, gravelly shorelines of fresh-water pools and their islets. Although they range from the coastal plains to areas 1,000 m (3,300 ft) above sea-level, most of these birds breed in lush, sheltered valleys with plenty of mossy bogs, damp grassland, and dwarf willow scrub. Some pairs even nest on improved grassland close to human habitation.

The nest itself is a shallow depression, which the female lines scantily with grass and a few leaves. Breeding involves bigamy by both sexes in a rapid, double-clutch system. Each male pairs with two females and fertilizes one clutch of eggs from each. Each female pairs with two males and lays a clutch of four greenish eggs with dark markings in each territory. The males then incubate and tend the chicks of the first clutch and the females look after the second. Incubation lasts three weeks and the young fledge a little over two weeks later.

The southward passage of Temminck's Stint is quite leisurely. It begins when the adults leave in July and continues until the juveniles reach their wintering grounds in October. Juveniles leave the breeding areas two or three weeks after the adults. The main passage through western Europe occurs between late July and early October. Temminck's Stints migrate overland, pausing at all kinds of inland waters, washlands, and irrigated areas. They are much rarer on the coast, but are occasionally encountered in sheltered, muddy backwaters and on saltmarshes.

Similar habitats are frequented throughout the winter. The main wintering areas are in the northern tropics, but a few remain in Europe, occasionally as far north as England. In America, the species has been recorded as a vagrant in both spring and fall on the Aleutian Islands and in western Alaska, St Lawrence Islands, the Pribilofs, and Vancouver, British Columbia.

Insects and their larvae, especially beetles and flies, are the birds' main food. These are taken from vegetation or the surface of mud with a deliberate pecking action. Temminck's Stints seldom probe. When feeding, they run and walk less than Little Stints, but cover less ground more slowly and methodically. When approached they often crouch, which adds to their small, mouse-like appearance. Although less gregarious than either the Little Stint or the Red-necked Stint, one or two hundred Temminck's Stints may gather at favoured feeding sites with plenty of mud. Generally in Britain though, Temminck's Stints are only seen singly or in very small groups.

▷ A Temminck's Stint on its display post.

Least Sandpiper
Calidris minutilla

Marginally the smallest shorebird in the world, the Least Sandpiper is usually easily distinguished from both the Western and the Semipalmated Sandpipers by its lack of partial webbing between the toes and, more importantly, in the field, by its pale legs. The Least Sandpiper forms a species pair with the similarly pale-legged Long-toed Stint of Asia, which is a vagrant to western Alaska and Oregon and regularly appears in the western Aleutians.

The Least Sandpiper breeds from western Alaska through northern Canada south to north-west British Columbia, northern Ontario and Novia Scotia, and east to Southampton Island and northern Labrador. It avoids very dry tundra or areas far from trees, and favours marshes within spruce forests, sedge meadows, flat sandy islands, and boggy tundra with moss hummocks and grass tussocks. The bird's spring passage across the U.S.A., is quite late, peaking in the first three weeks of May. The birds move over the Caribbean to the Gulf of Mexico and Florida, before flying up the Atlantic coast, arriving on the breeding grounds in early June.

The male advertises his territory by flying up at a steep angle to about 15 metres (50 or 60 ft), giving a series of short calls. The bird then performs a prolonged undulating flight, alternating fluttering wingbeats with glides on outstretched wings. All the time the song is given, a monotonous repetition of single notes at half-second intervals. Finally the male stoops or parachutes to earth.

The females are attracted to the territory by this display, and mating soon occurs. The nest is a shallow depression lined with dry leaves or grass, and is usually sited on a small hummock or at the base of a willow. Four eggs are laid, which are pale buff in colour, spotted and blotched, sometimes very heavily, with brown. The male takes the major share of incubation, which lasts for 19 to 23 days, and cares for the young birds.

The species winters from the southern

OTHER NAME: American Stint
LENGTH: 130-150 mm (5-6 in)

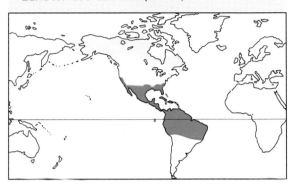

U.S.A., to central South America, occurring on both coasts from Oregon and North Carolina southwards, down to northern Chile and central Brazil. The migrants move south in a broad front from mid-July onwards, peak numbers occurring in August and September. Many move south-east out over the Atlantic from the Maritimes and New England to the Lesser Antilles and north-east South America; others move across central North America to arrive farther west in South America or to winter in the Gulf of Mexico and the Caribbean. The Least Sandpiper is a vagrant to Japan and Western Europe.

The Least Sandpiper is less coastal in the winter and on migration than other peeps, occurring in the upper reaches of salt-marshes, as well as inland on the margins of fresh water and in wet grazing meadows. The closed confines of the bird's habitat are reflected in its escape behaviour: when flushed, it 'towers', that is, rises steeply from the ground.

The Least Sandpiper has a short, fine bill, which curves down gradually throughout its length. Its short neck and hunched posture give it a creeping, mouse-like appearance. Like all peeps it has a white wingbar and sides to the rump. The call is a shrill, high, rolling 'kreeep' or disyllabic 'kre-ep', as well as a lower pitched, vibrant 'prrrt'.

In breeding plumage this species looks dark

◁A Least Sandpiper takes a rest during its migratory flight.

▷A Least Sandpiper on its Canadian breeding ground.

brown at a distance, with a dingy, well-streaked head and breast. Closer inspection reveals a fine pale V at the sides of the mantle and a rusty tone to the crown, ear-coverts, and upperparts. There is no prominent supercilium.

In winter plumage the species is a dark brownish-grey, much browner than the Semipalmated Sandpiper or Western Sandpiper. Its dark feather centres produce a slightly blotchy effect. There is a neat dusky breast band and quite a prominent pale supercilium.

In juvenile plumage the Least Sandpiper is rather brighter, and may recall the Little Stint or a tiny Pectoral Sandpiper in its general plumage pattern. The dark upperparts and complete breastband are noticeable, and in fresh plumage there are two white Vs on the upperparts.

The pale legs – yellowish, greenish, or brownish – distinguish Least Sandpiper from the other North American peeps, but it is easy to misidentify birds with their legs covered in mud. The Temminck's Stint and the Long-toed Stint both have pale legs, and the Least Sandpiper has to be carefully distinguished from the latter.

The Long-toed Stint is much brighter in breeding plumage, with broad rusty-orange fringes to the feathers of its upperparts. Its broad whitish supercilium sharply sets off its rufous-streaked 'cap'. In juvenile plumage it is more similar, but the Least Sandpiper's wings look warmer and browner. In winter the dark centres to the upperparts are more diffuse on the Least Sandpiper compared with the neater blackish centres and wider pale fringes on Long-toed Stint. In all plumages the head pattern is subtly different. The Least Sandpiper has a duller supercilium which meets over the bill, a dark line across the lores, and an isolated dark area on the rear border of the ear coverts.

Before the general clarification during the past ten years of the characteristics of stints and peeps, this species was successfully identified in the British Isles rather more often than the Semipalmated Sandpiper. Between 1958 and 1976 there were 15 acceptable records of the Least Sandpiper and only five of the Semipalmated Sandpiper. But in the ten subsequent years this pattern has changed dramatically and the corresponding figures were eight and 42. Thus, the Semipalmated Sandpiper averaged more than four records per year in the decade up to 1986 while the Least Sandpiper remained less than annual. Much better understanding of the field characteristics of Semipalmated Sandpiper is undoubtedly the main reason for this change. It may be that the appearances of Least Sandpiper are increasing, for it occurred in six of the last ten years and four of the last five, with three sightings in 1984. The most recent of these records involved an individual in

Cornwall from February 9 to April 10, 1986 – it had presumably wintered on this side of the Atlantic.

Of the grand total of 29 individuals, 12 were recorded in Devon or Cornwall, seven in Ireland, and two in Scotland. For such a rare visitor, it is notable that three of the records were well inland, in Berkshire, Cambridgeshire and Staffordshire. As with nearly all American waders, the vast majority of birds arrived between August and October but, as well as the apparent February arrival noted above, there were single birds in May, June and July.

△ *A Least Sandpiper on its northward spring migration. It was photographed on a Florida beach.*

However, the sighting at Marazion, Cornwall, on June 7 and 8, 1970 is currently being re-examined as it has subsequently been claimed as a Long-toed Stint.

White-rumped Sandpiper
Calidris fuscicollis

Although often grouped with the 'peeps', the White-rumped Sandpiper is noticeably larger and longer-winged, and is more logically compared with Baird's Sandpiper. It is generally greyer than Baird's Sandpiper, with more colourful breeding and juvenile plumages. Notably, its white rump helps to distinguish it at all times from both Baird's Sandpiper and the various peeps.

Slightly smaller than a Dunlin, the White-rumped Sandpiper has a long, low outline as a result of its relatively short legs and its long wings that project well past the tail-tip when the bird is at rest. The short, straight bill is blackish in colour, often with a dull green or yellow base. The legs are black. The bird has a narrow whitish wingbar and the white 'rump' is in fact a white band on the uppertail, not the true rump. The bird's call is a strange, quiet, high-pitched squeak, a 'jeet', often given in a couplet, and usually likened to the squeak of a mouse.

In breeding plumage the White-rumped Sandpiper is mottled with buff, grey, and black above, with a rusty tinge to the crown, ear coverts, and scapulars. The throat and breast are streaked and spotted with black, the streaks becoming larger black Vs on the flanks. In winter plumage it is dun-grey above, and much greyer and with a more prominent supercilium than Baird's Sandpiper. The breast is washed grey, with fine darker streaking.

The juvenile is scaly above, but less evenly patterned than Baird's Sandpiper: there are prominent splashes of chestnut on the fringes of the feathers of the back and crown, a white 'brace' on the sides of the mantle, and a contrastingly grey hind-neck and breast. The latter is well-streaked, and a few of the streaks extend on to the flanks. A whitish supercilium sets off the chestnut cap.

The White-rumped Sandpiper breeds in Arctic Canada from northern Mackenzie to southern Baffin Island, and occasionally in northern Alaska. Spring passage northwards is more westerly than the bird's movement in the

OTHER NAME: Bonaparte's Sandpiper
LENGTH: 150-180 mm (6-7 in)

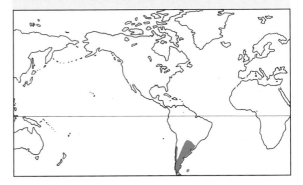

△ *A White-rumped Sandpiper in breeding plumage.*

fall. The birds overfly the Greater Antilles and Gulf of Mexico and cross the Great Plains. The species is very rare on the Atlantic coast in spring, and it is an infrequent visitor to the interior of the Pacific states. Peak passage is in late April and May.

The birds arrive on their breeding grounds in late May or early June, when these are still largely snow-bound. The breeding areas are on wet lowland and upland tundra with plenty of grassy tussocks and hummocks, near a river, lake, or group of pools. They are also usually near the sea – the White-rumped Sandpiper feeds mostly on sea-beaches.

The male has several displays to attract females to his territory, including a 'Sharp-tailed Grouse dance' in which he runs around on the ground, with the rump exposed, the tail slightly raised, and the wings held stiffly out-ward giving a low buzzing or growling call. Aerial displays include a horizontal flight 15 to 25 metres (50 to 80 ft) above the ground, followed by a period of shallow wingbeats. These are accompanied by a reeling call interspersed with a pig-like 'ng-oik', and followed by a glide back to the ground.

Once mating has taken place, the pair splits up and the male takes no further part in family life. The species is polygamous, and the male will mate with as many females as he can attract to his territory. The female sites her nest on a tussock or mound, well-concealed in a deep depression in soil or moss, and lined with grasses and dead leaves. Four eggs are laid, greenish to olive-buff, blotched and spotted with brown. They are incubated for 21 or 22 days, and the young fledge after a further 16 or 17 days.

◁A vagrant to Britain, this adult White-rumped Sandpiper was photographed in Cornwall, England in 1982.

▷A White-rumped Sandpiper broods its newly hatched youngster on its North American breeding grounds.

The White-rumped Sandpiper's eventual departure from the breeding areas is leisurely. The males leave early in July, but the juveniles do not arrive in the U.S.A., until late September and may still be passing through in December. Most of the birds move through interior North America, then along the Atlantic flyway and across the west Atlantic to northern South America. There is a strong south-east movement across Canada to the Atlantic coast, with low numbers north of New England and no fall records for the Pacific states. On passage to the winter quarters, lake shores, wet pasture, sea beaches, and even stubble fields are used.

The White-rumped Sandpiper winters in South America, mainly east of the Andes and south of the equator, mostly from southern Brazil to Tierra del Fuego and the Falkland Islands. A few are found north to Venezuela. Lagoons, brackish swamps, and fresh-water margins are frequented, and the species can occur in large flocks on mudflats in winter. The bird is a vagrant to western Europe, recorded annually in Britain in the fall, and there are also records from Spitsbergen and Franz Josef Land. In Britain and Ireland it had been recorded on 293 occasions up to 1986, with as many as 29 records in 1984, making it the third most regular Nearctic wader appearing in Britain. The increase between 1958 and 1986 is slightly above average. It seems probable that a number of White-rumped Sandpipers that crossed the Atlantic in earlier years are now regularly migrating north and south on this side of the Atlantic. Of the 155 individuals recorded since 1977, at least 47 (30 per cent) were adults on the east coast of Britain.

Baird's Sandpiper

Calidris bairdii

Slightly larger than a stint or peep, and smaller than a Dunlin, this bird has a long-winged, short-legged appearance and horizontal carriage that it shares only with the White-rumped Sandpiper. It is an uncommon migrant over much of North America, and is unusual among the smaller sandpipers in often favouring habitats away from water.

Generally buffer than a White-rumped Sandpiper, and lacking the bright tones of that species in breeding and juvenile plumage, Baird's Sandpiper always shows a neat, finely streaked breast band and unstreaked flanks. It is generally quite plain, with a less well marked supercilium than the White-rumped Sandpiper. At all times its fine-tipped bill and legs are blackish and in flight it shows a narrow wingbar and narrow white sides to the tail, but no white rump. The call is a low, raspy, trilling 'preeet' or 'kreeep'.

Summer adults are generally quite 'mealy' in appearance above, their plumage consisting of a mixture of buff, black, and grey, with large black centres to the central scapulars. In winter they are grey-brown above with fine pale scaling that is only obvious if you can get a good view of the bird. The juvenile is a dull grey-

LENGTH: 140-170 mm (5½-6¾ in)

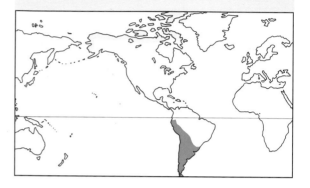

brown, with neat buff or whitish fringes to the features of the upperparts giving a distinctive scaly appearance. The larger Pectoral Sandpiper is also often found in dry-land habitats, but has a better defined and more heavily streaked breast band as well as paler legs.

Baird's Sandpiper breeds in the high Arctic, from the Chukotskiy peninsula in north-east Siberia across northern Alaska and Canada east to Baffin Island and north-west Greenland. The wintering range is in South America, south of the equator, from the high

◁A Baird's Sandpiper settles down to incubate its eggs.

▷A juvenile Baird's Sandpiper.

Andes in southern Ecuador south to sea level on Tierra del Fuego.

This bird has an unusual migration that is well inland and concentrated along the backbone of the continents – the Rockies and the Andes. The species begins to depart from its winter home in early March, and undertakes long-distance flights, passing over central America without stopping and moving northwards through the interior of North America in April and early May. It is therefore rare on the coasts in spring. The breeding areas are occupied from late May to mid-June. On migration and in winter Baird's Sandpiper favours fresh water margins and damp fields, as well as dry areas of short cropland and pasture, up to 4,000 metres (13,000 ft) above sea level. When found on the coast, it tends to be on the upper part of the beach. It pecks, rather than probes, when feeding, and is usually found in small flocks.

On arrival at its Arctic breeding ground, the species occupies the drier, more elevated section of the tundra, among the sand dunes or salt-water lagoons. Sometimes it is found on mountainsides well away from the coast. The males display in flight, rising up at a steep angle to 10 to 20 metres (30 to 60 ft) above the ground and giving the song, a guttural, frog-like trill, near the apex of the climb. The song is also given in the subsequent downward glide, when the wings are held high above the back.

The nest is placed in short vegetation – grass, moss, or lichen – and is a relatively exposed scrape lined with lichen and fragments of plant material. Four eggs are laid, and these are buff-coloured, rather thickly spotted with brown. The pair is monogamous, and both sexes incubate and take part in care of the chicks. The male is the most diligent, especially in the latter part of the chicks' development. Incubation takes 19 to 21 days and fledging 20 days.

The adults leave the Arctic in late July, moving south through Canada to the west of Hudson's Bay and on to the prairies of the northern U.S.A. Here they stop off to feed and put on fat to fuel a non-stop flight of some 6,500 km (4,000 miles), via a Great Circle over the eastern Pacific to the Andes. Most adults

have left the U.S.A., by mid-August, taking about five weeks to complete their journey of 14,500 km (9,000 miles).

The juveniles migrate at a more leisurely pace, peaking in the U.S.A., in late August and arriving in Patagonia in early October. They move south on a broader front than the adults. A few reach the Atlantic and Pacific coasts, and they are common in Texas and Arizona, though still scarce in Canada east of Hudson Bay, and very rare in the south-east U.S.A., and West Indies. The species is a vagrant to Hawaii, the Galapagos, Australia, New Zealand, Japan, Sakhalin, and the Kuril Islands, and in the east to South Africa, Senegal and western Europe, where it is annual during the autumn in Britain and Ireland. In fact Baird's Sandpiper is the seventh most-numerous of the American waders to be recorded in Britain and Ireland. Up to 1986 a grand total of 124 had been identified, of

△ *A vagrant to Britain and Ireland, this Baird's Sandpiper is one of the 30 or so noted in recent years. It is an adult moulting into its winter plumage.*

which 60 were since 1977. It has occurred annually since 1969, though numbers varied from single individuals in several years to as many as ten in 1980 and 1982. The annual mean of six over the past ten years is twice that for the preceding twenty years, an increase in line with that for American waders as a whole.

Of the 31 individuals recorded between 1982 and 1986, nine were in Ireland, six in south-west England and five in Scotland. All but one (a May record from Norfolk) arrived between August and October, with 23 (74 per cent) in September. One which appeared at Staines Reservoir, Surrey, on October 14, 1982 remained until April 24, 1983, a remarkable event as this species normally winters in South America south of the equator.

Pectoral Sandpiper

Calidris melanotos

The Pectoral Sandpiper breeds from eastern Siberia to Hudson Bay, and nearly the entire population winters in South America. It is, however, the most frequent transatlantic vagrant in Western Europe, with birds almost certainly crossing all of North America and the Atlantic rather than using the shorter, direct route from Siberia. As it breeds in the U.S.S.R., as far west as the Taimyr Peninsula, however, it is possible that some of the birds recorded in Britain have approached from the north-east across Eurasia.

The Pectoral is a medium-sized sandpiper, the males being significantly larger than the females. At all times it is marked by a neat, well-streaked breast or pectoral band, which is characteristically sharply cut-off from the white underparts. This feature, together with the olive to yellow legs, distinguishes this species from other birds, except for Cox's Sandpiper. The Pectoral Sandpiper's bill is of medium length and slightly down-curved. The basal third of the bill is olive-coloured.

Adults in breeding plumage have a mixture of black, grey, and buff upperparts, with black scapulars neatly fringed with buff. There is a white V at the sides of the mantle. The head is rather plain, with little or no supercilium. The males have a sooty-brown breast, mottled with white. In winter plumage, both sexes have duller brown feather centres with dingier, ill-defined fringes. The juvenile is similar to the summer adult, but has rather darker feather centres and better defined white, russet, and buff fringes, giving a neater and crisper effect. There are usually two prominent white Vs on the side of the mantle and scapulars.

In flight the Pectoral Sandpiper has a narrow white wingbar. It has a black centre to the rump and tail and shows a prominent white area at the sides of the rump. The call is a harsh, reedy 'churk' or 'prrp'.

The Sharp-tailed Sandpiper is regularly seen on passage in western Alaska and is a rare fall migrant to the west coast, with well over 100 records. Similar in size and structure to a

LENGTH: 190-230 mm (7½-9 in)

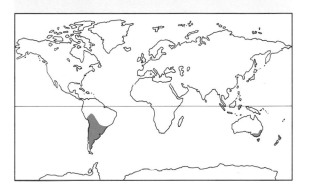

△ A North American breeding bird, the Pectoral Sandpiper is now recorded annually in Britain.

Pectoral Sandpiper, it always ·lacks the crisply demarcated breast band. The breeding birds have chevrons all the way over their under-parts, while the juveniles have a virtually unstreaked breast washed with bright buff, a conspicuous white supercilium, and bright rusty cap. Cox's Sandpiper, described for science as recently as 1982 from birds collected in Australia, was recorded in Massachusetts in fall 1987. It shows similarities with the Pectoral Sandpiper including a neat breast band and a long, dark, curved Dunlin-like bill.

The Pectoral Sandpiper breeds in Siberia from the Taimyr Peninsula eastwards, and in North America from northern Alaska to Southampton Island, the western shore of Hudson Bay and Banks, Victoria and Prince of Wales Islands. Wet, flat tundra is its favoured breeding habitat, both on the coast and in the foothills. Areas with prominent mounds or hummocks, low ridges adjacent to ponds, and marshy basins are popular.

The birds move northwards through North America from March to early June, mostly in the interior and to the west of Hudson Bay, but not on the West Coast. On arrival the male establishes his territory with a remarkable display, making use of a pendulous, fat-filled sack on his breast. He uses this to produce a hooting 'oo-af' call, given at the rate of four per second for up to 40 seconds. The male produces this call on the ground, with drooped wings and raised tail, and in a low-level display flight. The Pectoral Sandpiper is promiscuous – the males will mate with as many females as they can attract to their territory, but take no further part in family life.

The nest is on the ground, well-hidden in grass or a sedge tussock, substantially made of grasses, leaves and lichens. Four greenish-to-buff eggs are laid, heavily blotched with browns. Incubation takes 21 to 23 days, and the young fledge after about three weeks.

Most of the population follows a route south-eastwards over North America, via south-east Canada and the Gulf of St Lawrence, out over the Atlantic on a Great Circle to South America. The species is uncommon in the west in the fall. Passage spans the period late July to September. The wintering grounds are mainly in South America, from southern Bolivia and northern Argentina to Paraguay. Small num-bers also winter regularly in Australia and New Zealand. The bird also occurs as a vagrant in Hawaii, S. Africa, and W. Europe, where the bird is annual in autumn in Britain and Ireland.

▷ This Pectoral Sandpiper clearly shows the typical white V markings on the side of the mantle and scapulars.

Curlew Sandpiper

Calidris ferruginea

This Palearctic sandpiper is similar in size to a Dunlin, but more delicately built and elegant in behaviour. Its long, decurved bill, slender neck, and long legs produce a characteristic outline. Breeding birds are striking and distinctive, but non-breeding adults and juveniles are superficially similar to the Dunlin. However, their stance is more upright and their actions are more graceful. In flight, the Curlew Sandpiper's white rump also distinguishes it from all but the White-rumped Sandpiper and the Stilt Sandpiper.

The breeding adults have rich chestnut heads, necks, and underparts, apart from their undertail coverts, which are white. The scapular feathers are black with chestnut fringes and white tips, while the wing coverts are grey-brown with whitish fringes. Females have paler underparts with some white feathers and dark brown barring on the belly. The non-breeding plumage is much drabber, being grey-brown above and white below, except for some light streaking on the sides of the breast. Consequently they closely resemble Dunlins at this time, but can be distinguished by their long, white supercilium and cleaner appearance.

LENGTH: 180-230 mm (7-9 in)

Their longer legs and more evenly decurved bill also provide distinguishing features. The bill is black as are the legs at all times. The characteristic rippling 'chirrup' call is also distinctive. Juveniles are similar to non-breeding adults, but have browner upperparts that are decidedly scaly in appearance and a buff wash on the neck and breast. Unlike young Dunlins,

▽ A juvenile Curlew Sandpiper showing the more defined scaly appearance of the upperparts, the head and body having a buffish-coloured wash.

◁A *Curlew Sandpiper photographed in Oman.*

▷A *winter-plumaged Curlew Sandpiper reveals its distinctive white rump as it stretches its wings.*

they are also unspotted beneath. Curlew Sandpipers fly swift and low, and as they twist and turn in tight flocks, they show their white wing-bars and distinctive white rumps, both of which are broader than those of the smaller-bodied White-rumped Sandpiper. The similar Stilt Sandpiper lacks any wing-bar and has a straighter, blunter bill, flatter forehead and longer legs that project beyond its tail in flight. The Curlew Sandpiper's northwards movement during late April and May follows a direct route from the African wintering grounds to the Arctic. This takes the birds across Italy and south-eastern Europe, so in Britain very few adults are seen in their spectacular breeding plumage.

By early June, the birds are back on their breeding grounds. These are restricted to a very small area of arctic tundra from the Yenisei River eastwards to the Kolyma delta. Breeding has also occurred very occasionally in northern Alaska. Curlew Sandpipers exploit the seasonally rich boggy pools and hollows that are fed by melting snow on the edge of the permafrost. Most of these birds nest on south-facing slopes, which are the first to become free of snow. They are not especially territorial and several pairs may nest close together and in association with Grey and Pacific Golden Plovers. Their display consists of a song flight with slow wing-beats and glides, which is performed by the male birds.

The nest is usually in a tussock of grass or moss on a dry hummock. A few lichens are used to line out the shallow depression before the clutch of four eggs is laid. They are olive-buff or greenish-grey in colour, with bold brown blotches and spots. Information on the breeding of this bird is sparse, but incubation is apparently undertaken by the females. In the short Arctic summer breeding has to be quick and there is clearly only time to raise a single brood. Indeed, by mid-August juveniles will be flocking ready to migrate.

During fall, Curlew Sandpipers are regular visitors to western Europe. The males leave their summer arctic haunts first, with some beginning their departure as early as late June. The females follow next and during July and August adults of both sexes gather south of their breeding range to moult. The juveniles are last to leave in August. In western Europe the first birds usually arrive about the third week of July. These are adults, many of them still with remnants of their colourful breeding

plumage. From mid-August onwards most of the birds to arrive are juveniles. In some years relatively few appear, but in others they are plentiful. It has been argued that such fluctuations correspond to the three- or four-year population cycles of the lemming, with low lemming numbers causing Arctic foxes to take more Curlew Sandpipers.

While breeding success markedly affects the overall population, in western Europe, which is well to the west of any direct route between the Arctic and Africa, weather is also a major influence on numbers. In Britain, autumn flocks of twenty or so Curlew Sandpipers are quite regular at favoured staging posts. But easterly winds are always liable to drift any birds travelling south-westwards on to the east coast and during such conditions flocks of several hundred may occur. Curlew Sandpipers are also rapid migrants, well known for covering long distances in a single flight, and this would increase the likelihood of their being drifted off course. In any event, highly variable numbers of juveniles appear in Britain during August and September. By October most have left for their winter quarters farther south, but occasionally one or two individuals remain throughout the winter. Curlew Sandpipers also appear as rare vagrants in North America, with records inland as well as from both coasts.

The species' main wintering area extends from west Africa through to India, south-east Asia, and Australasia. Within this range most of the birds winter on the coasts, but in Africa many also occur inland along rivers and lakes. Outside the breeding season their favoured haunts are muddy and sandy shores, tidal creeks and the muddy margins of fresh-water pools, particularly those with little marginal vegetation. Curlew Sandpipers are very gregarious and often form large flocks. They also join readily with other species of small waders to feed or roost.

When feeding, Curlew Sandpipers will walk, run, wade, or swim with equal grace. Crustaceans, molluscs, insects, and some vegetable matter form their main diet. These are mostly taken by pecking, jabbing, and probing exposed wet mud or the bottoms of shallow pools in a similar manner to the Dunlin. In so doing, Curlew Sandpipers frequently wade up to their bellies in water, taking advantage of their long legs and bills to take prey that is beyond the reach of other small waders.

Purple Sandpiper
Calidris maritima

At all times the Purple Sandpiper looks like a dark-plumaged, portly and fairly large-sized 'Calidrid' with quite a long yellow-based drooping bill and short yellow legs. Outside the breeding season it is nearly always found on rocky shores, often in the company of Ruddy Turnstones. It can be seen scurrying around on the rocks or roosting nonchalantly amidst the spray and heaps of rotting seaweed – its typical pose is with its head buried in its back feathers. In winter, the birds are a dark slaty grey on the head, neck, back, and wings, and on much of the upper breast. On closer inspection, slim paler fringes are evident on the coverts and tertials, while the adults show a small white chin. The belly and undertail coverts are whitish, and are often flecked with grey at the sides. Sometimes you can make out a purple hue on the upperparts, the colouration that gives the species its name.

In flight the dark tail is bordered by bright white lateral upper tail coverts and there is a rudimentary slim white wing bar. Although it looks dumpy on the ground, the Purple Sandpiper is quite slender in flight with long pointed wings. A fairly quiet species, it does have a 'whit' or 'tit' contact call which is uttered when it takes wing. In summer the basic plumage remains dark, but takes on a browner tone with the crown and scapulars becoming more scaly-looking, being edged with gold, chestnut, and. white. At this stage an indistinct pale supercilium is evident.

Purple Sandpipers spend the whole winter on low rocks that receive vigorous wave and tide action. Here they move quickly among the crevices and seaweed in agile pursuit of food. Small molluscs and crustaceans are the main fare, with algae, worms, and insects supplementing the diet. On the breeding grounds similar items are taken, but the proportions of each vary according to availability. In the breeding areas, the diet frequently includes more non-marine invertebrates, which are often found among the lichens and mosses that abound in the tundra habitat.

LENGTH: 200-220 mm (7¾-8¾ in)

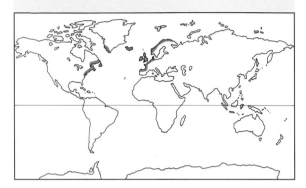

Wintering Purple Sandpipers can sometimes be found on artefacts such as piers, jetties, and breakwaters, where they are normally quite tame and approachable. But they are not always easy to spot, as their cryptic camouflage blends in with the backdrop of dark rocks. Very occasionally they will resort to sandy or muddy shores. The first I ever saw were a group of five on an estuary in Lancashire, England, one September, miles from their typical rocky habitat.

The breeding range of the species is quite extensive, stretching from the Canadian islands to Siberia, and including Iceland and upland Scandinavia. The nesting site chosen is invariably tundra with little vegetation. It may be from sea level up to higher mountain plateaux, but is often within sight of the sea. The birds pair up in early May, performing chase and wing lifting displays on the ground. After this a small cup-shaped nest is made and four eggs are laid. These are generally greenish, blotched and spotted with dark browns and with some fine blackish lines. The males carry out most of the incubation and the young hatch out after three weeks. The female departs before hatching, leaving the male to tend the young until fledging takes place.

The juvenile plumage is not unlike the adult's summer dress, but the upperparts have smaller feathers which are edged with buff, while the more finely streaked breast can have a brownish wash. After the young have fledged both adults and juveniles spend time on the coast adjacent to the nesting grounds before migration. Purple Sandpipers, however, do not undertake the long-distance movements typical of other sandpipers and tend to spread out over suitable habitat, perhaps less than 1,600 kilometres (1,000 miles) south of the area in which they bred. Most Canadian birds winter on the north-east coast of North America, though a few turn up inland at the Great Lakes and farther west. Few Palearctic birds move farther south than Portugal, with Britain, Iceland, and Scandinavia providing the winter home for most European birds.

In favoured locations, the Purple Sandpiper occurs in small groups of 20 to 30 or sometimes more; some roosts have held 100 individuals. In coastal Norway Purple Sandpipers are the commonest winter wader. In Britain the best areas to look for the species are the rocky coasts of north-east England, Scotland and the Northern Isles, where they remain until the end of April. The total winter population in Britain and Ireland is estimated to be around 25,000 birds.

▽ *Purple Sandpipers in winter plumage perched on coastal breakwaters.*

△ *A Purple Sandpiper in first-year non-breeding plumage.*

Rock Sandpiper

Calidris ptilocnemis

Closely related to the Purple Sandpiper, the Rock Sandpiper is the north Pacific equivalent of that species. Indeed, it is so closely allied that it has often been considered to be the same species and in many plumages is difficult or impossible to distinguish from the Purple Sandpiper. Fortunately for ornithologists, the two birds do not overlap in range. The Rock Sandpiper is a regular winter visitor to the west coast of America, south to California.

The species is resident in the Kuril and Commander Islands off the Kamchatka peninsula of eastern Siberia and in the Pribilof Islands and the Aleutian chain off Alaska. It is a summer visitor to the Chokotskiy peninsula of far-eastern Siberia and the southern Alaskan mainland. The latter populations move south in winter as far as northern California and to the Tokyo area in Japan (but not the intervening areas on the coast of Siberia). The bird is a late migrant in autumn, rarely arriving in the south before mid-November, and departs by early April. It is very rare away from the coast, with one record inland in British Columbia.

A medium-sized, stocky sandpiper with comparatively short legs and a long, slightly drooping bill, the Rock Sandpiper occurs in four races. Three of these, those breeding on the Commander and Kuril Islands, the Aleutians, and the Siberian and Alaskan mainland including all those wintering on the west coast of America, are nearly identical to the Purple Sandpiper. They are sooty black with a purple sheen in winter and more variegated with chestnut above and whitish below in breeding plumage. But they show more sharply defined spotting on the underparts than the purple sandpiper in their non-breeding and juvenile plumages. They also have a brighter, buff-brown neck and upper breast as juveniles and in breeding plumage they have darker chestnut fringes to the upperparts and often a blackish patch on the lower breast; they have a broader wingbar. Juveniles moult out of their breeding plumage after September, so all birds on the American West Coast are in winter plumage.

OTHER NAMES: Aleutian Sandpiper, Pribilof Sandpiper
LENGTH: 200-230 mm (7¾-9 in)

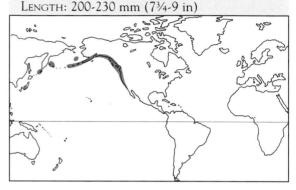

The fourth race, resident in the Pribilof Islands, is rather more distinct from the Purple Sandpiper. It is slightly larger, and shows more white on the wing in flight, a product of its broader wing-bar and the white on the fringes of its inner primaries. It also has whiter underwings. The breeding adults are rather paler and whiter than the respective plumage of the Purple Sandpiper, especially on the head and breast. They have much paler and sandier-buff fringes to the feathers of the upperparts, contrasting with the greyer wings. The dark lores and ear-coverts and a dark 'shield' on the lower breast are consequently obvious. The legs and bill are dark. The bird is vaguely similar to a dunlin, but that species has a black patch on the belly, not the lower breast.

In winter plumage this race is a pale grey above, mottled grey and white on the breast with a short supercilium, on the whole far paler than any winter-plumaged Purple Sandpiper. The legs and bill are yellowish. Juveniles have a neatly streaked and mottled breast, chestnut cap, and white, buff, and rusty fringes to the feathers of the upperparts.

The breeding biology of the Rock Sandpiper is rather similar to that of the Purple Sandpiper, though it uses mainly coastal tundra, and is apparently not so frequent at altitude. As the birds arrive on their breeding grounds, they feed on large boulders and rocky shelves

△A Rock Sandpiper in summer plumage.

covered with seaweed, sometimes moving on to mudflats at low tide. The pair-bond is formed in the winter, so the birds arrive already paired. When the snow melts in early May they move on to territories on the tundra among reindeer moss and low dwarf willows. They also occupy beaches, among the debris above the tide-line.

The male has a song-flight in which he rises 10 to 15 metres (30-50 ft) into the air before fluttering down, giving the song, which is reminiscent of a toad's trill. Four eggs are laid and are incubated by both sexes for about 20 days.

The young remain on the tundra for a few days, and after they fledge, they group together to form flocks on the coast.

The winter habitat is similar to the Purple Sandpiper's, consisting of rocky shores and stony beaches. The birds move in and out of the waves, often in water up to the breast; they can swim readily. They are usually found in small flocks, often with Surfbirds, Wandering Tattlers and Black Turnstones. Their voice is very similar to a Purple Sandpiper's.

Dunlin
Calidris alpina

This rather small, dumpy, and highly active 'Calidrid' is perhaps the most familiar of all birds along coastlines throughout the Northern Hemisphere. Often encountered in large numbers, the Dunlin is generally considered to be the yardstick against which many other small waders can be compared.

Named after the colour of its winter dress, the Dunlin is between a stint and a Curlew Sandpiper in size. It has medium-length black legs and a rather long bill, which is drooped at the tip. Appearing rather hunched and 'neckless' it appears an unremarkable dull grey-brown bird for much of the year. The upper-

OTHER NAME: Red-backed Sandpiper
LENGTH: 160-220 mm (6¼-8¾ in)

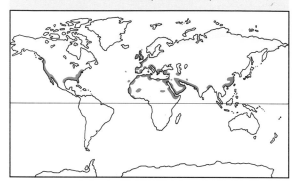

◁*Dunlin in summer plumage.*

▷*A Dunlin in winter plumage.*

parts are rather plain while the breast is lightly streaked grey and the remainder of the underparts white. In its breeding plumage, however, the Dunlin is unmistakable. Its large black belly patch contrasts with the white vent and flanks and the darker streaked breast, while the black-centred mantle and scapular feathers show varying bright chestnut, grey, and white borders. The wing coverts are greyish brown with paler fringes, and the flight feathers are dark grey. The crown is generally brown, lightly streaked with chestnut, contrasting with a whitish supercilium and paler ear coverts. These features vary from one area to another and six races have been recognised.

1. The nominate race *alpina*, which breeds in northern Scandinavia and north-west U.S.S.R., wintering in western Europe and the Mediterranean, eastwards to western India.
2. The race *schinzii*, which breeds in southeast Greenland, Iceland, Britain and southern Scandinavia, wintering mainly in west Africa.
3. The race *arctica*, which breeds in northeast Greenland and winters mainly in west Africa.
4. The race *sakhalina*, which breeds in northeast U.S.S.R., and northern Alaska, wintering in China and Japan.
5. The race *pacifica*, which breeds in western Alaska and winters along the west coast of the U.S.A., and Mexico.
6. The race *hudsonia*, which breeds in central Canada and winters in south-eastern U.S.A.

Of the six races, *schinzii* and *arctica* are the

smallest, *alpina* and *sakhalina* are intermediate in size, and the two American races, *pacifica* and *hudsonia*, are the largest. The two American races are also the brightest and richest red on the upperparts hence the bird's other common name of Red-backed Sandpiper.

In flight all races show a conspicuous, though narrow, white wing bar, white sides to rump and upper tail and a white underwing. The flight is fast though somewhat erratic, and individuals and small groups frequently utter a shrill 'treep' or 'kreee' call. As part of a larger flock, the birds are generally silent, but they can display amazing aerobatics as they wheel and turn as a single unit, always maintaining a small distance between each individual.

Dunlins prefer extensive areas of tidal mud flats, although they are also found inland in low-lying fresh-water areas, flooded fields, and lakes and reservoirs wherever there is a muddy fringe. Within these habitats the birds search energetically for food, either picking items from the surface or probing deeper into softer mud with a 'stitching' action of the bill. The diet consists mainly of inter-tidal invertebrates including many rag worms, bivalves, small molluscs, and planktonic crustacea. On the breeding grounds the diet changes to include adult and larval insects (especially dipteran flies), small beetles, spiders, mites, and earthworms. Seeds may also be taken, but this is evidently only when other animal matter is in short supply when the birds first arrive in Spring.

The Dunlin has a circumpolar breeding range and will nest in a variety of habitats from upland peat moorland to salt marsh in the south, and high Arctic tussock tundra in the north. In Britain, between 4,000 and 8,000 pairs of the race *schinzii* breed in areas from Dartmoor to the flows of northern Scotland. This is the most southerly breeding race of all Dunlins and is probably a relic from the last ice age, when the whole population occupied areas further to the south than at present.

On arrival at its breeding grounds in April and May, the male Dunlin carries out frequent song flights in order to attract a female and lay claim to a territory. The size of this territory is very variable and depends to some extent on food availability when the birds arrive. Where insect life is abundant, pairs may nest in a semi-colonial fashion, but with a cold or late spring, the birds may occupy territories of quite a considerable size. Pairs, however, are often 'site-faithful', and may return to nest within a few metres of the previous year's nest scrape. This is a small depression usually concealed in vegetation, and invariably it is very difficult to locate. It is usually lined with grass and a few leaves. The average clutch comprises four eggs of variable colour and markings; they range from pale greenish to olive-buff with grey spots, overlaid with many small spots or blotches of dark rich brown. The eggs are laid from April to late May, or sometimes in early June, depending upon the latitude. They are incubated by both adults for about 22 days, and the downy young are sometimes brooded for a few days after hatching. At this time the parent birds are vigorous in defence of their offspring and will often employ a distraction display if predators such as skuas, gulls, crows, or foxes appear. The juveniles fledge after about 20 days, by which stage they resemble the non-breeding adult, but have generally warmer plumage tones. The parent birds may remain within the area after the young have fledged in order to moult their wing feathers, but probably all but the North American races will suspend this moult before completion, in order to head south.

Passage may involve long and continuous flights between staging areas, but often also includes short movements along a coastline or overland. The birds winter along many coasts in the Northern Hemisphere, but they are generally scarce south of 15 degrees north. About 500,000 birds winter along the shores of Britain. These are birds that have bred farther to the north, and they represent about half of the west European mid-winter population.

In the U.S.A., Dunlins winter along the whole of the east coast, and from California southwards in the west. In spring the general move northwards begins during March or April. The birds reach their arctic-boreal breeding grounds about mid May to early June. Birds taking the west coast route may cut across the Gulf of Alaska; others move up from the southeast via Hudson Bay.

After nesting has been completed, adults leave their tundra summer home in late July or August. Both make a protracted southward journey, which lasts through to September, October, or even into November before both the adults and the birds of the year are established in their winter quarters.

Dunlins may roost in vast numbers on shingle spits and sand bars left exposed at high tide, often packing very close and intermingling with other wader species. Once in the roost, many individuals balance on one leg and tuck their bills into their scapular feathers. They look as if nothing would disturb them, but there are always a few alert birds that are ever-vigilant for the first sign of danger. Whether these birds are observed feeding on open mud flats, flighting in huge clouds, or settling into a roost, they are always entertaining to watch and prove a major attraction whenever and wherever they are to be found during the winter months.

△ A juvenile Dunlin.

Broad-billed Sandpiper

Limicola falcinellus

LENGTH: 160-180 mm (6¼-7 in)

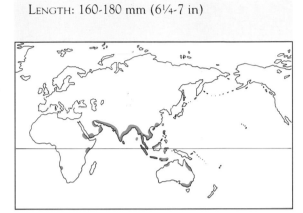

A small, stint-like wader that is somewhat enigmatic to European birdwatchers, this species occurs as a rare migrant in most of the continent. It is a familiar winter visitor to tropical Asia, where it can be found in quite large flocks. Although it was often confused with the dunlin in the past, the Broad-billed Sandpiper has a distinctive appearance and is usually easy to identify.

The Broad-billed Sandpiper breeds in south-central Norway, central and northern Sweden, northern Finland, and adjacent areas of the U.S.S.R. There is another population found in three widely separated areas of northern Siberia. These two populations have different wintering areas. Siberian birds are found in winter around the shores of the Indian Ocean, south and east through Indonesia to Australia. They occur on open shores and mudflats in mixed flocks with Stints and Sand-plovers, as well as in coastal lagoons. The wintering area of the Finno-Scandinavian birds is less well documented. They move south-east across Europe and the Middle East and are rare west of a line from the western Baltic to Italy. However, westward vagrancy appears to be increasing and the species is a rare but regular migrant in May on the east coast of Britain. The autumn passage spans the period from July to the end of October; muddy, vegetated fresh-water margins and salt-marshes are frequented. Most western birds probably winter in eastern or southern Africa. A few non-breeders spend the summer in the wintering areas. The species is also a vagrant to the western Aleutians, New Zealand, and Morocco.

The birds arrive comparatively late on their breeding grounds, from late May to mid-June. The breeding area can be in both lowland and montane marshy tundra, often in boggy areas with adjacent swampy meadows surrounded by coniferous forests. The habitat is rather reminiscent of that used by the Jack Snipe. Broad-

◁A *Broad-billed Sandpiper photographed in Oman. This bird is moulting into winter plumage.*

△A group of Broad-billed *and right are in summer*
Sandpipers on passage *dress though the middle bird*
through Eilat, Isreal during *is still in non-breeding*
May. The birds on the left *plumage.*

billed Sandpipers nest in the wettest and least vegetated parts.of the bogs, in loose colonies of three or four pairs. They are generally scarce, and during the breeding season they often skulk like a rail.

The male has a territorial song-flight. He flies slowly along, 10 to 20 metres (30-60ft.) above the ground, alternating periods of shivering wings with glides, and giving a rhythmic buzzing trill. He may switch to a high-speed flight and speed the song up to a wheezier or whirring 'virrirrirrirri . . .'. This change may be caused by the approach of another song-flighting male, and an aerial chase may follow.

The male makes two or three scrapes, from which the female selects one in which to lay. The nest, on the ground or the top of a tussock, is a shallow cup lined with leaves, dried grass, and sedges. Four eggs are laid; they are pale buff to pale fawn, heavily speckled with russet. The species is monogamous, and both parents take part in incubation over a period of 21 or 22 days, and in the care of the young, although the female may leave the male in charge after a few days.

The Broad-billed Sandpiper is slightly smaller than a Dunlin. Its black bill is long, with a distinct downward kink near the tip, but the breadth which gives its name can only be appreciated when the bird is in the hand. The legs are rather short and usually appear dark. The

bird's feeding behaviour in winter and on passage is also reminiscent of a Dunlin, but it holds its bill more vertically and has a more 'heads-down' stance. The bird may be tame, and may crouch if approached.

In all plumages the Broad-billed Sandpiper shows a double supercilium, splitting just in front of the eye, with the upper fork weaker and less well-marked. There is also a prominent dark eyestripe. The breeding adult generally appears dark with a well-defined breast band of arrowheads and streaks, extending on to the flanks. The upperparts are well striped; each feather is blackish, fringed with white on the coverts and white and rufous on the scapulars; the latter form two white Vs on the sides of the mantle and scapulars. When fresh, early in the season, birds may have a pale, 'floury' look, but when the fringes of the feathers are worn off, they appear very dark.

In winter the species is grey above with fine pale scaling and some darker feather centres producing a mottled effect. There is a darker area at the bend of the wing. The upper supercilium may be faint and difficult to see. Juveniles resemble breeding adults, but have the breast washed with buff and finely speckled. There are no streaks on the flanks, resulting in a neat pectoral band. The upperparts are also rather neater.

In flight the Broad-billed Sandpiper shows white sides to the tail and a narrow white wingbar. The call is similar to that of the Dunlin, a dry, buzzing 'chrrrreet', but is more of a trill, recalling Temminck's Stint.

Stilt Sandpiper
Micropalama himantopus

This rather small, though long-legged, American shore bird is a close relative of the 'Calidrid' group and shares many features with members of that genus. It does, however, display a number of subtle behavioural and plumage differences that set it apart and make it a most interesting and challenging bird for the ornithologist to study.

Always enjoyable to watch, the Stilt Sandpiper may remind you of a dowitcher as it feeds, or of a Lesser Yellowlegs as it takes to the wing. At times it resembles a Curlew Sandpiper, its Palearctic 'cousin', in terms of its shape and general appearance. As its name suggests, it has rather long legs, and these are ochre-yellow. The longish bill is marginally thicker and only slightly decurved compared with the Curlew Sandpiper, and it always appears to be more blunt-tipped. Non-breeding birds look mainly greyish at a distance, but closer views reveal white fringes to the upperpart feathers and a distinct white supercilium contrasting with the darker lores and crown. The underparts are whitish, with fairly fine darker grey streaking on the breast and flanks. From March the adult birds moult into their distinctive breeding dress. Once it is acquired, this distinguishes the species from all other waders. A dark barred lower breast and belly with a dark streaked neck develops, while the black upperpart feathers show rufous and white borders. The white supercilium becomes more conspicuous, contrasting strongly with a darker crown and warm chestnut lores, ear coverts, and nape.

If flushed, or often as the bird settles to land, the white under wing coverts are revealed. These contrast with the greyer flight feathers, and in summer with the barred belly. From above the fairly uniform greyish brown upper wing shows little or no trace of a wing bar and contrasts strongly with the white upper tail coverts which, as on the Lesser Yellowlegs, are cut square in line with the trailing edge of the wings. The Stilt Sandpiper, though, is markedly smaller than the Lesser Yellowlegs

LENGTH: 180-210 mm (7-8¼ in)

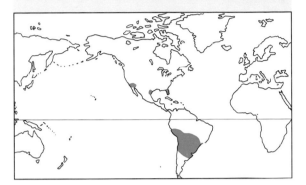

△ *A Stilt Sandpiper at its nest site.*

◁A Stilt Sandpiper in non-breeding plumage. This species is a vagrant to Britain. The photograph shows an individual which turned up in Lancashire in 1984.

▷A Stilt Sandpiper on its breeding ground in Northern Canada.

and has a longer bill. On the wing its long legs are particularly evident, with the feet trailing well behind the tail tip. The fairly easy, slightly flicking flight action shows similarities with that of both 'Calidrid' and 'Tringa' sandpipers. It is also while the bird is in the air that the soft trilled 'Krrrr' or 'grrrrt' call is most often heard.

The species shows a clear preference for shallow grassy pools, flooded marshes, and the shores of ponds and lakes. It is found much less frequently on hard sandy beaches and tidal mud flats. It habitually wades up to its belly just offshore, where it feeds deliberately, frequently plunging its head into or below the surface of the water in a manner reminiscent of a dowitcher. The Stilt Sandpiper, however, covers more ground, moving steadily around its selected feeding area; it can also be seen, less frequently, probing wet mud. The bird's diet is composed mainly of adult and larval beetles, small molluscs, and larval insects, with probably a few seeds and berries also taken.

The adults' spring passage is largely concentrated in the North American interior. Birds pass through fairly quickly from mid-March, arriving on their breeding grounds during late May. The species' range extends from northern Alaska to north-eastern Ontario, and the males quickly establish territories on arrival here. These territories are generally of 6 to 8 hectares (15 to 20 acres), although sometimes they are only a quarter of this size. The male carries out prolonged display flights over the chosen site at heights of between 20 and 60 metres (70 to 200 feet). This courtship ritual involves a fluttering flight with the tail well spread, interspersed with occasional long glides and frequent singing. Interestingly, birds show a strong degree of site fidelity with up to 50 per cent of pairs reuniting on their same nesting territory in succeeding years.

The nest, a rudimentary depression, is often sited on fairly well exposed areas of relatively dry tundra, but occasionally on damper areas more favoured by species such as the Pectoral Sandpiper. Surprisingly, pairs have been recorded reusing nest scrapes from the previous year, these being well preserved in the hard ground through the long northern winter. It appears that this behaviour allows an earlier start to the breeding cycle by more experienced pairs. The average clutch of four buff and brown flecked eggs is incubated for about twenty days. Apparently the male occupies the day-time and the female the night-time shift. Territorial defence declines at this stage with the non-incubating adult often straying a few miles from the nest to feed on small tundra ponds. On hatching, the downy young are led to wetter areas where there is a greater abundance of food. They fledge after 17 or 18 days, having already been abandoned by their parents. At this age the juveniles resemble the winter adults, but show a darker crown and

more prominent white supercilium, while the upper parts have a neatly scaled pattern and the lightly streaked breast has a pale buff wash.

The birds of the year head southwards from mid August – some two or three weeks later than the parent birds. The majority head through central Canada and the U.S.A., but rather more reach the Atlantic seaboard than in the Spring, although occurrences on the Pacific coast remain scarce. Some individuals winter in the southern United States, Mexico, and the Caribbean, but most pass farther south to spend the non-breeding season in cental South America. Here they rejoin the few, probably first year birds, which have remained there all year.

The Stilt Sandpiper is mainly encountered in small numbers away from its wintering and migration stop-over places, and is often found in the company of dowitchers and Lesser Yellowlegs. This, along with its generally confiding nature, has allowed the bird to become a familiar and well studied species throughout much of its range.

The Stilt Sandpiper was first recorded in the British Isles in 1954, the same year as the first Wilson's phalarope. The latter species has subsequently proved to be a regular visitor, but the Stilt Sandpiper has remained a true vagrant with no more than 17 officially accepted occurrences up to 1986. After the first in 1954, there were seven during the 1960s, five in the 1970s, and four between 1983 and 1985. The geographical distribution of records is rather surprising for a transatlantic visitor. There has never been a record from Scilly nor from mainland Cornwall (though there is a claim for 1987 awaiting ratification), and there have been only two in Ireland. As many as eleven (65 per cent) were in eastern England between Sussex and Humberside, two were in north-west England, and two in Scotland. Nor was the monthly distribution typical. Seven arrived in the spring or early summer, with four in July, and only ten were in the traditional period for American waders of August to October. Undoubtedly the most well-known bird of recent times was the individual that remained in Cheshire from April through to October in 1984.

Buff-breasted Sandpiper

Tryngites subruficollis

This quite small and rather active Nearctic sandpiper is one of the least aquatic of all waders. It is commonly found in its favoured habitat of dry, open grassland, actively searching for food. A fairly distinctive species, the Buff-breasted Sandpiper is roughly the size of a Common Sandpiper. In North America it has been likened to a diminutive, short-tailed Upland Sandpiper, but in terms of plumage and general shape, confusion is more likely with its larger Palearctic relation, the Ruff. The Buff-breasted Sandpiper, however, always appears more delicate, with a shorter, straight bill, a small rounded head, a long thin body, and moderately long legs. Like the Ruff, the male birds are up to ten per cent larger than the females and this fact is normally obvious in the field. Adults have a fairly bright apricot-buff coloured face and underparts that are unmarked apart from a few darker spots at the sides of the breast. The crown is flecked darker giving a capped effect at times, while the remainder of the upperpart feathering is grey or black, with buff fringes. The bill is generally dark and the legs a fairly bright ochre yellow colour. The small black eye surrounded by a paler orbital ring stands out on an otherwise plain-looking face and gives the bird a rather docile expression.

In flight this species appears fairly long-winged and the lack of any white wing bar or paler sides to the tail distinguish it from all

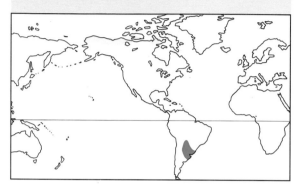

LENGTH: 180-200 mm (7-7¾ in)

other sandpipers. Additionally, the under wing is noticeably white, with a contrasting smudged dark trailing edge to the flight feathers, and a conspicuous blackish crescent along the greater primary coverts. These birds are normally reluctant to take to the wing, but if flushed, they tend to fly low for a short distance before re-alighting. It is at these times that one may hear the 'prrreet' alarm call.

The Buff-breasted Sandpiper is a fairly gregarious species, frequently occurring in small groups and sometimes larger gatherings, especially on migration. Generally found on short grassy plains, it often also visits golf courses, airfields, and stubble fields, but tends to avoid wet and marshy areas and coastal shorelines. It is a fairly active feeder, walking briskly on flexed legs with a slight bobbing movement of its head, while picking randomly at any potential food item it sees. The diet comprises largely terrestrial insects and invertebrates, especially the larvae of beetles and the larvae and pupae of dipterans.

The birds move northwards through the southern United States from mid-March to May and concentrate at traditional resting places in Texas and later Alberta en route. Sightings of individuals or groups on either Pacific or Atlantic coasts at this time of year are unusual. The species' breeding range is fairly restricted, but the density of pairs within

these areas can be quite high. The main range extends from northern Alaska to western Canada, with a few pairs also found in eastern Siberia. By late May, most birds will have arrived on these nesting grounds and will be preparing to mate. Like the Ruff, male Buff-breasted Sandpipers indulge in spring 'lekking' behaviour in order to attract one or more females. The 'lek' comprises between two and ten males which defend areas of approximately 10 to 50 metres (30–160 ft.) in diameter – a much larger area than that held by the Ruff. The display itself involves much wing-flashing and waving, with either one or both wings raised above the bird's back and with 'sparring' males at times jumping or fluttering into the air to a height of several metres. Most of this activity is carried out at dawn and dusk when the light intensity is low and the exposure of the under wing is most conspicuous. The successful males, having mated with one or more females, appear to take no further part in the breeding cycle.

The female excavates a shallow scrape on the drier slopes of grass or lichen tundra in which she lays an average of four buff-coloured and brown-spotted eggs. Most clutches are laid in June with the majority of young hatching

◁ *A Buff-breasted Sandpiper on its nest.*

▷ *Buff-breasted Sandpipers perform their courtship display on their breeding grounds in Alaska.*

out from mid to late July. They remain close to the female until they fledge a few weeks later. By this stage they bear a close resemblance to the adults, but have broader pale fringes to the feathers, thus looking rather more scaled on their upperparts. At this time many of the males have already assembled in flocks and, having suspended their moult, are preparing for the long migration south.

The main autumn passage through the prairies and central U.S.A., takes place between August and September. The birds converge on a narrowing front before crossing the Gulf of Mexico and flying on to their wintering grounds. The journey from the southern states to the Argentinian and Paraguayan pampas appears to be made with few stops, although birds will continue to arrive in areas near Buenos Aires from September through to mid-October. It seems that a small element of this passage, mainly juveniles, heads farther south and eastwards, cutting across the Great Lakes and through New England before making the longer sea crossing to north-eastern South America. It is almost certain that individuals from this secondary passage are recorded annually in western Europe. It also accounts for the greater numbers of birds recorded along the Atlantic seaboard at this season, although even here the species is never abundant.

It is perhaps surprising therefore that the Buff-breasted Sandpiper has become the second most-numerous American wader to cross the Atlantic to the British Isles. Since 1967 it has been an annual visitor to the Isles of Scilly usually to be seen on the airfield or golf course. In 1975, 1977, and 1980 there were major transatlantic flights which affected all parts of the British Isles and involved at least 67, 67, and 48 individuals, respectively; in 1977 at least 15 reached Scilly alone. By the end of 1982 the all-time total had reached at least 445 (nearly twice as many as the White-rumped Sandpiper, the next most-numerous species) and the Buff-breasted Sandpiper was removed from the list of species vetted by the British Birds Rarities Committee. This was perhaps unfortunate, as there is some evidence of a decline during the past few years. In the Isles of Scilly, the traditional stronghold, none were recorded in 1986, the first blank year for two decades.

As with several other Nearctic wader species, the Buff-breasted Sandpiper suffered extensive persecution at the hands of the shooting fraternity during the nineteenth and early twentieth centuries. Thankfully numbers have now recovered and this long-distance migrant is again a regular sight in the central states of North America during the spring and autumn migration periods.

▷ *The second most numerous American wader to cross the Atlantic to the British Isles, the Buff-breasted Sandpiper is an annual visitor to the Isles of Scilly, though this picture shows a juvenile in Cornwall.*

Ruff

Philomachus pugnax

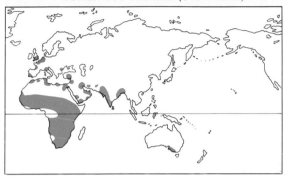

The Ruff is a bizarre wader, unique in the group in having a spectacular, ornate breeding plumage in the male, and one of the most remarkable mating systems to be found in the world of birds. Out of breeding plumage the ruff lacks distinctive markings but nevertheless has a unique and easily learned appearance.

A medium to large bird, the Ruff has a small head, long neck, medium-length slightly decurved bill, and long legs. The long body often has a hunchbacked appearance, which is heightened when the long, loose scapulars are raised by the wind. Male Ruffs are much larger than females – the size of a Greenshank compared to the size of a Green Sandpiper – and can be identified at all times. During the breeding season, they are particularly distinctive. They have an 'Elizabethan' style ruff and ear tufts, varying in colour from white through buff and rusty to black, either barred or plain.

OTHER NAME: Reeve (female only)
LENGTH: Male 260-320 mm (10¼–12½ in)
Female 200-250 mm (7¾–9¾ in)

There are patches of the same colour on the scapulars and flanks. The bill and legs are yellow to red.

Females in breeding plumage are variable in appearance, but have a dark brown head,

▷ *A female Ruff on its nest in Finland broods its recently hatched young.*

breast, and upperparts, with many dark feather centres and dark spotting on the breast and flanks. The males may also look like this while moulting out of their breeding plumage. Non-breeding adults of both sexes are a dun-grey colour above with darker feather centres and fine pale fringes. The lores are white, the crown and sides of the neck a pale dirty-greyish colour, and the underparts white with a grey wash on the breast. Some males may be largely white around the head and neck. The bill is black and the legs variable in colour, often fleshy or dull orange.

Juvenile Ruffs have neatly scaled upperparts, with blackish feather centres (especially on the scapulars) fringed buff to white. They have a sparse supercilium and the face, neck, and breast are variably buff, fading to a white belly. The bill is black and the legs greenish. They may be confused with the Buff-breasted Sand-piper, but that species is smaller, and has chrome yellow legs, a distinctive bare-faced expression, and short bill. In flight Buff-breasted Sandpipers have a plain rump and wings, while Ruffs show prominent white ovals at the sides of the rump and have a white wingbar. The Ruff is generally silent, even during the courtship display.

The species breeds across northern Europe and Asia, from the British Isles to eastern Siberia. It has decreased markedly in numbers, especially on the southern fringes of its breeding range, but remains an abundant and familiar wader. In Britain, it bred regularly until the last quarter of the nineteenth century but, as a result of drainage and later egg collection, was wiped out by the 1920s. But it returned to breed in the 1960s, and small numbers are now regular, notably on the Ouse Washes in East Anglia.

In the north of the range, the breeding habitat is low-lying tundra with lakes and marshes, as well as drier, raised areas for lekking and mating. To the south damp grassland, meadows, and fresh-water marshes are favoured.

Virtually the entire Ruff population winters in Africa, mostly in a strip from Senegal and Gambia to Sudan, where individual concentrations of over a million birds have been recorded at several locations. Smaller numbers are found in the Mediterranean and on the shores of Saudi Arabia, the Indian subcontinent and southern Australia. The Ruff is rather scarce eastwards to the Philippines. A few birds winter in western Europe, nearly all males; in Britain a notable wintering flock is found at Martin Mere in Lancashire. Many birds also spend the summer in the 'winter' quarters.

The Ruff is a common migrant throughout Europe, though the numbers in the west during spring are small. The northward passage is early, from February to May, and the autumn movement involves the usual protracted passage of males from early July, followed by females and juveniles from late July to early October. The species is a vagrant to Bermuda, Madagascar, South America, and regularly to the U.S.A., and Canada where it occurs on both coasts and in the interior. It nested in Alaska in 1976. The habitat on passage and in winter is grassland, fresh-water margins, paddies, and coastal lagoons; it is seldom found on the open seashore.

Ruffs arrive on the breeding grounds in western Europe in mid-April, though not till later to the north and east. The sexes are segregated most of the time. Males congregate at the traditional sites, known as 'arenas', some of which may have been in use for over 100 years. These are on dry mounds or dykes, or flat marshy areas near water. The males are divided into two groups, 'independent' males, which generally have dark plumes, and 'satellites', which are usually white. Each independent male occupies a tiny territory within the arena, known as a 'residence'. The residence is defended by both threats and actual fighting from the other males, in a display known as 'lekking'. Satellite males do not defend territories or fight.

The males spend most of the day at the arena, but the females visit only briefly to mate. The males pose with head and neck horizontal, tufts raised, and wings spread and fluttering. They periodically crouch with their bills touching the ground and bodies shivering. Independent males holding central positions in the arena are most successful in terms of the number of females they can mate with, and satellite males are the least successful. However, there is a complex and as yet unclear relationship between the two groups. In large arenas, only independent males will mate, but in smaller arenas the presence of satellites increases the chances of mating for all the males.

The Ruff is polygamous. Males mate with as many females as possible, but take no further part in breeding. Once they have mated, the female Ruffs move off to nest, often in small groups, and become very inconspicuous. The nest is a shallow scrape, lined with grass, and well concealed in the ground-vegetation. Four eggs are laid; they are greenish-olive, blotched and streaked with brown. The female sits for 20 to 23 days, and feeds the chicks for the first few days after they hatch. The fledging period is 25 to 28 days.

◁ *A juvenile male Ruff.*

△ *A male Ruff resplendent in breeding plumage.*

Jack Snipe

Lymnocryptes minimus

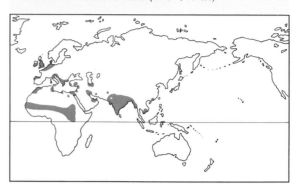

Each Autumn many hundreds of thousands of wading birds arrive in Britain, to spend the winter on estuaries, mud flats, marshes, and other watery habitats, proclaiming their presence as they feed between the tides in noisy, swirling flocks. In complete contrast and shunning the limelight, is the Jack Snipe, probably one of the least known and most unobtrusive waders to set foot on these shores.

In any fresh-water marshy area, with longish grass interspersed with small areas of water, one might come across one of these small mysterious birds. Probing the soft ground with its short stubby bill, it searches for insect larvae, worms, and freshwater molluscs. At other times it will use a 'jabbing' action to catch water beetles and insects. It will also resort to feeding on the seeds of aquatic plants, especially when the ground is frozen.

Unless you know exactly where to look, you usually encounter the Jack Snipe by accident. When walking in a suitable marshy area you may be startled when a small dark bird takes flight from almost beneath your feet. By the

OTHER NAME: Half Snipe
LENGTH: 170-190 mm (6¾–7½ in)

time you have composed yourself, the bird has already landed, sometimes just a few yards in front of you. You tread warily across the marsh to where it landed, hoping to snatch a rare glimpse of it on the ground. You arrive at the site, and look hard but nothing can be seen. You take one step more and the bird takes flight from the place where you are standing. This frustrating sequence of events can continue indefinitely. With patience, you will be rewarded when you see a small, dark bird with bright yellowish stripes on its back, which, compared to the Common Snipe, has a relatively short bill.

The Jack Snipe is indeed a master of concealment, hiding itself in the sparsest of vegetation, its cryptic coloration blending into the background. Sometimes its reluctance to fly can be its undoing, as occasionally it is trodden on and squashed. There are even records of birds being caught by hand and by dogs.

Jack Snipes return to their breeding grounds between April and mid-May. It is here that this shy unconfiding little bird, which you never get to know in winter, comes to life. It performs high acrobatic manoeuvres, twisting and then diving vertically to the ground. As it does this it calls incessantly, rising again to circle high above the ground in a continuation of its demonstrative courtship display, far removed from its shy antics in Britain.

The bird's breeding habitat is in the marshy wetlands, usually amongst conifer forests, from northern Norway eastwards across Scandinavia through to Siberia in a thick belt stretching to the Arctic tree zone. The nest is a shallow cup lined with grass. It is sited in a tussock, just above the water line, or on a hummock surrounded by floating swampy bogs. The eggs, up to four in number, are olive to dark brown, heavily blotched with chestnut. These are incubated solely by the female for up to 24 days. As with much of its behaviour, the Jack Snipe's breeding biology is little known, but it is thought that the young are fledged after 3 weeks. By early September as the snows approach, the breeding area is abandoned, and the birds move south and south-west in search of warmer climes.

On their fall migration, the birds begin to appear at the end of September throughout Britain. It is at this time that this most secretive of waders can surprise the birdwatcher by showing itself in the open. At such times it performs an almost comical feeding action, in small patches of mud at the edge of a reed- or grass-fringed pool. This consists of making slow vertical bouncing movements as if its legs were springs while it probes the mud for food. This open display is possibly only performed by passage migrants. By November most of the birds have taken up their winter quarters where they resort to their solitary lifestyle deep in the grass and well away from other species. Britain is one of the particular winter strongholds of this species. An estimated 100,000 Jack Snipe are present during winter.

▷ A Jack Snipe photographed in Oman.

◁ The short bill of the Jack Snipe is evident in this photograph.

Common Snipe

Gallinago gallinago

This bird is equally familiar to sportsmen and birdwatchers, if only through the evasive zigzag flight that is characteristic of the species whenever it is disturbed. Normally a secretive and mainly solitary bird, the Common Snipe is adept at hiding from view in the marshy locations if favours, where it probes deeply for worms with its long straight bill.

Usually one sees no more than a silhouette of a Common Snipe as it explodes from its feeding site to fly erratically and rapidly away over the ground, quickly covering a considerable distance, then gaining height and either disappearing completely from view, or dropp-

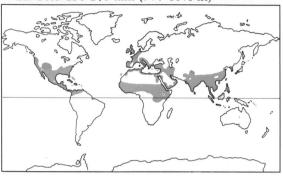

OTHER NAMES: Snipe, Fantail Snipe, Wilson's Snipe
LENGTH: 250-270 mm (9¾–10½ in)

▷A pair of Snipe feeding.

◁A Common Snipe stands on a fence post, behaviour typical of this species in the breeding season.

ing back to earth again. Invariably the bird calls with a harsh 'scaap' note as it makes good its escape from gun or binoculars. At the times when it is seen well (for there are occasions when one might catch sight of it feeding out in the open) the rich browns, blacks, and yellows of its plumage are visible. The upperparts are heavily mottled and barred with those colours, producing the effect of longitudinal yellow stripes. This pattern provides effective camouflage as the bird crouches and 'freezes' to avoid detection in the long grass when it believes it is under threat. The crown is black, with central buff streaks above and below the eyes. The latter are set high up in the head, thus allowing the bird to retain all-round vision as it probes to the full length of its bill. The neck and breast are buff with dark edging, while the flanks are whitish with some well defined vertical brown bars. The remainder of the underparts are predominantly white. The legs and feet are pale green and the bill is mainly brown and about 65 mm (2½ in) long. Like that other 'sporting' bird the Woodcock, the Snipe has a sensitive bill, its tip equipped with nerve endings that enable it to feel for worms in the soft ground. The upper mandible is slightly longer than the lower one and can be raised independently of the rest of its length. Though soft mud provides a preferred feeding condition, the more liquid the situation the better

for the snipe, and so 'old style' sewage farms are much favoured by this bird. In winter especially, such places can attract quite good concentrations of these birds, perhaps 50 or 60 individuals, or even more on some occasions.

The Snipe has a rather vigorous feeding action, driving its bill into the mud or ooze in a series of jerking movements of its head and neck. As well as worms, it takes a wide variety of insects, larvae, and other invertebrates. At times seeds are also taken. A widespread species, the Snipe breeds in North America and north-east Africa. It also nests in Iceland, in Britain, and across Europe, Russia and Siberia northwards to above a line 70 degrees north. To the south it extends to the Danube valley, France, and Portugal.

There are three races. The nominate race *gallinago* is to be found throughout most of the palearctic, while *faeroeensis* breeds in Iceland, the Faeroes, Orkney, and Shetland. The race *delicata*, or Wilson's Snipe, breeds throughout North America and is the most distinctive. Typically it has eight pairs of tail feathers (as opposed to seven on the nominate race), while the axillaries show wider brown bars. Also the white trailing edge to the wing is marginally narrower than in *gallinago*.

Snipe are usually on their breeding grounds by April. This territory might be some lowland marshy area or in more elevated places, boggy

◁A *Common Snipe at its nest site; this is usually located in dense vegetation.*

moorland. Sometimes quite dry heathery locations are selected, however. Here the spring 'chip-per chip-per chip-per' call is uttered with monotonous regularity night or day, the birds freely perching on whatever vantage point is available – fence posts, stone walls, tree tops, or raised hummocks. But it is the Common Snipe's aerial display which is so distinctive. It is known as 'drumming' or 'bleating' or, in America, 'winnowing'. The bird rises quickly on rapidly beating wings to a height of 150 metres (500 ft) or more. It then dives at great speed at about an angle of 45 degrees. During this dive the tail is fanned and the two outer tail feathers are projected outwards. The passage of air past these feathers causes the drumming sound. This can be produced for several seconds during each dive and the display may go on for some time, the bird diving and climbing again and again to repeat the performance. Both sexes perform this display, though presumably it is the male that is mainly responsible. The Snipe nests extensively in Britain and Ireland but is sparse in south-west Wales, south-west England and central England. The total breeding population in Britain and Ireland is probably in the region of 100,000 pairs.

The nest is a scrape lined with grasses, usually well hidden in a tussock. The eggs are pointed and olive grey in colour, blotched with dark brown and black. The usual clutch numbers four. Incubation is carried out entirely by the female and lasts for about 18 or 19 days. The chicks leave the nest as soon as they are dry and are looked after by both parents during the early days of their life.

In Britain the winter distribution of the Common Snipe is widespread, but it is determined by suitable habitat and greatly dependent on the severity of the weather. Generally more concentrated in the southern half of the country and Ireland, the bird's numbers are augmented by migrants from areas around the Baltic. Estimates of the total number that pass through north-western Europe in late summer have been put at 20–30 million birds. In Britain and Ireland equally, numbers can be no more than approximations. However, about 85,000 Snipe are reckoned to be shot each year, so the wintering population in Britain must be well into the hundreds of thousands.

In North America Wilson's Snipe breeds from sub-arctic Alaska southwards, though only very locally in California, Arizona, and Colorado east into New Jersey. The birds winter in the Americas from southerly parts of the breeding range south into Colombia and Venezuela. As in Britain, this bird is widely shot for sport, but legal limits are imposed and so its numbers are perhaps not too greatly depleted by the gun.

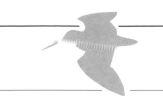

Great Snipe
Gallinago media

The Great Snipe formerly bred as far west as West Germany and perhaps Holland, but it is now restricted to the mountains of Scandinavia and from eastern Poland to the River Yenisey in Siberia. Habitat and climatic changes and hunting have all been suggested as causes of the decline. In Scandinavia the species breeds on boggy ground near the treeline. Further south and east many sorts of marshland are chosen; often there will be trees nearby and in Siberia the species may nest in quite dry woodland.

The Great Snipe is unique among snipe in having a communal display. This begins within a few days of the birds' arrival on the breeding grounds in May and continues for six to eight weeks. Display arenas, or leks, are situated in extensive areas of flat, boggy ground, and are often used year after year; over 60 years' continuous use has been recorded. In the past, leks of over 100 birds were noted, but now 10 to 20 is a good total. The males gather on summer evenings and their display may continue until dawn. The older males each hold a territory within the arena. As darkness falls they take to mounds of *sphagnum* moss, standing erect with their chests out, tails cocked, and bills open, all the while uttering an amazing song. This is impossible to render on paper, but has 'bibbling', 'drumming' and 'whizzing' phases. Every so often the males perform little flutter-jumps into the air, and the display is broken up with bouts of fighting.

Females only visit the arena to mate and, like many birds with a communal lekking display, the male Great Snipe is polygamous, successful males mating with several females. The males take no further part in family life once they have mated. The nest is a shallow depression on the ground, hidden in thick vegetation, with a meagre lining of grass or moss. The eggs vary from fawn to buff, with dark brown blotches and spots concentrated at the broad end. The clutch usually totals four, and is incubated for 22 to 24 days. On hatching the young can walk and feed themselves, and are independent after three to four weeks.

OTHER NAME: Double Snipe
LENGTH: 270-290 mm (10½–11½ in)

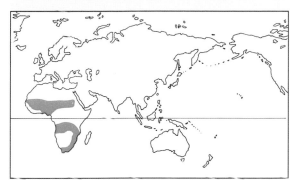

△ A Great Snipe calling on its nesting grounds.

▷*A Great Snipe on migration, photographed in the Seychelles.*

The breeding areas are deserted from mid-August onwards, with birds passing through Central and Eastern Europe en route to Africa. The Great Snipe is rare on passage in Western Europe and also east of Turkey. Most of the birds winter south of the equator, especially in Zambia and Malawi. Great Snipe favour drier habitats than Common Snipe on passage and in winter. During the day they remain concealed in cover, but before dawn and at dusk they fly to feed on open mud, in wet grass, or even on puddles on dirt roads. They probe less than Common Snipe, and less frequently enter water. Their diet consists of earthworms, small snails and slugs, a variety of insects, and the seeds of various marsh plants.

The Great Snipe is very similar in appearance to the Common Snipe, both on the ground and in the air. Most views of the bird will reveal a bulky, deep-chested, broad-winged snipe seen in flight for a few seconds. The flight is characteristically short, low, unhurried, and direct, compared to the frantic, zig-zag 'towering' typical of the Common Snipe. Another distinguishing feature is that the shorter bill is carried nearer the horizontal. If it calls at all, the Great Snipe utters a low, weak 'urrgh', rather than the common's incessant 'scaap'.

Points to look for on the wing are the adult's dark mid-wing panel (made up of the greater secondary and primary coverts), bordered by lines of striking white spots, and conspicuous white corners to the tail. Juveniles are duller: the upperwing can even look quite uniform and the white corners to the tail are more restricted and often only show as the bird changes direction or on take-off and landing. The Common Snipe has a white belly and a mainly white underwing, but the Great has only a small unbarred area in the centre of the belly; the flanks and the rest of the belly and underwing are heavily barred.

On the ground it can often be seen that the Great Snipe has a bulkier, ball-shaped body, a larger head, and a shorter bill than the Common Snipe. The head has a less prominently striped, generally 'mealy' appearance. On adults the white spots on the wing coverts are conspicuous, forming parallel rows across the closed wing, but on juveniles these are less pronounced. The flanks and most of the belly are barred with dark chevrons, a clear difference from the common snipe.

In Britain, the Great Snipe was formerly a rare but regular autumn visitor, the number of records no doubt inflated by the popularity of snipe shooting. Only about 50 have been recorded in the 30 years since 1958, mostly in autumn along the East Coast and on Fair Isle, with just a handful in the winter and spring. Vagrant Great Snipe have been recorded as far west as Madeira and east to Burma, but have only reached North America once – New Jersey in September 1963.

Short-billed Dowitcher

Limnodromus griseus

Dowitchers are medium-sized, stocky shore-birds with a long, snipe-like bill and relatively short legs. They feed on open mud or in shallow water, with a distinctive head-down sewing-machine-like action, rapidly jabbing the bill up and down into the mud or water, and often submerging the whole head. The Short-billed and Long-billed Dowitchers are very similar and were only finally recognized as distinct species in 1950.

In size, shape, and colouring the two species are nearly identical. At all times the bill is dark with a dull olive base, and the legs variably dull olive. In flight the birds have a distinctive shape, with a plump body and comparatively narrow wings, as well as the long, straight bill. There is a lozenge-shaped white wedge on the rump and lower back, and the tail is barred dark and white, generally appearing grey. There is an indistinct wingbar and a fine whitish trailing edge to the secondaries.

OTHER NAME: Red-breasted Snipe
LENGTH: 250-290 mm (9¾–11½ in)

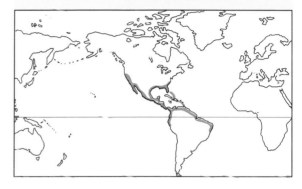

In breeding plumage both species are rusty or orange-red below, and a mixture of black, buff, rufous, and white above. This is a pattern shared only by the godwits, which are considerably larger. In winter the dowitchers are dull grey above and white below, washed grey

<1A Short-billed Dowitcher
moulting into summer
plumage while on migration
during April in Florida.

on the breast and flanks, with a distinct white supercilium. It is only in the juvenile plumage that there are any appreciable differences between Short- and Long-billed Dowitchers. Full details of these are discussed in the section on the Long-billed Dowitcher.

The best distinction between the two at all times is provided by their calls. The Short-billed Dowitcher gives a mellow 'tu-tu-tu', recalling a Lesser Yellowlegs, in flight and when it is alarmed; the Long-billed gives a shrill, slightly Oystercatcher-like 'keek', sometimes in an excited series, when it is alarmed.

The Short-billed Dowitcher breeds in three distinct areas of northern North America: eastern Canada (northern Quebec), northern Canada (eastern British Columbia, northern Alberta, Saskatchewan and Manitoba), and southern Alaska. These three populations are often separable in breeding plumage (eastern birds retain a white belly in full summer plumage, central birds are entirely rufous below, and Alaskan birds are variable below and typically darker and less well marked above). The three populations also have different migration routes and wintering areas.

In spring, the birds pass through the U.S.A., from early March to early June, stopping off at a wide variety of wetlands, both inland and coastal, including prairie lakes and sloughs. They arrive on their breeding grounds from late May onwards. The nesting habitat is swamps and open marshes, quaking bogs with low scrub, and forest areas on the surrounding drier ridges. Swampy coastal tundra is sometimes also used.

The male gives his song, a repetition of liquid, musical, gurgling 'cha' notes, in a hovering flight over the territory. This is defended by both sexes, often together. Little is known about the birds' courtship behaviour, but the males indulge in a woodcock-like strut on the ground. The nest is well hidden in a depression on or near a hummock, lined with grasses and mosses, usually within 100 metres of a lake or pool, or sometimes in a small forest clearing. Four eggs are laid, and they are greenish to olive-buff in colour, spotted with brown. Both sexes incubate the eggs for about 21 days.

Once the chicks have hatched, the female often leaves the breeding area to begin her journey southwards. Sometimes this is as early as late June. She is followed by the male a few weeks later, the juveniles forming a third peak in the southward migration, appearing from late July onwards. The Short-billed Dowitcher is a comparatively early migrant, another way of distinguishing it from the Long-billed.

Alaskan birds follow the Pacific coast (with some moving inland in the western states) to winter on the coast from California south to Peru. Central Canadian birds follow the Great Plains and Mississippi valley to winter on the Gulf coast and both the east and west coasts of Central America as far south as Panama. A few also move south-east from the breeding grounds and down the Atlantic coast from Long Island southwards. Birds from Quebec follow the Atlantic coast southwards, wintering from North Carolina to Florida and around the shores of the Caribbean islands and South America south to Brazil. They are scarcer on the Atlantic coast in spring. Unlike Long-billed Dowitchers, the short-billed species is largely coastal in winter, occurring, often in large flocks, on intertidal mud and sometimes on saltmarsh pools.

During the migration periods, the birds put on a considerable amount of fat, allowing them to make prolonged flights, each leg of their journey being up to 4,000 km (2,500 miles) long. In the spring, for example, birds wintering in South America make a non-stop crossing of the outer Caribbean from the Guianas to Florida.

The Short-billed Dowitcher is a vagrant to the Galapagos, and there are several records from Western Europe. It remains an extremely rare visitor to the British Isles. There are only five currently accepted records, of which four (a sight record from Norfolk in 1957 and specimens from 1862, 1872, and 1902) are in some doubt. The most recent and unequivocal individual was a juvenile at Tacumshin, County Wexford, Ireland, between September 30 and October 2, 1985.

▷ *A Short-billed Dowitcher in summer plumage on its*   *Canadian nesting grounds.*

Long-billed Dowitcher

Limnodromus scolopaceus

LENGTH: 270-300 mm (10½–11¾ in)

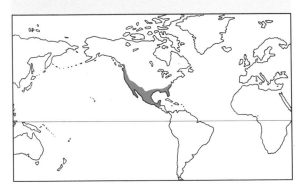

A close relative of, and very similar to, the Short-billed Dowitcher, the Long-billed Dowitcher has a rather different breeding distribution and pattern of migration, and is a more regular transatlantic vagrant. The general characteristics of dowitchers have been described under the short-billed species, and only the details of the plumage differences between the two birds will be dealt with in this section.

The Long-billed Dowitcher breeds on the coast of north-east Siberia from the Chukotsky peninsula west to Vankarem Bay, and in the Anadyr basin. In North America it breeds on St Lawrence Island and coastal northern and western Alaska, and probably also in north-west Mackenzie and the northern Yukon.

The bird's wintering grounds are in the southern U.S.A., from South Carolina and Florida west to central California and then south through Mexico to Panama. In the main therefore, it winters to the north of Short-billed Dowitcher. It prefers fresh-water or brackish pools to intertidal mud, though it will make use of the latter. It often occurs

in smaller flocks than does the short-billed species, and a few non-breeding birds spend summer in the winter quarters.

This bird's spring passage through the U.S.A., is from late March to mid-May. In spring it is rare on the Atlantic coast, mostly occurring to the west of the Mississippi. The birds arrive on the Alaskan breeding grounds in late May but do not reach Siberia until June. The breeding habitat is the tundra beyond the tree-line, in grassy or sedgy swamps, and often near a small lake. The dowitchers arrive as the snow is melting and feed around pools of melt-water on insects, seeds and even moss, moving on to feed on cranefly larvae in sedgy swamps later in the season.

The breeding pair defend a comparatively small territory, and the male delivers his song in a low-level display flight, hovering on quivering wings and giving a rapid series of 'pee-ter-wee-too' notes. The nest is usually placed in a small clump of low sedges, or on a small mound covered with moss and sedge, frequently on damp ground. Four eggs are laid, and they are brown or occasionally olive in colour with many elongated spots of brown, grey, and olive. Both sexes incubate, the male often standing guard near the nest in the early stages to ward off intruders. Incubation takes 20 or 21 days and, as with the Short-billed Dowitcher, the females often take no further part in the care of the family, forming flocks from late June onwards and moving south. The males do not leave until late July or early August.

Because of its more distant breeding grounds, the Long-billed Dowitcher usually passes through the U.S.A., on a schedule that is five or six weeks behind the Short-billed Dowitcher. It is scarce on the Atlantic coast until mid-August, and the juveniles do not appear until mid-September. The birds move south-east across North America to the Atlantic coast south of New England, with only small numbers occurring along the Pacific coast and in interior North America from the Rockies to the Mississippi valley. The species is a rare but regular migrant in Japan, and a vagrant to Novia Scotia, Bali, Brunei, and Thailand. Its route from Alaska south-eastwards takes it on a Great Circle over the North Atlantic and it is a vagrant to Western Europe, annual in Britain from late September onwards.

Only about 15 per cent of Long-billed Dowitchers are noticeably longer-billed than the short-billed species, with the bill twice the length of the head. A plumage feature that is useful for identification all-year-round is that the white bars on the tail of the Long-billed are usually narrower than the dark ones, and never wider, whereas on the Short-billed, the white bars are usually wider than the dark.

The two species are nearly identical in non-breeding plumage and can only be distinguished in ideal conditions. The Long-billed is a slightly darker grey, and its throat and breast are not speckled; there is an abrupt division between the grey of the breast and the white of the underparts.

In breeding plumage some Short-billed Dowitchers have a white belly, a feature never shown by the long-billed in full plumage, and the red of their underparts is paler and more orangey. The foreneck of the Short-billed is lightly, rather than densely, spotted, the centre of the breast is spotted, not barred, and the belly is lightly spotted, rather than unmarked.

It is in juvenile plumage that the two species can be readily distinguished. Long-billed Dowitchers are washed with buff below, often with a distinctly greyer head and neck. The upperpart feathers have narrow rusty fringes and solidly dark centres. Juvenile Short-billed Dowitchers are much brighter; all the underparts and head are washed with buff and the

◁An adult non-breeding Long-billed Dowitcher.

▷A Long-billed Dowitcher photographed in October feeding along a Florida shoreline.

△ *A Long-billed Dowitcher in non-breeding plumage.*

feathers of the crown and upperparts have broad orange-buff fringes and irregular orange markings within the dark centres, notably on the 'tiger-striped' tertials. However, the best distinction at all times is the voice, described in the section on the Short-billed Dowitcher.

Of 242 dowitchers recorded in the British Isles up to 1986, 113 were successfully identified as Long-billed and only five (not always unequivocally) recorded as Short-billed. As the former species has a much more westerly breeding distribution and is much scarcer along the Atlantic coast, this might be considered surprising. But the Long-billed Dowitcher is a relatively late migrant along the Atlantic coast, having moved south-east from as far as Alaska, and arriving at a time when autumn storms make it more susceptible to transatlantic displacement. In fact, dowitchers as a whole (and it seems clear that the vast majority

of dowitchers not specifically identified were in fact Long-billed) are the fourth most-commonly recorded of the American waders on the British side of the Atlantic. Recently, one was recorded as far afield as Oman, and I saw one in Tunisia in October 1987.

During the last decade an average of over ten dowitchers per year has been recorded in Britain and Ireland, with 17 in both 1977 and 1985. The numbers of positively identified Long-billed Dowitchers varied from as few as three in 1982 to as many as 14 in 1985. Of 34 recorded in the five years 1982–86, 16 were in Ireland or south-west England, eight in east or south-east England, and seven in Scotland. Increasingly, individuals have appeared in the summer months and several have wintered. Most remarkable of all was a Long-billed Dowitcher which arrived at Ballycotton, County Cork in October 1980 and, apart from brief absences, remained in the area until March 1984.

Woodcock

Scolopax rusticola

This secretive, terrestrial wader is well adapted to its woodland home. The bird's large eyes, set curiously high in its head, give all-round vision; strong legs enable it to spring into the air if danger threatens; and broad, rounded wings carry it swiftly away, dodging and weaving through the trees. This makes the Woodcock an attractive quarry for the sportsman, although the birds do not flush readily but sit tight on the forest floor, where their mottled and barred rufous-brown plumage provides perfect camouflage among the leaf litter and dead bracken fronds.

In outline a Woodcock resembles a heavy Snipe, with a similarly long, straight bill. Confusion is unlikely, however, as the Woodcock is bulkier, with broad, rounded wings.

▽ *A Woodcock prepares to bathe in a small woodland pool.*

OTHER NAME: Eurasian Woodcock
LENGTH: 330-350 mm (13-13¾ in)

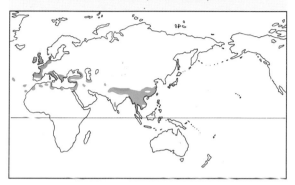

Superficially, the plumages show the same mixtures of rufous browns, buffs, and blacks. But the Woodcock's head has transverse black bars whereas the Snipe has lateral buff ones,

and the Woodcock lacks the Snipe's distinctive buff stripes on its back.

Wet lowland woods and forests with a good shrub layer or an understorey of bracken are the Woodcock's preferred habitat. The bird particularly favours natural birch, oak, or pine woods, with a mixture of dry areas for nesting and damp ones for feeding. Woods with wide rides, glades, or open canopies are also favoured, and some birds frequent moors, heaths and even open fields. During winter there is less affinity with woodland and birds occur in scrub, young plantations, and even hedgerows in Ireland.

Woodcock are largely active at dusk. This may explain why, despite being so numerous and widespread, they remain something of an enigma. For example, we still do not fully understand their breeding ecology. Most are solitary, so the occasional 'pair' feeding or migrating together in early spring suggests a pair bond. Yet many are polygamous, with the males using their characteristic roding flights to advertise themselves and locate females that are ready to breed. Having mated, the male remains with the female for three or four days, but then resumes his roving flights in search of another mate.

The breeding range of the Woodcock extends right across the temperate forest zone of Eurasia. In Britain there are probably between 10,000 and 50,000 'pairs', but these figures are based on roding birds, which may conceal the true numbers. Woodcocks occur in most areas, but are scarce or absent in Cork and Kerry in Ireland and from south-west England, the fens, and the Essex-Suffolk border. 'Pairs' – if such they are – begin to form in late February, but breeding continues into July. Although skirmishes between males do arise, Woodcock are apparently not territorial and their roding flights do not always cover the same ground.

The roding flight is slow, deliberate, and owl-like, with the bill pointing downwards at 45 degrees. It takes place just above the tree-tops at dawn and more especially dusk and lasts about twenty minutes. While roding the male utters a strange song of up to five 'snores' followed by a 'sneeze'. Roding increases until the summer solstice, then subsides quickly.

Nests are usually made on the ground in woodland, often near a tree, and concealed by vegetation. The female lines a shallow depression with dead leaves, dry grass, and a few feathers before laying her clutch of four eggs. Most laying occurs in March and April. Incubation lasts for about three weeks and is undertaken by the female, who also tends the young once they have hatched. Fledging takes another two or three weeks, but it is five or six weeks before the young are truly independent. Occasionally females fly from danger carrying their young between their legs. During the breeding season the birds roost in clearings or fields by night and feed by day, mostly on earthworms.

Woodcock are migratory, wintering in frost-free areas to the south and west of their breeding range. However, the breeding and wintering ranges overlap in Britain, Ireland, and France, and many Woodcock are resident all the year round in these areas. Autumn dispersal is prompted by hard weather and takes place quite late – many birds do not reach Britain until October or November, and numbers in Ireland are still increasing in December. This westerly migration has also led to vagrancy across the Atlantic, with records from Newfoundland and Quebec south to Alabama and even inland in Ohio. The British winter distribution is widespread and excludes only the higher ground of northern England and Scotland. Elsewhere the wintering range includes Iberia, North Africa, and from Asia Minor to Japan.

During winter Woodcock roost singly during the day and feed at night. Most fly out to feed in the hour after sunset and return in the hour before dawn. Weather permitting, they are faithful to both their roosting and feeding sites. Feeding occurs in wet pastures, puddles, muddy ditches, and streams – anywhere in fact where the birds can probe for worms and insect larvae. If the ground is too hard to probe, other prey is taken and many birds resort to plant food when snow is on the ground. Migrant birds leave their wintering grounds in March and early April, the females returning to their former breeding areas, but the males showing less fidelity to particular sites.

△Woodcock at the nest site from which its young have just hatched.

▷A Woodcock displays at its nest site.

American Woodcock

Scolopax minor

Like its European counterpart this bird is also largely noctural and is only usually seen on its dawn and dusk display flights or when flushed unexpectedly from thick cover. The American Woodcock is the smallest of the world's six species of woodcock and in general plumage pattern is similar to its Eurasian counterpart – rusty-brown above, intricately barred and mottled with black and grey. Also like the Eurasian Woodcock, it has broad black cross-bars on the crown and large eyes placed high up and well back on the head, giving it good all-round vision. The tail feathers are black on the underside with prominent shining-white tips that are conspicuous in display.

In flight the American Woodcock can be distinguished from other American shorebirds first of all by habitat – it is the only species to be regularly found in woodland. When flushed from cover during the daytime, it jumps up and flies off, twisting and turning through the trees. It is about the same size as a snipe, with a bulky body, short tail, broad rounded wings, and a long bill. The outer three primaries are uniquely pin-like, being shorter and narrower than the rest. They produce a whistling or twittering noise in flight. There are also two clear grey Vs on the edge of the mantle and scapulars, and the underparts and underwing are a uniform rusty-buff colour, lacking any trace of dark barring. These are both clear differences from the Eurasian Woodcock.

American Woodcocks breed in mixed or deciduous woodland with plenty of under-growth and areas that are moist, but not too wet, for feeding. They will also use adjacent damp fields or marshland. The birds feed at night, resting in cover during the day. Their diet largely comprises earthworms, though beetles and fly larvae are also taken. Wood-cocks are common, but tend to be local, occurring only when conditions are just right. In the winter they are less selective in their habitat, being also found in more open wood-land and gardens as well as pastures, burnt fallow fields, and pine uplands.

OTHER NAMES: Woodcock, Mudbat, Timberdoodle
LENGTH: 265-295 mm (10½–11½ in)

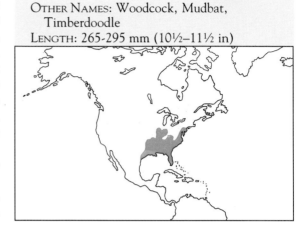

The breeding range of the American Wood-cock lies in the eastern half of North America, north to southern Ontario and Quebec, New Brunswick, Novia Scotia, and south-west Newfoundland. It extends as far west as the eastern Dakotas, Nebraska, Kansas, and Oklahoma. The northern birds are migratory, being resident from late March to October, but the species is present all the year round south of Arkansas, Tennessee, and Virginia, although it is only a winter visitor to southern Texas, Louisiana, and Florida. It is a vagrant west to Montana and Colorado, and has occurred on Bermuda.

The breeding season begins in January in the southern parts of the range, though not until April in the north. The male Woodcock defends a territory centred on a clearing or located on the forest-edge. This is known as a display station or singing ground. Display takes place mainly at dawn and dusk in the breeding season, but also occurs on warm winter nights. The male stands upright on the ground with breast puffed out and bill held horizontally, giving a nasal 'peent' call, interspersed with a quiet, cooing 'tuko'. The call is similar to that of a nighthawk and is often confused with it. Every few minutes the male will take flight and circle high overhead, producing wing-twitter-ing noises before hovering and giving the 'song', a number of liquid chirping notes,

▷An American Woodcock
on its nest.

which continues as he plummets back to earth in a series of zig-zags with his wings whistling. The song flight of the American Woodcock lasts from two to three minutes.

Females are attracted to the display station and once they are there, the male displays to them on the ground with his tail raised and spread and his wings drooped. Males are promiscuous, mating with as many females as they can attract to their station, but after mating they take no further part in family life.

The nest is a rudimentary structure on the forest floor. The female lays four buffy eggs, sparingly spotted with brown and grey, and sits tight during the day, relying on her superb camouflage to avoid detection. At dawn and dusk, she will leave briefly to feed. Incubation takes 19 to 21 days and, once hatched, the young develop rapidly. They can fly short distances in just two weeks and are fully grown after four. Like the Eurasian Woodcock, the female American is reputed to be able to carry her young between her legs in flight, and this has been reliably observed.

Black-tailed Godwit

Limosa limosa

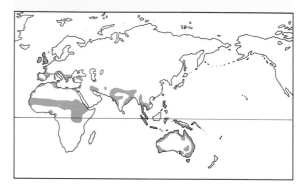

With its long bill and legs this is not only the larger of the two Palearctic godwits, but also the taller and more graceful. It nests in small colonies among damp vegetation, but at other times occurs around the muddy margins of fresh water, in flooded fields, and in favoured estuaries or river valleys in winter. Whether displaying over their breeding territories, feeding in flocks or roosting together, Black-tailed Godwits are always delightful birds to watch.

There are three separate races. The European and western Asiatic race breeds in an area stretching from England across to central Russia and winters mainly in Africa and India.

LENGTH: 360-440 mm (12-17 in)

The Icelandic race breeds in Iceland and winters in western Europe, especially in Britain and Ireland. The third race breeds in eastern Asia and winters south to Australia, passing through the Aleutian Islands in spring. The species has occurred as a vagrant to the eastern seaboard of the U.S.A.

At all seasons the Black-tailed Godwit is a striking bird in flight with a strong white wing-bar, contrasting black and white tail, and white underwing. Its long bill and legs – the latter projecting well beyond the tail – also give it a distinctive, elongated appearance. By comparison the relative with which it is most likely to be confused, the Bar-tailed Godwit, is very much more uniform. The Hudsonian Godwit (a very rare visitor to Europe) shows mainly black underwings and the Willet (another American vagrant to Europe), has a boldly marked black and white underwing.

On the ground more care is needed as confusion is possible between all three godwits. However, there are some useful structural differences. The Black-tailed Godwit has proportionately longer legs, neck, and bill as well as a more upright stance. Its bill is also straighter than those of the other two species. Plumage differences between the species are more subtle and depend on the time of year and the sex of the particular bird.

Northward migration to the breeding territories takes place between February and April, with European birds arriving from Africa a month or so before birds wintering in Britain leave for Iceland. At this time many of the birds are moulting into their breeding plumage. The males begin to sport rich, chestnut-red heads, necks, and upper bellies; chestnut, black, and grey blotches on their backs; and dark bars on their flanks and bellies. The females are similar, but less strongly marked, paler, and more diffusely coloured.

Once back on their breeding territories among damp, tussocky grass, marshy moorland, blanket bog, wet heath, or reclaimed land near to fresh water, Black-tailed Godwits become very conspicuous and noisy. The males indulge in switch-back displays of agile tumbling and rolling, accompanied by strident 'weeka-weeka-weeka' calls.

The western European population is centred on the low countries and West Germany. In Britain the species became extinct about 150 years ago, but began to recolonize the Ouse Washes in East Anglia in the 1950s. Since then it has established a firm foothold there and has spread to new areas, though with no more than 80 pairs at a dozen widely scattered sites it remains scarce and local. The British migrant population has also increased.

▷ *A newly hatched Black-tailed Godwit chick.*

◁ *Black-tailed Godwits in winter plumage.*

△ *Like many waders, the Black-tailed Godwit will perch freely on posts during its nesting period.*

Once paired, a shallow scrape is made on the ground or in short vegetation and this is lined with grass stems or leaves before the three or four olive brown eggs with dark markings are laid on it. Incubation, which is undertaken by both adults, lasts about three weeks, but the young are tended by their parents for another month or so. Juveniles have a warm pink or buff tinge to their upperparts and breast, which is reminiscent of a pale adult in breeding plumage.

The return passage southwards begins in late June, when the adults start to leave their breeding quarters. Juveniles follow soon afterwards and by the end of August the breeding grounds are mostly deserted. Migration peaks between mid-July and October, by which time the adults have lost all of their warmly coloured plumage and are uniformly pale grey-brown above and grey-white beneath. Juveniles, however, may still retain some of their warmer colouration.

Some 5,000 Black-tailed Godwits winter in Britain. The largest gatherings occur in the estuaries along the southern coasts of Ireland and England, on the Stour and Hamford Water in eastern England, and on the Ribble and Dee in north-west England.

Black-tailed Godwits generally feed apart from other species in tight flocks that may number several hundred. Often they are seen up to their bellies in water, probing into the mud with a rapid action while their heads are totally submerged. On land they peck food from plants as well as probing the soil. Their diet consists chiefly of invertebrates, particularly earthworms from inland, and both lugworms and ragworms from around the coast. Where Black-tailed and Bar-tailed Godwits share the same estuary, the Black-tailed tends to probe for its food in the muddy channels of the inner estuary, whereas the Bar-tailed prefers the sandier outer estuary.

Hudsonian Godwit
Limosa haemastica

LENGTH: 355-405 mm (14-16 in)

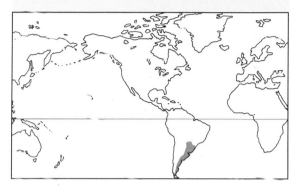

Once thought to be a rare and endangered species, the Hudsonian Godwit was, and still is, an elusive guest for many American bird-watchers. However, quite recent discoveries of regular 'staging posts' and migratory flight lines along narrow corridors, have shown it to be less rare than was previously believed.

Arguably the best place to see the Hudson-ian Godwit is on road-side flooded fields along the Gulf of Texas during April. Here they are in their element, feeding in close association with each other, wading belly-deep in water, and frequently swimming when out of their depth. On these occasions they immerse their heads in a series of rapid probing motions, moving from side to side to seek out worms, molluscs, and crustaceans. The birds often lift their heads totally clear of the water as they struggle with larger prey. The Hudsonian Godwit is equally at home in a variety of aquatic habitats from estuaries and tidal beaches, to fresh-water and saline lagoons. Here birds will strut about stiff-legged, toes outstretched and heads and necks lowered in a hunched posi-tion. At other times, if alarmed, they shoot up erect with necks fully stretched, revealing the full majestic beauty of their breeding plumage.

▽ *A Hudsonian Godwit on its breeding ground.*

In bright sun the deep chestnut red breast and belly, and light grey head and neck, contrast markedly with the black and yellow spangled back, giving the bird a regal look. The long orange bill with a black tip is slightly upturned, while the longish legs are dark grey. Normally a shy, unapproachable bird, the Hudsonian Godwit is easily disturbed and quickly takes flight, revealing narrow white wing bars, a black and white tail, and protruding legs. At such times it bears some resemblance to the European Black-tailed Godwit, but the Hudsonian Godwit is a more slender looking bird with less extensive areas of white on wings and tail. At rest when in winter plumage, however, both species look similar, with greyish upperparts and a white breast underneath. But the Hudsonian Godwit has only to raise its wings, revealing jet-black under-wing linings to preclude any doubt as to its identity if the two species are encountered together. The bird has these black feathers at all times of the year. In flight its ordinary call is a modulating trill reminiscent of the Whimbrel.

Spring stop-over feeding sites hold these birds for only a day or two as they move quickly north through the Great Lakes towards their breeding grounds of north-western British Columbia, parts of Alaska and northern Canada from the Mackenzie river valley to Hudson Bay. Here at the edge of the tree limit, this godwit chooses the extensive sedge marshes, bogs, and meadows in the vicinity of lakes and coasts in which to raise its young. In such settings, the male bird attracts its mate and defends its territory with elaborate aerial displays and song flights, whilst on the ground the black underwing features in its display.

As soon as the pair bond has been formed, a scrape is prepared, which is no more than a depression in a tussock of grass, to which a lining of grass and dead leaves is added. This is usually near to dry hummocks or dwarf trees, which serve as lookout posts during the nesting period. The four eggs are light olive buff, sparingly spotted with dark markings. Incubation takes 22 to 25 days and is carried out by the female during the day and by the male at night.

▷ This Hudsonian Godwit is using a tree top as a lookout in defence of its breeding territory.

◁ A Hudsonian Godwit on migration.

The fledging period is around 30 days, during which time the young are closely guarded by both parents. At the end of this time the young birds strangely disappear for around 10 days to reappear suddenly, fully feathered and in a free-flying state on a nearby shoreline.

From the end of July, the birds mass on the east Canadian coast around the James's Bay and Hudson Bay areas, where almost the entire population of this species passes through prior to their flight south to Tierra del Fuego. During this long migratory movement there are at present no known regular feeding and resting places where these birds might be found, so that it is still one of the more difficult north American shore birds to locate, certainly in the autumn.

The first Hudsonian Godwit to be recorded in the British Isles was an adult, accompanying four Black-tailed Godwits, at Blacktoft Sands, Humberside, from September 10 to October 3 1981. On November 22 of the same year what has been assumed to be the same individual appeared at Countess Weir, Devonshire, again accompanying four Black-tailed Godwits. It remained in that area until at least mid-January 1982. After an absence of more than a year, a Hudsonian Godwit visited Blacktoft again, between April 26 and May 6, 1983. So although there have now been three appearances in Britain, it seems that only one individual has been involved. Given that this species is thought to make a long oceanic migration over the western Atlantic between Canada and South America the bird might be thought a candidate for regular transatlantic displacement, but it is clearly well adapted to its offshore flight.

Bar-tailed Godwit

Limosa lapponica

This, the smaller of the two Palearctic godwits, can typically be found in its favoured winter habitat, the tidal shoreline. Whether probing the exposed surface for food, flying in loose skeins over an incoming tide, or roosting on a high sandbank in the company of other waders, it is always an interesting bird to observe.

Confusion with its near relative the Black-tailed Godwit is possible, but once the Bar-tailed is seen in flight the rather uniform grey-brown wings, barred tail and contrasting white of the rump and lower back make identification easier. Curlew and Whimbrel share a similar plumage pattern in flight, but the long straight bill of the Bar-tailed Godwit distinguishes it from these two species.

At rest, separation from the Black-tailed Godwit is less easy, but careful observation will reveal a Bar-tailed Godwit in winter plumage to be a slightly browner bird with more heavily streaked upperparts and dull white underparts. Further, the shorter all-dark legs, slightly up-tilted bill and more dumpy appearance are useful differences.

By late March, Bar-tailed Godwits start to moult into their breeding plumage. The male at this season develops a deep rufous-cinnamon or chestnut coloration on the underparts and around the head, with the darker centred mantle and scapular feathers showing orangey-buff edgings. The wing coverts remain a duller grey-brown, but this bird in full plumage is arguably the smartest wader to be found along the shore line. The female remains duller looking, only developing a warm buff wash down the throat and breast.

From autumn through the winter the species can be found in loose flocks along both muddy and sandy shores, often feeding close to the water's edge, where prey is more active beneath the ebb and flow of the tide. Here it can usually be observed walking briskly in search of food before stopping to snatch surfacing worms, or on occasions probing deeper by rotating its head and bill in an effort to capture more elusive items. The bird's diet typically consists

LENGTH: 370-410 mm (14½-16 in)

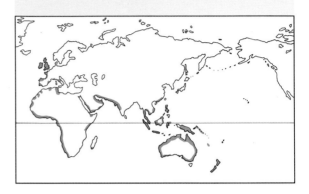

of annelid worms, crustaceans, and molluscs. In the breeding quarters, seeds and berries are an important additional element of the diet, especially before the main hatch of beetles, caterpillars, and other insects has taken place.

By late May most breeding adults will have arrived back on their Arctic nesting grounds, which stretch from northern Scandinavia eastwards to the westernmost part of Alaska lying close to the Arctic Circle between latitudes 65° and 75° north. The birds prefer large open tracts of low-lying swamp tundra over which the male will stake out a territory by performing an aerial 'skydance', accompanied at times by a short song. The nest is a shallow depression, which is lined with a few twigs and dead leaves. The three or four eggs have a light background colour with sparse grey markings and brown blotches. These are incubated by both sexes for about three weeks, rather a short period for a wader of its size. After hatching, the young will remain near to the adult birds until they fledge, about four weeks later. Juveniles resemble the adults in winter plumage, but show a slightly warmer buff wash down the breast and a greater contrast between the brown-centred and buff-edged feathers on the upperparts.

Adults depart the breeding grounds in late June and July, with the birds of the year following on soon afterwards. Migration southwards to traditional autumn moulting grounds such as the Ribble and the Wash estuaries in Britain, and the Wadden Sea in the Netherlands, is fairly rapid. Some birds will fly straight through to their wintering areas, instead of stopping over for a few weeks to complete their moult before heading further south once again. At this time of year, as well as during spring passage, a few birds may be seen inland, but the majority fly straight over or along the coast. Occurrences even a few miles from the seaboard are generally rather irregular.

The Bar-tailed Godwit can be found wintering along the shores well to the south in Africa with a spasmodic distribution eastwards from here around coastal India and south-east Asia and into Australasia. Concentrations of up to 600,000 are recorded around Mauritania, north-west Africa, whilst perhaps 60 per cent of the 100,000 remaining in western Europe can be found on the mud flats of Britain and Ireland.

Feeding flocks of Bar-tailed Godwits may be large, but are usually quite well spread, and often intermingled with other species of shorebirds. However, as the tide flows in, groups of birds will take off and gather together in large numbers. They fly, often for several kilometres, to favoured roost sites on isolated sand bars or shingle ridges. As the birds head inshore they are more frequently heard to call – usually a sharp 'kak-kak' or 'kirrick'. On approaching a high tide roost they fall spectacularly towards the ground, braking at the last moment before alighting on the chosen site. Godwits in a roost are evenly spaced with a couple of birds' lengths between each individual and even when all appear to be asleep they remain alert to the slightest disturbance.

It is the sub-species *Limosa lapponica baueri* that breeds in Alaska. In winter plumage it might be mistaken for a Marbled Godwit as it appears sparingly on migration along the North American Pacific coast. The European bird is a rare visitor on the Atlantic coast with only a handful of records.

▽ *Males in winter plumage at a spring tide roost.*

◁ *A female Bar-tailed Godwit on the nest.*

▽ *A male Bar-tailed Godwit on the nest.*

Marbled Godwit

Limosa fedoa

The largest member of the godwit family, the Marbled Godwit differs from its relatives in not attaining a distinctly obvious bright orange or red plumage in the breeding season. Like the other godwits, however, it does at times look awkward and ungainly, waddling along the shoreline on its extremely long dark legs, with its head tucked into its shoulders, seemingly only at ease while belly deep in water. At such times it uses a rapid sewing-machine-like nodding action in its relentless pursuit for food. When doing this, it keeps its head almost permanently submerged, only occasionally lifting it clear of the water to swallow large prey, which includes molluscs, crustaceans, worms, leeches, and larval insects. At other times it will probe in soft mud and on occasions it will rapidly run along the shore, catching food washed up by the incoming tide, like a giant Sanderling.

By April it has attained breeding plumage which, if not strikingly bright, has a warm subtle beauty of its own with the dark brown and black upperparts heavily spotted and streaked with buff, white, and chestnut. These give the bird a 'marbled' effect, hence its name. The underparts are tawny brown, barred darker brown on the neck, breast, and flanks.

Throughout May, the Marbled Godwits return to their breeding grounds, which extend from Canada's central prairie provinces to Montana, North and South Dakota, and western Minnesota. Preferred locations seem to be prairie wetlands close to ponds, streams, or fresh or saline lakes. Amongst the grass of a short- to medium-length grassy meadow, the male stakes out his territory, with other marbled godwits close by as neighbours in a semi-colonial existence. His display involves raising the wings, revealing bright orange and cinnamon under-wing feathers and axillaries. Circling flights are also undertaken, accompanied by musical 'ger-whit' calls.

The nest, formed by the male, is a depression on a raised area of an otherwise damp terrain. Here the four buff-olive, slightly

LENGTH: 405-510 mm (16-20 in)

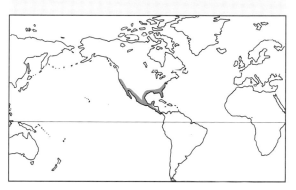

△ *This Marbled Godwit was photographed in Florida on its northbound spring migration.*

△ A Marbled Godwit
stretches its wing revealing
the conspicuous cinnamon-
coloured flight feathers.

spotted eggs are laid on a grassy lining. The female incubates for the majority of the 23 days, during which time she sits tightly and will not move until almost stepped on. The male incubates the eggs throughout the night. During the nesting period the adults feed on insects, especially grasshoppers. They catch these by stalking them in the grass or occasionally by catching them in flight. As well as foraging close to the nest site, birds can be found farther afield on dry uplands, open ponds and at times roadside ditches.

The young are vigorously defended by both adults, but it is the female who is usually the first to respond to danger. As if by signal, the rest of the colony react in a mass show of protection, and on such occasions the air is filled with strident 'ker-rek' alarm calls, as the birds whirl in pursuit of the foe. After about 3 weeks, the female is left to tend the, by now, well grown young, while the males gather to form large pre-migratory groups in nearby fields. Four weeks after hatching, the young are ready to migrate.

By the end of July, the birds head south-west to the California coast, with smaller numbers flying south-east to the Gulf of Mexico. At their staging posts the Marbled Godwits mix with other migrant wading birds. At this time this species might be confused with the larger Long-billed Curlew, although the godwit's long slightly upturned two-toned pink and black bill should make it possible to identify it.

Confined to the North American continent as a breeding species, it also formerly bred in Nebraska, Iowa, and Wisconsin, but due to over-hunting its numbers have dramatically decreased in recent decades.

During the winter, the vast majority of the population is found on the Pacific coast of California through to Mexico and Panama. Others frequent the Gulf coast south to central America, where they will congregate on estuaries, beaches, flooded fields, and marshes, usually separate from other shore birds.

Eskimo Curlew

Numenius borealis

The Eskimo Curlew formerly darkened the skies of North America on its spring migration across Texas and the Great Plains, and was as common, if not more so, on the coast of Labrador and New England in the fall. In the period from 1850 to 1890, however, the species was ruthlessly slaughtered, and by 1929 it was thought to be extinct. Fortunately, this was not quite true. Although it is teetering on the brink of extinction, one or two are still occasionally seen on migration, most regularly on the coast of Texas at Galveston Island. In addition, two specimens were seen in possible breeding habitat to the west of Hudson Bay in August 1976.

The Eskimo Curlew performed spectacular Great Circle migrations to and from its breeding areas on the barren-ground tundra of the Northwest Territories of Canada (and perhaps also Alaska). In the fall, the flocks would head via south-east Canada to the coastal marshes of Labrador, Newfoundland, and Nova Scotia, where dense concentrations of the birds spent a few days fattening up on berries and small snails. Then they headed out over the Atlantic and across the southern Caribbean to their wintering grounds on the pampas of South America, from southern Brazil to central Argentina. There is unfortunately no record of the habits of the species in its winter quarters.

In the spring, the Eskimo Curlews returned north on a different route, flying over Central America and then following the Mississippi and Missouri valleys north across the tall-grass prairies of the Great Plains, feeding largely on grasshoppers. Not surprisingly for such a powerful migrant, vagrants reached Bermuda, Greenland, and even Ireland and Britain. Of those that reached Britain, two were recorded in Suffolk in 1852, and individuals were sighted in Grampian in 1855, 1878 and 1880, in Dublin in 1870 (found at a market and said to have been shot at Sligo), and the Isles of Scilly in 1887. Sightings have also been reported in the Falkland Islands, the Pribilof Islands and the extreme eastern U.S.S.R.

LENGTH: 290-340 mm (11½-13 in)

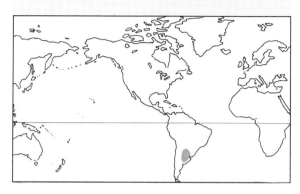

The demise of the Eskimo Curlew was at the hand of man. They were slaughtered in the fall on the East Coast and, as settlers moved west, they were also killed in large numbers on the Great Plains in spring. This hunting was at first for food, but later degenerated into the pointless destruction that was to decimate so many of the animals and birds of the mid-West. Even in the winter, they were not safe from Argentinian hunters. From being extraordinarily abundant, like the Passenger Pigeon, they came close to suffering the same fate as that gregarious and ill-fated species. Indeed, they were known by early settlers as 'prairie pigeons', and Audubon, visiting Labrador in July 1833, compared the Eskimo Curlew to the earlier flocks of Passenger Pigeons. There were great clouds of them, flocks a mile square in the air and covering 16-20 hectares (40-50 acres) on the ground. Now there are none, and it is a lucky birdwatcher indeed who gets the chance to try to identify a single individual.

At three-quarters of the size of a Whimbrel, the Eskimo is a tiny curlew and much smaller than any other American curlew. However, great care must be taken in its identification. The Eskimo shares a dark rump with the North American race of Whimbrel, and its striped head is also similar, though the pattern is less well-defined. An important distinction is the cinnamon tone to the underparts and underwing of the Eskimo. In addition, its inner primaries are plain rather than notched and barred with off-white, as in the Whimbrel. Its voice was described as a rippling 'tr-tr-tr' (the Inuit name was an onomatopoeic 'pi-pi-pi-uk') and a whistled 'bee-bee', and calls resembling the Upland Sandpiper have also been reported.

The Eskimo Curlew is very closely related to the Little Curlew of Siberia. Indeed, it has even been suggested that it is the same species. Whilst it may seem an academic exercise to distinguish the two, a Little Curlew was seen in California in 1984 and the Asian species may be more likely on the West Coast or in Alaska than the native Eskimo Curlew. The Eskimo is slightly larger, longer-winged (the wingtips project well beyond the tail at rest), shorter-legged (the toes do not project beyond the tail in flight) and cinnamon (rather than buffish) on the underparts and underwing. Notably, the Y-shaped chevrons along its flanks are a good clue to identification.

Little is known of the breeding biology of the species beyond the fact that the clutch of four, occasionally three, eggs, is laid in the second half of June. All the eggs now held in museums were collected by one man, Roderick MacFarlan, between the Mackenzie and Coppermine rivers. Though there are no records, the fledging period is probably very short, with the birds leaving for their winter quarters immediately after fledging.

Whimbrel

Numenius phaeopus

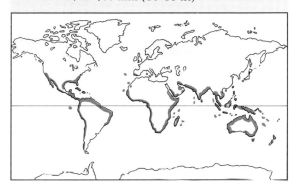

This smaller northern relative of the Curlew is the most cosmopolitan species in its family. Known in some localities as the seven whistler, its distinctive whistling call as it passes overhead is often the first indication of its presence.

At first glance this species appears rather similar to *Numenius arquata*, but on closer inspection the boldly patterned head, shorter, more sharply decurved bill and smaller size, all suggest that it is a different species. The combination of a pale buff central crown stripe and eyebrows, contrasting strongly with darker sides to the crown and eye stripe are particularly distinctive. The upperparts appear slightly darker brown than the Curlew with variably marked paler feather fringes giving a more mottled appearance at a distance. The white upper tail, rump, and back contrast with the rest of the upperparts and the tail, which is grey brown with darker barring. The underparts are buffish white, variably streaked with darker brown on the breast. In flight, confusion is possible with the smaller Bar-tailed Godwit until the Whimbrel's distinctive downcurved bill is revealed.

The Whimbrel can generally be found feeding singly or in small parties. It tends to use its keen eyesight to pick at visible prey more than

OTHER NAME: Seven Whistler
LENGTH: 400-460 mm (16-18 in)

its larger relatives, though it will also be seen making 'test-probes' with its bill. The bird's wide diet is dependent to a certain extent on seasonal availability, but generally includes molluscs, crustaceans, and annelids along the shore line, with a corresponding terrestrial diet of snails, beetles, and earthworms. As a supplement or even a main constituent, various berries and seeds may be taken on more northerly breeding grounds.

▽ A Whimbrel (of the eastern race, Hudsonicus) on its nest in Manitoba, Canada.

As a breeding species the Whimbrel has a virtually circumpolar distribution. Within these upper-middle latitudes preference is shown for bare open areas of tundra or comparatively dry moorland that has perhaps the occasional stunted tree. The birds arrive during May and quickly claim territories. Both males and females will display over the chosen ground with a bubbling song flight rather similar to that of the Curlew. The nest is selected from one of a number of small scrapes that are excavated and is usually found amongst short tussocky vegetation. This is sparsely lined with dead grass and maybe a few feathers. The four eggs are olive brown, blotched and spotted brown and lavender. These are incubated for 27 to 28 days, largely by the female. At this time the male is very protective of his territory and often stands sentinel on a nearby rock or boulder. Many nests are robbed by Arctic Skuas, while gulls, crows and perhaps the odd fox also take their toll. The appearance of any such threat normally drives the Whimbrel into a noisy defence of its eggs or young, when it will fly low and straight, aiming for the head of the intruder.

The juveniles take five or six weeks to fledge, thereafter quickly becoming independent. They are similar in appearance to the adults, but the crown is darker, showing less contrast with lateral crown stripes and eyebrows. The wing coverts are also slightly darker and the breast markings smaller and more rounded.

From late July, the passage birds head south. Icelandic, North European and central Siberian breeders winter in the Afrotropics and along the coasts of the west Indian Ocean. Farther east, Whimbrels head for the shores of south-east Asia and Australasia, while Alaskan breeders winter along the coasts of South America as far south as Tierra del Fuego. Movement is generally along a broad front, although travelling Whimbrels are most frequently observed along the coast. In Britain most inland records are of birds heard calling as they pass overhead – frequently at night. Many more probably fly through undetected.

Very small numbers of Whimbrels winter in western Europe. Usually no more than thirty are seen in Britain and Ireland in any one season. These may be individuals that have bred in the Scottish Highlands and islands, although more probably they are birds returning from nesting grounds farther to the north.

In North America Whimbrels move up the Pacific coast in spring and can also be seen locally inland, passing through the interior to northern Alaska and parts of the western Canadian Arctic. The fall route is the reverse of this. On the Atlantic side the birds arrive

◁Newly hatched Whimbrel chicks and egg shells in a nest.

▷A Whimbrel calls as it approaches its Shetland nesting site.

via the West Indies, generally migrating along the coast up to Chesapeake Bay, sometimes as far as New Jersey, then inland to James Bay and west Hudson Bay. In the fall, some birds cross the Ungava Peninsula to the outer part of the Gulf of St Lawrence; others cross from James Bay to the Gulf then all follow the same course to the Maritimes. From there they fly over water to the New Jersey area to continue the spring route in reverse.

The Nearctic race of the Whimbrel (the so-called 'Hudsonian Whimbrel' or 'Hudsonian Curlew') breeds in Alaska and areas west and south of the vicinity of Hudson Bay. It has a brown lower back and rump, uniform with the rest of the upperparts, whereas in the nominate race these areas are contrastingly white. American individuals are, therefore, identifiable in the field, and have been recorded in Britain on four occasions up to 1986. The first was on Fair Isle, Shetland, in May 1955 and this sighting was followed by a number of others: in County Kerry in October 1957, Out Skerries, Shetland, in July and August 1974, and County Wexford in September 1980.

▷ A migrant Whimbrel wades along the margins of an inland pool.

Curlew

Numenius arquata

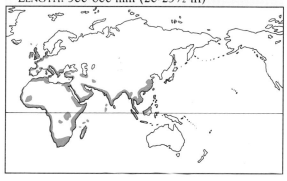

It is customary when writing about this bird to commence with reference to its call. There is good reason for this, since the far-reaching cry of this species (which gives rise to its name) is the very essence of the wild and lonely places that are the usual domain of this majestic wading bird.

The largest of the European shore birds, equalled only in size by the Long-billed Curlew and the Far Eastern Curlew, 10 to 15 cm (4 to 6 in) of its length are taken up by the distinctive curved bill, the longest-billed birds being females. Not as dramatically patterned as some species, the Curlew's head, neck, and breast are light brown with dark streaking, while its underparts are whitish with streaks and transverse barring to the flanks. There is brown barring on the tail, and the long legs are greenish grey. When flying, which it does much more slowly and in a more gull-like fashion than most other waders, the whitish rump extending up the back is a distinctive feature, for there are no wing bars. When travelling over any distance a flock will fly at some considerable height in long lines or in V-formation. At such times the frequent 'cour-

OTHER NAMES: Eurasian Curlew, European Curlew, Common Curlew
LENGTH: 500-600 mm (20-23½ in)

lee' contact cry, with emphasis on the first syllable, draws attention to the birds' presence as they pass overhead.

A bird of temperate and sub-arctic regions, the Curlew breeds from Britain eastwards to Siberia and from Scandinavia and Russia in the north to France through to the Balkans and beyond to the Kirghiz Steppes. The winter range extends from northern Europe to the Atlantic Isles in the west, south to South Africa and Madagascar, and east to India, and south-

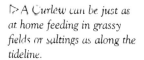

▷ A Curlew can be just as at home feeding in grassy fields or saltings as along the tideline.

east Asia. A widespread breeding bird in lowland Britain, inhabiting river valleys, meadows, and crop fields, it is better known as a bird of upland areas where indeed it is still a typical summer inhabitant. However, densities of nesting birds are generally lower at these moorland sites.

Most British Curlews return to their nesting grounds early in the year, many during February in lowland areas, though some upland locations may not ring to the stirring bubbling trill which is uttered by both sexes until early April. Most birds are usually paired on arrival and once territories are staked out these are delineated by territory marking flights. The birds rise steeply on trembling wings to hang

suspended before planing earthwards, trilling as they do so.

The male makes several scrapes in the grass or heather, and the female lays four eggs in the one of her choosing. The eggs are pear-shaped, glossy, greenish to dark brown, and have speckles, blotches and streaks of brown. There is only one brood. Once the eggs are laid the pair become very secretive. Regular incubation begins on completion of the clutch and lasts about four weeks. Both parents take turns, changing over twice daily. The chick is basically tan in colour with black and brown markings. It has a short straight bill. It grows quickly and within six weeks is fully fledged with its bill half-grown. The curve is fully developed by the

time the bird is 18 or 19 weeks old.

By the end of July most of the breeding grounds are deserted and family parties wander in search of suitable feeding areas. They finally move to the coasts and estuaries for the winter, where they feed between the tides on ragworms, molluscs and small crabs. In late fall particularly, this latter prey forms a major part of the Eurasian Curlew's diet. When feeding, the Curlew walks sedately making frequent shallow jabs with the bill; sometimes it will extract its prey from sand, mud, or tidal pool by agile neck movements. At times it will wade deeply and is invariably the last to leave any feeding area as the tide rises.

At high tide large numbers will roost together. In late fall particularly, numbers are at their greatest. As well as using uncovered sand banks, rocks or islands, some will resort to nearby fields to preen and rest or to continue feeding.

In England and Wales there are some inland areas which traditionally hold wintering flocks with 1,000 or so birds in favoured places. In Ireland inland feeding is widespread particularly in the west. The British winter population of Curlews is supplemented by migrants from central and eastern Europe including some from Russia, though many of these birds are merely passing through on their journey to France and the Iberian peninsula.

Whereas the British breeding population of Curlews is possibly in the region of 50,000 pairs, winter totals are probably in excess of 200,000 birds. In the Nearctic the Curlew is a vagrant to Massachusetts, New York, Jan Mayer, and Bear Island. The Long-billed Curlew is the counterpart of the Eurasian bird in North America and this is the next species to be dealt with in this book.

◁ *A group of Curlews on the Red Rocks in the Dee Estuary await the turn of the tide.*

▽ *A Curlew at its nest with newly hatched young.*

Long-billed Curlew

Numenius americanus

The largest of the North American shore birds, the Long-billed Curlew closely resembles its relative the Curlew, although it has a much larger bill. In summer dress, however, the drab brownish grey becomes a rich buffish orange, lessening any similarities with the Eurasian bird. Surprisingly, though, it could be confused with the unrelated Marbled Godwit in this form, particularly if observed from a considerable distance, when the shape of the bill is not apparent. Seen clearly, though, it will be noted that the Long-billed Curlew's head is small and grey, and almost unmarked except for an inconspicuous white eyebrow. Its long thin neck, breast and belly are a bright orangey buff colour with fine dark streakings and spots. The mantle and wing coverts are black, uniformly spangled with buff and orange. The beautiful orangey body plumage is further enhanced by brighter orange underwing linings and axillaries, giving the species an even more striking appearance when in flight. Additionally, the darker coverts and outer primaries contrast markedly with the bright orange trailing edge of this bird's very long wings, a further aid to its identification even when viewed from a long way off.

The strikingly long curved bill is of course a major feature of this bird and can vary in size from twice the head length in some males and most juveniles to three times the head length in females. This formidable tool is used in the bird's unremitting search for food in a variety of ways. Typically it will probe for prey such as crustaceans and worms. It works along tidal beaches and mud flats, relentlessly pursuing its prey with rapid twisting probes until it is dislodged. The victim is then juggled into an acceptable position before it is swallowed.

Other food is gathered by the Long-billed Curlew when wading belly-deep in water, the head totally submerged, probing frantically with a quick nodding action. It can sometimes also be observed casually stalking crabs (it has a fondness for Louisiana fiddler crabs) across

Other Name: Sicklebill
Length: 510-660 mm (20-26 in)

open mud flats or chasing them with elegant gait as the situation dictates. Small fish, amphibians, and insect larvae additionally help to sustain this bird as particular feeding circumstances allow.

Throughout the winter the Long-billed Curlew can be found in a variety of haunts other than those described above and these can include saline and fresh-water lakes, flooded fields, and farmland. In such circumstances it is often solitary, when it is invariably shy and unapproachable, but along the coast it is a gregarious species when it freely associates with other species – especially with Marbled Godwits.

Long-billed Curlews return to their breeding grounds early in the year, at which time its eerie echoing 'cour-lee' call draws attention to the often high-flying V-formations as the birds pass overhead, northward bound.

Over the last century this bird's breeding range has receded dramatically, due to over-hunting, and is now confined to south-west and southern central Canada, California, Utah, Nevada, northern New Mexico, and coastal and northern Texas. Within this area two races of Long-billed Curlew are now recognized. The 'Lesser' Long-billed Curlew breeds in the northern part of the species range including Canada, South Dakota, and Wyoming, through to California. The 'Greater' Long-

◁A Long-billed Curlew takes flight revealing the long wings with orangey-coloured trailing edges, an orangey rump, and a tail barred with dark brown.

▽A female Long-billed Curlew with a bill that is three times as long as its head, wades in flooded grassland, a favourite haunt.

billed Curlew is restricted to Nevada, Utah, New Mexico, and Texas. Between the two races there are, apart from some slight size variation, only subtle and insignificant differences of plumage, making distinguishing them in the field almost impossible.

By the end of April, most of these birds have arrived back on their nesting territories. Preferring prairie and rolling grassland (though sometimes quite arid locations are chosen), they are faithful to their chosen site, returning year after year unless disturbed. Not a great deal is known about the Long-billed Curlew's breeding behaviour, but its pre-nesting display comprises song and flight activity similar to the bird's Eurasian counterpart. The nest site is a hollow or depression created by the male, usually in shortish open grassland situations. This is lined with a certain amount of dry grasses. The four eggs are whitish buff to deep olive, overlaid with spots and blotches of various dark brown shades. The clutch is usually complete by mid-May, and both parents take it in turns to incubate. After around thirty days the eggs hatch. Two weeks later the female vacates the area, leaving the male to look after the young until they are fully fledged, about six weeks later. During this time a great deal of the birds' food comprises berries and insects, particularly grasshoppers. Astonishingly, it also acquires a taste for nesting birds and their chicks.

After nesting has been completed, Long-billed Curlews remain to forage on farmland and around inland waters, though most move to the coast. The preferred wintering grounds are California, South Carolina, and Texas. Some birds move out of the U.S.A., by October, making their way southwards to Mexico, Guatemala, Venezuela, and Panama.

The Long-billed Curlew has unfortunately gone into decline over the last century through over-hunting and habitat destruction. Sadly it has ceased to breed in many areas where it was formerly common. Now fully protected, it has, since the 1950s, shown appreciable improvement in its status though it is doubtful if it will ever return to its former abundance.

▷ *A Long-billed Curlew*
with a shorter-length bill is
more likely to be a male.

Upland Sandpiper

Bartramia longicauda

Plover or sandpiper? The choice of common names indicates something of the popularity of this dry-land wader. It feeds like a plover, and looks similar to the curlews in some ways, to the shanks in others, but is probably not closely related to either.

The Upland Sandpiper is very distinctive. About the size of a yellowlegs, its long tail projects beyond its wingtips when it is at rest, and the small head is supported by a neck which, when fully stretched, can look ridiculously thin. The short, straight bill is yellow with a darker ridge and tip. The species has a high-stepping gait: the head and neck are pumped backwards and forwards and the tail flicked or wagged. When feeding, the Upland Sandpiper hunts by sight, executing little runs before stopping and rapidly picking up small items. It often perches – on rocks, walls, trees, and fenceposts – and holds its wings up for a couple of seconds on landing.

OTHER NAMES: Batram's Sandpiper, Upland Plover
LENGTH: 280-320 mm (11-12½ in)

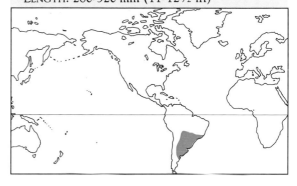

The general appearance of this bird recalls a very small Curlew or Whimbrel. Notably, the crown is blackish with an indistinct buffish crown-stripe. Otherwise the face is very plain, and the large eye is consequently prominent and staring. Confusion is possible with Little and Eskimo Curlews, but these are larger birds with clearly decurved (not straight) bills and greyish (not yellowish) legs. In addition, the Eskimo Curlew has a very distinct cinnamon tone to the underparts. The Whimbrel and the various other species of curlew are clearly much larger than the Upland Sandpiper.

In flight the Upland Sandpiper has a cross-like outline with long wings and tail. The centre of the back, rump, and tail are particularly dark, as is the outer wing, and there are no pale wingbars. From below, the heavily barred underwing coverts and axillaries are noticeable. The species often flies with shallow, fluttery wingbeats recalling the Spotted and Common Sandpipers. The flight-call is a liquid, fluty 'quip-quip-ip', reminiscent of a quail. There is also a more tuneful song.

The Upland Sandpiper breeds in interior North America from north-west Alaska south and east across western Canada and the central and eastern U.S.A., to Virginia and Maryland, at elevations up to 1,850 metres (6,000 ft). Most common in the western parts of its range, it is scarce and declining in the east. Its num-

△ *An Upland Sandpiper. This particular bird was one that turned up on the Isles of* Scilly *in 1983 and became so tame that it eventually took food from the hand.*

bers were severely reduced in the late nineteenth and early twentieth centuries by widespread hunting, but, following protection, the species has now largely recovered. The Upland Sandpiper breeds in a variety of grassland settings, including prairies, hayfields, rank grassland along sloughs, pastures and, more rarely, in fallow cropfields and cultivation. Farther north, clearings in spruce forests are used.

Spring migrants reach the southern U.S.A. in early March, with the first arrivals on the southernmost breeding grounds in late April, but not until June in Alaska. They are usually already paired on arrival, and move straight on to their nesting territories, which are often grouped into loose colonies. The song flight is spectacular. The bird slowly circles at a great height giving a drawn-out whistle, a 'rrrr-phee-oooo', and may then fall to the earth like a stone. They also give a bubbling 'quip-ip-ip-ip-ip-ip-ip-ip'. The nest is well-hidden, often in a clump of grass which totally conceals it from above. Four eggs are laid. These have a creamy or pinkish buff colour, speckled or spotted with reddish brown. Both sexes incubate over a period of 24 days and the young fledge after

◁An Upland Sandpiper perches on a post in its favoured prairie grassland breeding territory of North America.

▷An Upland Sandpiper pants in the heat as it incubates its eggs.

a further 33 days. The diet comprises insects (mainly grasshoppers, crickets, and weevils), and in the fall the birds also eat seeds and spilled wheat.

In the fall juveniles begin to move south down the Mississippi and central flyways in early August, and most have left the States by October, moving through eastern central America or across the Gulf of Mexico to Columbia and Venezuela and then south to the pampas of southern Brazil and Argentina or to the Rio Negro. The Ontario and New England populations move south across the interior of the eastern states and over the Greater Antilles, and may be those found wintering in small numbers in Surinam and north-east Brazil. The species is a vagrant to the west coast of America, occurring in both spring and fall. It also travels much farther afield – even to Western Europe. In Britain, there had been 39 recorded sightings up to 1986, 24 of them since 1958. The Upland Sandpiper appeared annually from 1970 to 1976 but in only six of the subsequent ten years. Of the records since 1958, eight (33 per cent) were in the Isles of Scilly, three each in Ireland, Scotland, and Wales, two in Cornwall, and individuals in five other English counties. The majority arrived in September (seven) or October (eleven), but there were two as late as December and singles in April, July, and August. The April individual, on St Kilda, Western Isles, in 1980, is the sole spring occurrence.

Individuals have varied markedly in their behaviour, some being extremely wary while others have been relatively confiding. One on the Isles of Scilly in October 1983 proved to be probably the most approachable American wader ever, taking food from the hand and, eventually, even an earthworm from one observer's mouth! This sandpiper has also been recorded in Tristan da Cunha, south to the South Shetlands and west to New Zealand and Australia.

On passage and in winter, Upland Sandpipers are to be found in a variety of short-grass habitats, such as airfields and even suburban gardens, as well as fields, pastures, or prairie-dog towns. They are generally found singly or in small groups, away from other waders.

Spotted Redshank

Tringa erythropus

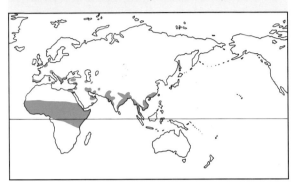

Compared to other 'shanks' this is the odd one out, on two counts. Firstly, it has no counterpart in America, and secondly, it undergoes a dramatic plumage transformation. It changes from its sober grey and white winter dress, to a majestic sooty black nuptial plumage evenly sprinkled with small bright white spots over its back and wings, this 'peppered' look giving rise to its name. This 'spotted' plumage is retained by most birds from late April through to June or July during which time it gives no cause for misidentification.

The Spotted Redshank breeds from northern Sweden eastwards to eastern Siberia, on a

OTHER NAMES: Dusky Redshank, Spot Shank
LENGTH: 290-320 mm (11½-12½ in)

slightly more northerly latitude than its relative the Greenshank, although both species breed on some open marshy areas in this region. The most favoured site is on a dry area, amongst forest marshes. Here it nests in a shallow depression lined with leaves, stems and feathers, usually close to a stone or dead branch, or occasionally below small trees. The four eggs are similar in colour and markings to those of the Greenshank but they are a slightly darker green. They hatch after 23 days or so, being incubated by the male alone. During this period the parents perch on a vantage point, usually a tree, and stand guard against would-be predators. After four to five weeks the young can fly. In some years when females are outnumbered by males, females will lay clutches for more than one male.

On passage the Spotted Redshank is for the most part a gregarious species, gathering in tight flocks of up to 30 birds, especially on coastal fresh-water lagoons. Occasionally in the fall, smaller flocks stop off at reservoirs and pools throughout inland Britain. At other times solitary birds are encountered, perhaps on a small reed-fringed pool, when they are wary and unapproachable. If disturbed they quickly take flight, uttering their characteristic, disyllabic, penetrating 'chu-it' whistle. In darting fast direct flight, they flash low across the reeds, to settle in another hidden pool.

When feeding, this bird takes full advantage of its slender bill and long red legs, probing in rapid sewing-machine-like fashion, with its head almost continually immersed in water as water beetles, newts, frogs, and small fish are all eagerly seized. On other occasions worms, crustaceans, and insect larvae are caught. In times of mosquito hatches, the Spotted Redshank frantically chases and snatches at these insects in flight. It rarely probes in open mud unlike most waders and might be considered as one of the more aquatic of its group. It is a frequent swimmer.

Identification of winter and fall birds is an annual cause of concern to most inexperienced birdwatchers. The problem is invariably the similar Redshank, as both this species and the Spotted Redshank are grey and white with red legs. Closer views however, will reveal subtle but obvious differences. The Spotted Redshank has a longer, more slender neck and long atten-

◁A moulting Spotted Redshank begins to lose the spotted appearance of its summer dress.

▷A Spotted Redshank in summer plumage.

△ A Spotted Redshank in
winter plumage.

uated rear end, as opposed to the more dumpy rounded redshank. The upperparts are much clearer in appearance, formed by a light-grey base, interspersed by uniformly white-edged feathers. A thick black stripe through the eye emphasizes a very obvious white eyebrow. The underparts are clearer, and whiter, with finer streaking. Bill and legs are much longer, the latter varying from red or orange through to pink. In flight, the lack of white secondaries is a clinching feature.

In Britain the species occurs as a spring and autumn passage migrant, being more in evidence inland, certainly during its return journey southwards. On average, 5,000 birds occur annually throughout the British Isles with the largest numbers noted on the south and east coasts. In the autumn most birds are juveniles and often these are seen well into October. In recent years it is reckoned that up to 200 individuals winter along the relatively warmer south coast of England.

The Spotted Redshank's main wintering area includes the Mediterranean region, Africa south to the equator, and occasionally South Africa. It is much commoner in west Africa than east Africa. Some birds move to southern Arabia while large numbers spend the non-breeding season in the Persian Gulf, northern Pakistan, south-east India, Sri-Lanka, Burma, southern China and Japan.

Redshank

Tringa totanus

At all times the noisy extrovert behaviour of this bird ensures that its presence is never overlooked wherever it is to be found. In Britain, estuaries and coastal marshes provide the suitable nesting requirements while at times drier situations in dune systems are favoured. Inland, damp marshland, grassy waterside meadows, the margins of lakes and reservoirs, sand and gravel workings, water reclamation works, and similar habitats are all used. Though many redshanks nest in the above-mentioned inland situations, the winter distribution of this bird is essentially a coastal one and, where there are suitable feeding areas, concentrations are quite considerable, especially at roosts, generally, however, the Redshank tends to feed singly or in small groups, well scattered over exposed mud flats and saltings. Rocky or shingly parts of the shoreline are normally avoided and flat sandy beaches offer no attraction to this bird at all.

When feeding, the Redshank picks and probes, finding most of its prey by sight. In coastal situations the food mainly comprises molluscs, crustaceans, and worms, which it will often wash before swallowing. At inland locations, earthworms, cranefly larvae, veget-

OTHER NAME: Common Redshank
LENGTH: 270-290 mm (10½-11½ in)

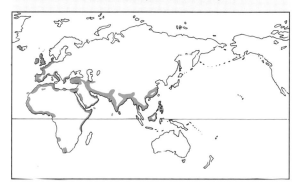

able matter, seeds, and berries are taken. As the occasion demands it will wade quite deeply, often up to its belly, swimming readily when out of its depth. In breeding plumage the rich brown upperparts of the back, head, and neck are strongly streaked with black, the white underparts closely streaked and speckled. (There is, however, considerable variation in the intensity of this colouring throughout its range). The vermillion red legs from which the bird gets its name are distinctive. The bill is also an orangey-red colour, tipped with black.

◁ *A Redshank broods its recently hatched young.*

In winter the Redshank loses its warm brown colouring and looks quite grey, while the red bill is duller and the legs become quite yellowish. Young birds also have yellowish legs and for this reason might be misidentified by the casual observer. However, no-one could mistake the species when it takes flight, which it frequently does, for it is a nervous and wary bird, its watchful ways earning it the reputation of 'watchdog' or 'warden of the marshes'. When on the wing the conspicuous white edges to the dark wings are revealed, which along with the white back and rump give a very black and white appearance, almost like an Oystercatcher, though the musical 'tuhu-tuhu' call is quite different to that of the Oystercatcher.

In the breeding season the Redshank perches freely on the branches of trees or shrubs, but also uses fenceposts from where it will launch itself into its aerial display flight, rising on quivering wings and producing a long trilling call. The nest is hidden in deep grass, often with longer stems interlocked to form a canopy, but equally it can be a mere scrape in the dunes, with only sparse marram grass as cover. The four eggs are whitish or creamy buff, and they are spotted, streaked, and blotched with shades of dark reddish brown.

Incubation lasts about 21 to 25 days and both sexes take their turn on the nest. The young leave the nest soon after hatching and quickly learn to find their own food. In the early days of their life they are brooded by the parents at night and sometimes also in the day if the weather is inclement. At any sign of danger the parents fly up, giving strident alarm calls. The young birds 'freeze' rendering them virtually undetectable.

△ A Redshank in winter plumage photographed in Oman.

▷ A group of roosting Redshanks in late autumn wait for the tide to recede.

In Britain birds wintering on the coast can return to their breeding grounds as early as January or February, though more typically they do so in March, depending upon the prevalent weather. In more northern climes it can be May before they arrive. By July nesting is usually complete and birds begin their drift back to the coast. Though the Redshank is less migratory than other *Tringa* species, there is evidence of some movement of European birds to Britain and Ireland. The breeding population of the British Isles may well be in excess of 50,000 pairs. But winter counts indicate at least half a million birds to be present, equivalent to approximately 75 per cent of Europe's Redshanks and around 15-20 per cent of the world's total population. There have been only one or two reports of this species reaching the North American continent, where the Lesser Yellowlegs takes its place.

Marsh Sandpiper
Tringa stagnatilis

This bird, the smallest of the 'Shanks', is possibly the most elegant of all shoreline waders. Although similar in size or general appearance to two or three other species, its structure and general behaviour give it an appearance which is distinctive even at quite long range.

Slightly larger than a Wood Sandpiper, the Marsh Sandpiper more closely resembles the larger Greenshank in its plumage patterns. However, the disproportionately long greenish legs and fine needle-like bill, combined with rather a small ping-pong-ball-like head, long neck, and slim body should preclude any confusion with this last species. In non-breeding plumage the crown and upperparts are a fairly uniform grey-brown colour, contrasting with whitish underparts. The bird's 'face' generally appears rather whiter than that of a Greenshank, while the streaking below tends to be rather fine, and restricted to the sides of the breast. In this plumage, resemblance is closest to a winter Wilson's Phalarope. The Marsh Sandpiper, however, lacks that species' rather pot-bellied appearance. It also feeds in a totally different way.

As the breeding season approaches, the Marsh Sandpiper acquires darker upperparts with wing and scapular feathers showing irregular greyish buff or fawn edgings. The breast develops dark spots with greyish chevron markings at the sides and down the flanks. The legs often turn a slightly brighter yellowish-green colour, although the bill remains essentially dark.

As a rule this species tends to be rather wary and will take flight fairly quickly at human approach. As the bird takes off, the white of the rump is revealed, extending to a point in the centre of the back. This feature contrasts with the darker wings and mantle. The long legs trailing well behind the lightly barred tail further add to the impression of a very long, thin-bodied bird. The Marsh Sandpiper's flight is slightly weak-looking and rather hesitant. While the bird is airborne, the 'teeoo-teeoo-teeoo' call is most often heard. This resembles

LENGTH: 220-250 mm (8¾-9¾ in)

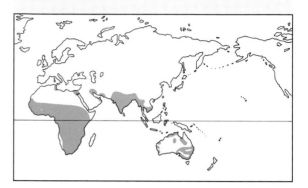

△ A Marsh Sandpiper. The long legs and needle-like bill characteristic of this species are shown well.

a Greenshank's call, although it sounds fainter and slightly higher in pitch.

The Marsh Sandpiper is usually only tolerant of fresh or sometimes brackish water and is generally to be found singly or in small groups at the edge of an inland lake or marsh. On the coast, occurrences tend to be restricted to smaller creeks, lagoons, and estuaries. The species favours using its long legs to the full, wading slightly offshore, sometimes up to its belly in water, while picking delicately to either side for food items. The Marsh Sandpiper seems to take most of its prey randomly from the surface of the water or exposed mud, and the prey is detected mainly by sight. The diet comprises mainly insect larvae, water and terrestrial beetles, molluscs, crustaceans, and amphipods. An interesting adaptation observed in this wader's wintering quarters is its close attendance behind ducks, egrets, and other waders, in pursuit of prey disturbed by these other birds' feeding activities.

Individuals may breed in their first calendar year, although many do not and remain to the south of their range in Africa and India. Breeding birds arrive on the nesting grounds from mid April to May. Preference is shown for river valleys and depressions adjacent to freshwater marsh land where there is a fairly good growth of grass. The exact range is difficult to define due to the presence of non-breeding birds in suitable breeding habitat, but generally extends from Austria eastwards through the warmer mid latitudes to northern Mongolia. As with most of the *Tringa* group, the male performs an aerial song flight; apparently this is done as much to attract a female as to lay claim to a territory. The nests may be found in solitary locations or in loose colonies, as close as 10 metres (30 ft) apart in some places. It is in fact fairly common to find nests in close proximity to marsh tern or Little Gull colonies. It may be that the Marsh Sandpiper derives increased protection from those species' greater aerial alertness.

The nest, as with many waders, is a simple shallow depression on the ground, usually among shorter vegetation. It is lined with a few dead strands of grass. The four, or occasionally five, eggs are heavily blotched with reddish brown on buff and are well disguised within the chosen habitat. The chicks hatch about one month after egg-laying and are able to feed themselves from an early age. The adults remain in fairly close attendance despite this early independence, and share the abundance of insect life that is present. The young tend to remain on their natal territories until fledged, when they gather to form small groups prior to migration. In appearance, the juvenile resembles a non-breeding adult, but the upperparts are generally browner with paler buff fringes.

Migration to the south takes place from late July onwards, with adults frequently having started or partially completed their moult into winter dress before departure. Movement is on a broad front and is relatively direct with few stops en route. Birds reach their wintering quarters during late August and September and can be found, sometimes in concentrations, throughout Africa, Madagascar, south and east Asia, and more sparsely in Australasia, until the following spring. There appears to be a north-east to south-west element during Autumn passage across north Africa and the Sahara, and it is probably offshoots from this movement that are seen as vagrants in Great Britain and western Europe each year.

Prior to 1976, the Marsh Sandpiper was an extremely rare visitor to Britain, with only 20 records in total and as few as eight between 1958 and 1975. It appeared annually from 1976 to 1985, however, and these ten years produced a total of 38 individuals, with a peak of 11 in 1984. This remarkable upsurge has been matched in western Europe, while in Finland breeding has been confirmed in at least two years since the mid 1970s. Not surprisingly, 23 (60 per cent) of the records since 1976 have come from eastern and south-eastern England. Marsh Sandpipers remain very rare in western Britain and there have been only two recorded in Ireland. The 38 individuals noted above all arrived between April and October; ten appeared in both July and August but there was also a good spring presence, with four in April, five in May, and five in June.

Greenshank
Tringa nebularia

It was one August many years ago that I was first introduced to the Greenshank. I well remember the small sewage marsh in the English midlands where I learned to recognise this fascinating bird. The species so impressed me, it has been one of my favourites ever since, epitomizing the autumn passage of migrating birds through the midlands particularly.

I can still recall that first sighting of an elegant grey-looking medium-sized wading bird nervously rocking on grey-green legs before it leapt into the air to streak away on dark pointed wings, showing its distinctive V-shaped white rump. These characteristics, along with its call, readily identified the species.

The Greenshank's triple flutey 'tchu, tchu, tchu' call is an unforgettable sound, and this haunting cry sets my blood tingling to this day whether I hear it drifting across a coastal marsh, or inland pastures, or at other times in the darkness of the night over some city or town, when a migrating bird calls for guidance and comfort to any other of its kind that happens to be within earshot.

I had earlier come to know the Redshank and could make comparison with this other *Tringa* wader. The Greenshank's appearance is similar in many ways, but it is slightly larger, taller and greyer-looking. Also its upturned, thicker-looking bill is quite different and, as I later learned, is used to obtain food in several ways including a side to side sieving motion which the Redshank uses only rarely. Another feeding method subsequently noted was the capture of small fish by making a rapid succession of high-stepping dashes through shallow water with neck extended and bill submerged to secure the prey. The Greenshank possibly takes more fish than most other shore birds, though it is just as likely to be seen picking and probing as the situation dictates in a manner more typical of wading birds in general.

Globally, the Greenshank breeds from Scotland in the west across northern Europe through Asia to the Kamchatka Peninsula in

OTHER NAMES: Common Greenshank, Greater Greenshank
LENGTH: 300-340 mm (12-14 in)

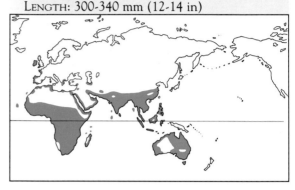

the east. Within this region it nests in marshes and swamps, clearings in the taiga, bogs and on the tundra. It is an abundant breeding species in Scandinavia and in the U.S.S.R. In Scotland a main stronghold of the 800-900 breeding pairs is the so-called 'flow country' of Caithness

△ A Greenshank juggles with a fish it has caught. Fish form a favoured ingredient of its diet.

▷ A Greenshank removes an egg shell from the nest; the rest of the clutch has yet to hatch.

and Sutherland. However, disturbances in recent years and afforestation in some of the Greenshank's breeding localities may well have reduced this total.

In Scotland nesting birds are back on their breeding grounds in April, but in Scandinavia and Siberia they return about a month later. When on territory the male indulges in a series of display flights, gaining height with a rhythmic lashing of wings, gliding down singing as it goes, then circling on fixed bowed wings before climbing again to repeat the performance.

In summer dress the Greenshank's dull grey upperparts are spotted, streaked and blotched with black and brown with the head and neck finely streaked. Along with the whitish underparts this provides good camouflage for the sitting bird. The nest is often no more than a scrape, but sometimes is quite a deep cup of grass, leaves, lichens, and pine needles, according to the locality. It is generally placed near some landmark such as a stone or log. Four eggs is the usual clutch. These are pale greenish, streaked and blotched or finely marked all over with reddish brown. The sexes take it in turn to incubate during the 25 days or so before hatching. There is a further period of 28 days before the young are fully fledged.

In fall, the Greenshanks are on the move by early August when Scandinavian birds and those that breed in U.S.S.R., migrate south to winter beyond the Sahara. In Britain and Ireland winter distribution is predominantly westerly with most of the 1,000 to 2,000 birds that stay to be found in Ireland, particularly the south-west. Most of these are thought to be from the Scottish breeding population.

American birdwatchers are not too familiar with this species in their home territory for it has occurred as a regular migrant only in the Aleutians and Pribilofs. There are alleged sightings on the Atlantic seaboard and reports of birds that have wandered south to Argentina and Chile.

▽ *A juvenile Greenshank photographed in Oman.*

Greater Yellowlegs

Tringa melanoleuca

In spring the Gulf coast of Texas offers one of the most awe-inspiring spectacles of the avian world to be seen in the Northern Hemisphere. Here, seething flocks of many species of shore birds mass together along the tidal beaches and mud flats, sweeping to and fro in an endless colourful procession, their movements dictated by the changing tides. Away from this relentless activity, perhaps tucked away in a muddy corner of a nearby field, you might find that large, wary and generally unsociable bird, the Greater Yellowlegs, feeding quietly by itself.

The largest of the *Tringa* waders, it is not dissimilar in character, call and overall appearance to its European counterpart, the Greenshank. However, if seen well enough, the long bright yellow legs that give Greater Yellowlegs its name are sufficient to prevent misidentification with the duller-coloured legs of the other bird. Both species, though, do have a long slightly upcurved bill, but in flight the Greater Yellowlegs shows a square white rump, whereas the Greenshank reveals a white rump that extends up the bird's back in a V-shape. As both birds are migrants on opposite sides of the Atlantic, there is little chance of these two species being found in the company of each other, so opportunities for comparisons in the field are unlikely.

A large, robust version of the commoner Lesser Yellowlegs, this bird's upperparts are generally dark brown with various lighter markings, including many small white flecks. The underparts are white, streaked dark on the throat and breast with barring on the sides; the sexes are alike. At the times when the size difference between Greater and Lesser is not immediately apparent, the ratio of head to bill is a useful guide to identification. The Greater Yellowlegs' bill is 1½ times as long as its head and is also broad at the base, whereas the thin, straight bill of the Lesser Yellowlegs is only just longer than its head. But this difference is only noticeable at close quarters and as the Greater Yellowlegs is invariably shy and unapproachable, it can rarely be put to the test. Easily

OTHER NAME: Greater Yellowshank
LENGTH: 320-380 mm (12½-15 in)

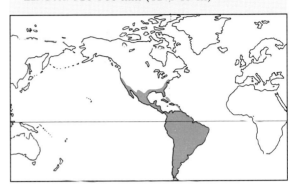

disturbed and put to flight, the 'chu chu chu chu' call will also remind Europeans of the Greenshank; another shared characteristic with this bird is its feeding technique of running through the shallows with bill open, sweeping from side to side in its attempts to catch small fish. At other times it can be found in a variety of habitats including fresh-water and brackish lagoons, coastal creeks, and especially flooded and muddy fields. At times the Greater Yellowlegs will feed in the company of other small waders and occasionally ducks, when it will wade belly-deep, snatching at surface aquatic insects. In soft mud it probes and picks for worms, insect larvae, crustaceans, and snails, while in dry conditions grasshoppers are pursued with a high striding gait.

By the middle of May, these birds have reached their breeding grounds, which comprise a continuous band from southern Alaska, through British Columbia, eastwards to Newfoundland and extending northwards into the sub-arctic tundra. In some areas it overlaps with the territory of the Lesser Yellowlegs, but where it does, it generally has a preference for wetter locations.

In such places it favours open areas amongst tall woodlands with sparse undergrowth interspersed with marshy pools for nesting. The actual site is usually a hollow lined with some dry vegetation. The four eggs have a buffish or

▷ A Greater Yellowlegs in breeding plumage pauses on its migration northwards along a Florida lagoon.

▽ Two Greater Yellowlegs moulting into winter plumage perch on a breakwater.

greenish background colour and are blotched with chestnut and darker browns.

The display of the Greater Yellowlegs involves a lot of running about with wings raised; at other times the bird engages in an undulating song flight over its territory. Incubation takes 24 days, during which period the nest site is vigorously defended by the male. At times it will perch precariously on the top of a nearby tall tree on the lookout for intruders. At the first sign of danger it flies up calling loudly, giving rise to its nickname of 'tell tale'. After hatching, the young are led to the nearest water, which might be at least a mile away. Here they feed up, and after 28 days or so they are fully fledged.

The fall movement of this bird is a rather prolonged one with some birds on the move by the end of July; certainly in August the movement is in full swing. As they move south, the birds come together in groups of 10 to 20 (much smaller numbers than the Lesser Yellowlegs). At such times they are wild, restless and decidedly noisy. Readily alarmed, they cause less easily disturbed species to take flight as well. If approached too closely, they adopt an upright alert posture, twittering nervously as they survey the scene. Suddenly, they leap into the air en masse and in a crescendo of noise spiral skyward on long pointed wings to resume their migration or find some other quieter, more acceptable feeding location.

By mid-October, most birds have cleared the U.S.A., (though a few winter in some southern states), being either en route, or established in their winter quarters. These include the West Indies and South America. Stragglers have been drifted eastwards to Baffin Island, Greenland and to Britain.

With an all-time total of only 28 records, the greater yellowlegs remains a true rarity in the British Isles, and its appearances remain distinctly less than annual. It occurred in only four of the ten years between 1977 and 1986, though three of these years (1978, 1983 and 1985) each produced two. The geographical distribution of records is much as expected, with eight of the eleven since 1970 being in the west (including four in Ireland) and only three in the east. The monthly distribution of these eleven individuals, however, was far from predictable, for only five arrived in the classic months for American waders of August and September. One appeared in July, two in November and, remarkably, as many as three in the spring (April or May), although one of these (in County Kerry in April 1983) was rumoured to have wintered in the area.

◁ A juvenile Greater Yellowlegs.

Lesser Yellowlegs

Tringa flavipes

This bird is often referred to as the American counterpart of the European Redshank. In reality, however, only vague similarities of plumage and call exist, offering no real reason for parallels to be drawn. Unlike the more sedentary Redshank, the Lesser Yellowlegs is a highly migratory species, undertaking long-distance flights between the northern and southern extremities of the Americas.

In spring the Lesser Yellowlegs is one of the most ubiquitous of American migrant shore-birds as it spreads northwards throughout the continent. Generally more numerous east of the Rockies, it has a tendency to be concentrated in the eastern and Gulf states. In these areas gatherings collect in loose association using a variety of habitats that include coastal beaches, mud flats, brackish lagoons, freshwater lakes, and pools. The species also has a fondness for flooded fields, wherever they may be. On arrival at such places the Lesser Yellowlegs is gregarious, and assemblies of 300 or more are found together. But they soon disperse, breaking up into smaller groups. They are also quite often encountered singularly when they might be found in the company of smaller 'calidrid' type waders. At preferred migration stop-overs the Lesser Yellowlegs feeds with a variety of techniques that include wading belly-deep in water, stalking surface insect prey, and chasing flying insects across open mud with long high stretching strides. Its most regular feeding method is a deliberate pecking action on the surface of soft mud or dipping in shallow water; it seldom probes deeply. Food consists of crustaceans, small fish, insects and their larvae, worms, and small aquatic life.

By the middle of April most birds are heading quickly for their breeding quarters with main migration routes taking them through the Mississippi valley northward to the Great Lakes. From there the birds fan out in a north and north-westerly direction to their respective nesting areas in north and central Alaska and adjacent Canadian provinces. These include

OTHER NAME: Yellowshank
LENGTH: 240-280 mm (9½-11 in)

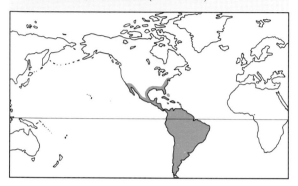

△ A Lesser Yellowlegs on its breeding grounds in Northern Canada.

▷ A Lesser Yellowlegs on passage through Florida in spring.

the Yukon and stretch southward through the prairies and eastward to northern Ontario and western Quebec, providing an almost even continuous distribution throughout the region.

The nest can be located on either hilly or flattish ground in the northern boreal zone amongst trees with little undergrowth. Preferred sites are often on hillsides with fallen or burnt trees strewn about the landscape. Less extensively used are open lichen-covered areas that are surrounded by forests. At all sites, however, marshes and muskegs are close to hand. The actual nest is situated in a hole or hollow below a small tree or bush with handily placed sentry posts for birds to perch on. The nest depression is lined with dry grass and leaves in which the four eggs are laid. They are olive to creamy buff, evenly spotted with dark red. Incubation is undertaken by both parents and lasts approximately 22 days. The cryptic coloration of the sitting birds renders them virtually undetectable. Highly protective of the nest and its contents, the birds will frantically dive-bomb intruders and fly from tree to tree in an attempt to distract and lure away man or animal. At such times they call with loud piercing 'kip kip' alarm notes.

Soon after hatching the young are led away to nearby marshy areas to feed, where they grow quickly. They are fully fledged in 23 to 25 days. Towards the end of July the birds vacate their breeding areas, moving in a south-easterly direction to gather on the Atlantic coast.

These pre-migratory birds assemble with other shore birds which can include the similar but larger, more robust Greater Yellowlegs, thus allowing opportunities for comparison. It will be seen that Lesser Yellowlegs is a medium-sized, slender, almost dainty-looking bird and though both species have long bright yellow legs, these appear proportionately longer on the Lesser Yellowlegs. The plumage of both species is otherwise much the same, being dark brown on the back and the coverts, which are spotted and edged with white. The head, neck, and upper breast are white and heavily streaked with grey, while the rest of the underparts are white and clean.

When encountered on its own the Lesser Yellowlegs is very confiding and approachable, at which time it nervously bobs its head and tail. Viewed in such close proximity the bird's gentle appearance is apparent, which is enhanced by the long needle-thin bill, the major difference between this species and the Greater Yellowlegs.

In flight, a square white rump is the most obvious feature along with disproportionately long wings, a grey and white barred tail, and projecting legs. Prior to taking flight, this delicate-looking bird can adopt a vertical stance, the stilt-like legs emphasizing its elegant proportions. It generally calls as it takes wing, when the distinctive 'tew tew' notes further aid its identification. The autumn migration is concentrated along the Atlantic seaboard as birds move south to winter quarters in the West Indies, Chile, and Argentina. At such times some of these birds get caught up in cyclonic weather conditions and a few are wind-drifted across the Atlantic to Britain and Europe.

The Lesser Yellowlegs has been recorded in the British Isles on at least 190 occasions and is thus the sixth most numerous of the Nearctic waders to reach the British side of the Atlantic. It has averaged just over six records a year during the past decade, compared with just under five between the late 1950s and the mid-1970s, and has thus not shown the recent significant increase demonstrated by several other of the more regular American visitors.

Given the increased observer coverage of recent years, and the fact that Lesser Yellowlegs is a relatively distinctive species, it seems likely that the species is in fact crossing the Atlantic less frequently than hitherto.

Records of Lesser Yellowlegs tend to involve individuals in widely scattered localities, and there has never been a major transatlantic flight or a concentration in south-west England. Indeed, there was not a single bird in Cornwall between 1983 and 1986, during which period there were five in Ireland and no less than eight in east or south-east England; this suggests that at least some of the more recent English records have involved birds which crossed the Atlantic in a previous autumn.

▽ *A Lesser Yellowlegs in Autumn; this is one of a handful which reach the British Isles every year.*

Solitary Sandpiper

Tringa solitaria

The Solitary Sandpiper lives up to its name, occurring singly or at the most in packs or groups of three. One of the most catholic of waders in its choice of habitat, passage birds can be found beside the tiniest piece of water, sometimes in surprising situations. A medium-sized wader, with the bill and legs neither exceptionally short nor long, dark above and whitish below, the Solitary Sandpiper needs to be distinguished from several other similar species in the field.

The adult's upperparts are blackish-brown, slightly paler and more olive on the head and neck, and finely speckled with white and buff. The breast is greyish-white, heavily streaked with dark brown, the streaking extending on to the flanks; the rest of the underparts are white. Birds in non-breeding plumage are a little paler and greyer with rather less spotting, while the juvenile is similar to the summer adult but a bit browner with buffer spotting. In all plumages the legs are grey-green and the bill blackish with an olive base. Importantly, there is a prominent white eyering and short stripe extending from the bill to the eye, bordered below by a dark line across the lores.

In America the Solitary Sandpiper has to be distinguished from non-breeding Spotted Sandpipers and the Lesser Yellowlegs. Compared to the Spotted, it is a little larger, much darker and usually finely speckled, and the legs are greyish-green. The prominent eyering and leg colour also serve to distinguish it from the Lesser Yellowlegs.

In Europe Solitary Sandpipers also need to be distinguished from Green and Wood Sandpipers. The Wood Sandpiper shows a strong supercilium extending well behind the eyes. It also has yellowish legs. The American counterpart of the Green Sandpiper, both in appearance and habits, the Solitary Sandpiper is slightly smaller and its longer tail gives it a long and tapering silhouette. It is paler and browner above with more spotting, and the eyering is usually more prominent, though Green Sandpipers can show prominent 'spectacles'.

LENGTH: 180-210 mm (7-8 in)

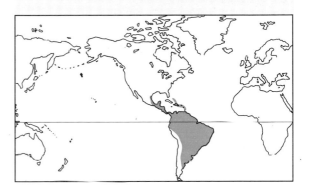

In flight, the Solitary Sandpiper has a unique combination of dark wings with no wingbar, dark underwings, and a dark rump and tail. There is barring at the sides of the tail, visible from both above and below. Rather than flicking low over the water like a Spotted Sandpiper, the Solitary will 'tower' into the air when alarmed. Its normal call is a thin, weak 'pip' or 'pip-pip'. Only in full flight will it give a 'pleet-weet-weet', sharper than a Spotted Sandpiper.

The species breeds from Alaska across Canada to Labrador, north to the treeline and south to a line from central British Columbia to central Ontario. Spring migrants pass through the U.S.A., in April and early May. The breeding habitat is open coniferous forest in the vicinity of water. Not surprisingly, the bird perches freely during the breeding season.

The display song is reminiscent of the call of the American Kestrel. It is given by both sexes, from the ground, a perch or the air, in normal flight as well as in the weakly undulating song-flight. Solitary Sandpipers breed in the disused nest of a small passerine, usually a thrush. Nests of Common Grackles, Waxwings, Grey Jays and others are also used. Both sexes search for a suitable nest, which is normally sited in a conifer close to water, though it may be as much as 200 m (650 ft) away. The female lines the nest and lays a clutch of four eggs. It is thought that both sexes incubate, but the

precise period, as well as the time the young take to fledge, is unknown. The species feeds on insects, small crustaceans, spiders and even small frogs.

On passage, the Solitary Sandpiper can turn up beside any patch of water, from woodland streams and lake and river margins to pasture ponds, puddles, and other transient patches. The birds are often tame and approachable. The winter habitat is similar, but includes coastal mangroves. The species is rarely found on the open shore. The first birds appear back in the U.S.A., in late June, though the bulk of the passage is from mid-August to September. It is a vagrant to Western Europe, with 24 sightings in Britain, where it has always been a very rare visitor. Its appearances have not shown the recent increase displayed by American shorebirds as a whole. With only seven records between 1977 and 1986, it remains a less-than-annual visitor and only in 1974 and 1984 has more than a single individual been recorded. The majority of records have been in the south-west, particularly the Isles of Scilly (six of the twelve since 1970), but there have been only two in Ireland. All occurrences have been in the period July to October, with half in September. Other individuals have been found in South Africa, the Galapagos and South Georgia.

The winter range of the Solitary Sandpiper comprises an area of inland South America south to Argentina and Uruguay. Smaller numbers are to be found in the West Indies and central America, with a few wintering in the southern U.S.A. All have reached the winter quarters by November, and a few oversummer in the Neotropics.

◁A Solitary Sandpiper photographed on spring migration in Florida.

∨ This photograph shows the more prominent eyering, heavier spotting and larger tapering tail of the Solitary, the American counterpart of the Green Sandpiper.

Green Sandpiper
Tringa ochropus

This medium-small, stocky sandpiper has a hunched, horizontal stance and the characteristic family habit of 'bobbing'. It is dark olive-brown above and white below, with heavy brown streaking on the head, neck, and breast. In flight the Green Sandpiper can be readily identified by its prominent white rump.

Close views of this bird will reveal a white eye-ring, a distinct white supercilium in front of the eye, and fine olive-brown streaks on the chin and throat. These become denser on the breast and flanks, where they merge into blotches. There are some subtle seasonal and age differences. In breeding plumage the bird's upperparts have whitish spots, but by August these have mostly disappeared, and any that remain are indistinct and buffish. In non-breeding plumage the head and breast are paler and more evenly coloured greyish brown. Juveniles can be distinguished by their paler, browner plumage. Although their upperparts are liberally spotted with deep buff, they lack the contrast of a breeding adult. Also their breast is evenly spotted with no blotches.

In flight the Green Sandpiper resembles a large House Martin, with dark back and wings and a startlingly white rump. The tail is also barred. This pattern closely resembles that of a Wood Sandpiper, but is always more contrasted. The Green Sandpiper can further be distinguished from the Wood in flight. It has broader wings, a dark underwing, and shorter legs that do not project beyond the tail. At rest it is larger than either Common or Wood Sandpiper and its upperparts and legs are darker. It further differs in lacking the Common Sandpiper's white wedges between the breast patches and the folded wings, and in being stockier than a Wood Sandpiper, with less speckled upperparts and a shorter supercilium. It most closely resembles its Nearctic equivalent the Solitary Sandpiper. However, the Green Sandpiper is again bulkier and shorter in the neck, wings and tail; in flight its broader, darker wings and prominent white rump allow identification. Green Sandpipers are noisy, with

LENGTH: 210-240 mm (8¼-9½ in)

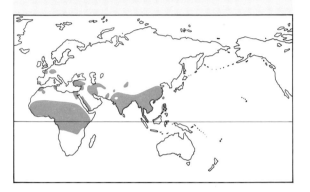

a variety of liquid, melodious notes that are freely uttered when the birds are migrating in parties or when flushed. The commonest calls are a loud, ringing 'klu-weet-weeta-weet' and a rippling 'tu-loo-ee'.

Northward movement through Europe peaks in late March and April, though some birds remain in their winter quarters until early May. Migration occurs on a broad front and Green Sandpipers can be seen at even the smallest area of fresh water. Numbers, however, are always small and passage is swift. By mid-May most of the birds are back on their territories in the forest swamps that stretch from Scandinavia and eastern Europe through to eastern Siberia. Breeding has occurred in Britain, but not since 1959. Some migrants are occasionally displaced much further east, finishing up as vagrants on the outer Aleutian Islands.

Once the female reaches the breeding grounds, the male begins to display. He flies over the territory in undulating circles, rising on vibrating wings, descending on bowed ones and uttering his distinctive 'titti-lool, titti-lool' song. The pairs are solitary and most nest inland along sheltered valleys with muddy fresh-water margins. Green Sandpipers are monogamous and produce a single brood each season. The breeding season begins in late April, but is later in the higher latitudes where it may not finish until July.

The nest is usually in a tree above water-logged ground with sparse vegetation. Generally the old nest of a thrush, pigeon or crow is used, or even a squirrel's drey. Less often the Sandpipers choose an old stump, a hummock, or a site between the tree roots. During the breeding season the birds move freely and easily about the branches, but at other times they seldom perch in trees. Mosses or lichens are sometimes added as a nest lining before the female lays her four cream or olive eggs with their dark streaks and blotches. Incubation is undertaken mainly by the female and lasts about three weeks. Shortly after hatching the chicks have to jump about 10 metres (30 ft) to the ground to be led away to a feeding area by their parents. Initially the young are tended by both adults, but the female often leaves before the four-week fledging period is over.

This early dispersal of females means that the Green Sandpiper is one of the first migrants to return southwards. Indeed, some birds will have spent barely a month on their breeding grounds when they leave in the first half of June. By the end of the month many have reached western Europe and it must surely be this early arrival that in the past led to some mistaken claims of breeding in Britain.

▽ A Green Sandpiper in Eilat, Israel on spring migration in April.

△ *A juvenile Green Sandpiper at a small pool in the English Midlands in late summer.*

Outside the breeding season, Green Sand-pipers visit a variety of shallow, inland fresh-water sites, no matter how small. In Britain the birds frequent streams, ditches, farm ponds, and gravel pits. They seem to prefer gently flowing to still water and show a marked aversion to coastal and tidal habitats. The main wintering areas are in central Africa, the Mediterranean basin, and from Turkey and Iran eastwards through India to China. However, some winter farther north in the more temperate parts of western Europe, including up to 1,000 in Britain, mostly in south-eastern England. At most times they are solitary or in very small groups, but gatherings of up to 30 can occur at favoured feeding sites. Concentrations of more than 50, however, are quite exceptional.

Green Sandpipers are secretive feeders. They seldom probe, but feed mostly from the surface, working around marginal vegetation with a slow, deliberate action as they take prey from shallow water, mud, and plants. In deeper water they sometimes swim while feeding and occasionally they submerge their heads and necks to get at deeper items. Their food consists principally of aquatic invertebrates such as beetles, flies, water bugs, and certain crustaceans and molluscs. Small fish may also be caught and brought to the bank for consumption.

Wood Sandpiper
Tringa glareola

This delicate bird is usually to be found around fresh-water shores where, given reasonable views, its identification poses few problems, in spite of its close resemblance to some other sandpipers. Breeding adults have grey-brown upperparts which are boldly speckled white, and white underparts, save for some brown streaking on the neck and breast. In winter plumage the upperparts are less clearly speckled and the breast is greyish with much finer streaking. Juveniles are warmer brown above with buff spots and fine brown streaks on the breast, which is initially washed buff but fades to white by late autumn. At all ages and seasons the white eyebrow is prominent.

Confusion is most likely with the Green Sandpiper, but the Wood Sandpiper is smaller, slimmer, longer-legged, and altogether more elegant. In flight it looks more slender and agile, with legs that project well beyond its tail, and it shows less contrast between the dark wings and white rump and finely barred tail than does a Green Sandpiper. Seen from beneath, there is also less contrast between the white belly and pale grey underwing of a Wood Sandpiper than there is in either a Green Sandpiper or a Solitary Sandpiper – a rare American vagrant to western Europe – both of which have dark underwings. The 'chiff-iff' or 'chiff- iff-iff' call is also characteristic. Wood Sandpipers have yellow or greenish-yellow legs, which might cause confusion with another American vagrant to Europe, the Lesser Yellowlegs. But the latter is larger and greyer and has legs that are proportionately longer and much deeper in colour. In autumn juvenile Common Sandpipers may also have yellowish legs, but they are smaller, more compact, browner, and plainer birds.

Wood Sandpipers in breeding plumage move northwards through Europe during April and May, but seldom linger long in any one place. By the end of May most have reached their breeding territories, which extend from Scandinavia across northern Russia and sporadically into the Aleutian Islands and

LENGTH: 190-210 mm (7½-8 in)

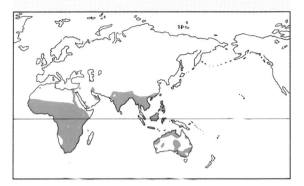

△ A Wood Sandpiper's nest and eggs.

Alaska. Breeding also occurs very sparingly in the north of Scotland, where most years see half-a-dozen pairs at three or four localities.

Once on territory, the pair engage in a distinctive display, during which the male glides downwards on bowed wings, repeating a mellow double-note. The nest is usually within a clearing in a damp conifer or birch wood, on boggy moorland or in a marsh. The pair make a scrape amongst dense ground cover, often on a rise or tussock, and line this with grass stems and leaves. Occasionally they use an old tree-nest of another species, such as Fieldfare, Great Grey Shrike or Waxwing. The normal clutch of four pale-green eggs with dark markings is incubated by both sexes for about three weeks. As soon as they hatch, the chicks are independent and the adult females leave shortly afterwards. It is another month, however, before the chicks fledge. During this time they are mostly tended by the males, which may become very excited and noisy in their defence, uttering a repeated 'chip, chip' alarm.

△ A newly hatched Wood Sandpiper chick.

▽ A Wood Sandpiper on its breeding grounds in Swedish Lapland.

▷ A migrant Wood Sandpiper stands alert, showing its slender neck and small rounded head.

Wood Sandpipers leave their breeding grounds very early. By late June the adult birds are beginning the long journey southwards to their winter quarters in the tropics and subtropics. The juveniles follow a month later and the passage through western Europe peaks in late July and August. By early October most have left for Africa, but occasionally one or two late stragglers are seen. Indeed, overwintering has occurred as far north as Britain, though this is exceptional. The species has also occurred as a vagrant along the eastern seaboard of the U.S.A.

While they are on their autumn migration, these birds quite often pause to rest and feed. Their favoured haunts are marshy areas, damp meadows and especially the muddy margins of open freshwater lakes and pools. Unlike the Green Sandpiper they seldom visit enclosed or overhung pools. Both avoid the littoral zone.

Wood Sandpipers generally feed in scattered groups, but may flock together during migration or in winter. In certain areas several hundred may be present at any one time, but in Britain the birds are usually seen singly or in very small groups. On their own, Wood Sandpipers are often confiding, but in flocks they become much more excitable and wary. If flushed they often tower, calling shrilly.

Their diet comprises mainly fresh-water and terrestrial insects, particularly beetles, which are taken by probing and pecking. When feeding, Wood Sandpipers walk with a distinctive high-stepping action, often wading up to their bellies as if swimming. They take morsels from the surface of the water, from the ground, or from vegetation, with a delicate action that typifies the species.

Terek Sandpiper

Xenus cinereus

Named after the Terek River, which flows east from the Caucasus Mountains into the Caspian Sea, the Terek Sandpiper breeds in an area of northern Europe and Asia that extends from the Baltic states eastwards to eastern Siberia. There are recently established outlying populations around Kiev and on the Baltic coast of Finland. An increase in the latter area since 1950 has been reflected by more occurrences in Western Europe and West Africa. The bird has also bred once in Norway.

The breeding habitat of the Terek Sandpiper comprises a mosaic of standing or gently flowing fresh water, soft moist bare ground, and dense patches of vegetation. This type of habitat is typically found along larger rivers and the shores of lakes in the taiga of Eurasia. In the Baltic, small islands and islets are also used.

Terek Sandpipers arrive on their breeding grounds from mid-May to early June, and are very noisy. The courtship song, a rich, melodious whistle made up of repeated 'per-rrrr-eeee' phrases, is given with raised tail and fluttering wings by the male on the ground, and in an aerial display: he calls repeatedly before taking flight, hovering briefly and then gliding back to earth.

The nest is a shallow cup placed on the ground in short vegetation. Four eggs are laid, pale buff to cream in colour, with dark brown blotches and a few scribble-like marks. The eggs are incubated for 23 days, probably by both sexes. After hatching, both parents tend the young, and fledging takes place after about 15 days.

The adults head south in the first half of July, but the juveniles do not follow until August or September. Terek Sandpipers often overfly the Mediterranean and Sahara deserts in one flight and are rare or scare migrants west of Iraq. Coastal in winter, they feed on sandy or muddy beaches, as well as on extensive mudbanks, mangrove creeks, and coral. Terek Sandpipers will roost on any area that remains dry at high water, including mangrove trees, often with other waders. Their winter quarters

LENGTH: 220-250 mm (8¾-9¾ in)

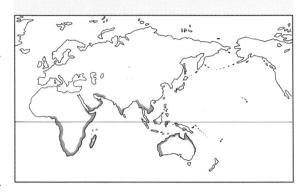

include the coasts of southern and eastern Africa and the shores of the Indian Ocean, but the species is most abundant in India, southeast Asia, Indonesia, and northern Australia. Many immature birds also spend the summer in these areas.

Giving the impression of a medium-large, pale, long-billed sandpiper, superficially similar to the Common Sandpiper, the Terek Sandpiper has a bulky body with a short, thick neck and rather angular head with a high forehead. Most notably, the bird sports a long, fine, gently upcurved bill, which taken together with the generally pale grey upperparts, white underparts and short yellowish legs.

The breeding adult is grey above, marked with an irregular dark line along the scapulars, which is most prominent rear- or head-on. The underparts are white with a paler grey wash on the sides of the breast, across which a band of fine streaks may join in the centre. The dark scapular line is lost in winter. The juvenile is browner with fine buff scales on the upperparts; it also has blackish scapular lines. The bird's bill is black, often with a yellowish base in the winter and juvenile plumages.

In flight, the Terek Sandpiper could be mistaken for a Redshank as its most distinctive feature is a narrow white trailing edge to the inner wing; but it lacks the Redshank's white vent. Also noticeable are the darker leading edge of the wing and darker primaries. The rump and tail are grey, and the tail has narrow white sides. The underwing is whitish. The flight is sometimes similar to the flicker of a Common or Spotted Sandpiper, but can also resemble that of a Redshank. The flight call is a tittering whistle, reminiscent of both the Common Sandpiper and the Whimbrel, while birds on the ground give a more Redshank-like 'du-du-du' or 'du-du' as well as a piping 'wit-e-wit' and 'to-li'.

When feeding the Terek Sandpiper makes use of a variety of techniques. It feeds singly or in small groups, often intermingled with other species. It frequently probes, but also picks items from the surface and can be extraordinarily dashing, moving rapidly with frequent changes of direction as it chases its invertebrate prey. Its short legs sometimes give the impression that the bird is about to topple over. Only occasionally does it use its upturned bill like an Avocet, head down with side-to-side sweeps. In the breeding season the chief prey is aquatic insects, but seeds are also taken.

This sandpiper is a rare visitor to Western Europe, though a familiar shorebird of tropical Africa, Asia and Australia. With only 28 records in total, the Terek Sandpiper remains a true vagrant in the British Isles. However, it has appeared more regularly since the mid 1970s, and half of the total (14 individuals) occurred during the ten years 1977 to 1986, with a peak of four in the latter year. Of these records, there were four in both May and June, and two each in July, August, and September. Three were in Hampshire, three in Norfolk, and two in Essex, with singles in Avon, Cleveland, Highland, Kent, Northumberland, and Suffolk: thus only three were north of a line from the Severn to the Wash.

△A Terek Sandpiper.

◁A Terek Sandpiper on its nest.

Common Sandpiper
Actitis hypoleucos

In Britain this is undoubtedly the best known bird with the common name of sandpiper. It probably provides most beginning birdwatchers with their first test of sandpiper identification, as it did for me at a small inland lake in mid-Warwickshire in the late 1940s. Along with the Green and Wood Sandpipers, this bird forms a trio of similar-looking species that at times can puzzle even experienced observers, particularly in the fall, when perhaps not all the distinguishing features of any of those species can be seen clearly. However, the constant up-and-down movement of the Common Sandpiper's tail is a sure means of putting a name to this bird. This teetering action is very emphatic, particularly when the bird becomes excited and agitated. The Green Sandpiper has a similar bobbing movement at times, although this is never as pronounced and characteristic as it is in the Common Sandpiper. Equally distinctive is this bird's

LENGTH: 190-210 mm (7½-8¼ in)

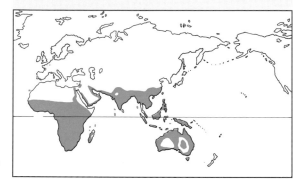

flight. It performs a regular flickering wing-beat with a momentary glide on down-curved wings, an action typical to the species. When disturbed it invariably flies out over the water returning to the shore in a wide arc, perhaps landing 40 metres or so from its starting point. On the

⊲A Common Sandpiper approaches its nest and eggs.

△A Common Sandpiper usually nests near water and particularly favours tumbling mountain streams or lakesides with stony rocky areas, as here.

wing it shows a well defined wing bar with white on either side of the tail. As it flies, the bird calls with a shrill piping 'dee-dee-dee-dee-dee', quite different to the voice of either the Green or Wood Sandpiper. This distinctive cry has earned the bird such names as 'Kittie-needie' and 'Dickie de-dee' in some areas of Britain. Its habitat preferences have brought about such other local names as 'sand snipe', 'shore snipe' and 'heather peeper'.

Breeding extensively in most parts of Britain and Europe, the Common Sandpiper is also to be found eastwards through Asia to China and Japan. While the majority of European breeding birds migrate to Africa south of the Sahara, those that nest in Asia move south to India, Thailand, Laos, Cambodia, Vietnam, the many East Indian islands, and also Australia.

The winter population in Britain is probably no more than 100 individuals, most of which are to be found south of a line from the Wash to the Severn with half of these at coastal sites and half at inland locations.

The favoured European nesting habitat comprises clear fast-running streams, and the borders of lochs, tarns and reservoirs in, or close to, hilly country. In more mountainous regions it has been recorded nesting at heights of 3,000 metres (10,000 ft). In lowland settings, river banks, small islets, and sometimes even sand and gravel workings are found to be suitable by the species.

The bird's nuptial display is dramatic. It begins almost as soon as the male reaches its chosen territory in late April and early May. Circling higher and higher it trills shrilly, after which aerial chases often take place. On the ground, the birds strut and run around with wings held stiffly upwards. Once pairing is completed, a nest is soon built. This consists of a depression lined with grass, moss, and leaves. It may be sited in thick vegetation, in the lee of a rock, among the roots of a tree, or in flood debris by a river bank or lochside. The clutch normally comprises 4 eggs, which are whitish to yellowish-brown in colour, spotted, streaked, or blotched with red-brown. Incubation lasts around 21-23 days with a fledgling period of about 4 weeks. Towards the end of summer, the adults are on their way south. The young birds are identifiable by their heavily barred brownish plumage. Common Sandpipers are among the first migrant waders to be noted at the inland waters of lowland Britain, often as early as July, though some birds, possibly failed breeders, might be seen in June. By August small parties can be found round the margins of reservoirs, lakes and other watery habitats. At times you can see as many as twenty, thirty, or even more. These larger concentrations, when observed late in the day, could well be birds gathering to roost together.

The Common Sandpiper obtains its food mainly by picking rather than probing. The bird takes insects, worms, small molluscs, and crustaceans from water margins. It also feeds along estuaries, inlets, and creeks.

At close quarters the Common Sandpiper's brown back, white belly and the streaked upper plumage on either side of the breast, form a white peak in front of the folded wing. The legs are greyish though in some juveniles they are yellowish, while their brown upperparts are quite heavily barred. In winter the Common Sandpiper is not dissimilar to the Spotted Sandpiper. However, the tail, which is longer in proportion to the wing, and the different call should prevent confusion with the North American species. Common Sandpipers are rare visitors to the outer Aleutions, the Pribilofs and St Lawrence Island. Vagrants have reached western Alaska.

◁A juvenile Common Sandpiper showing its yellowish legs.

Spotted Sandpiper

Actitis macularia

The Spotted Sandpiper is closely related to the Common Sandpiper and some authorities have considered the two birds to belong to the same species. The birds do look very similar, particularly when seen feeding slowly along the water's edge, constantly teetering and bobbing their rear ends up and down. If disturbed the Spotted Sandpiper flies off low over the water with a shallow, flickering wingbeat interspersed with frequent glides, giving a series of 'weet' notes. It has short, narrow wingbars and an unmarked rump and tail.

In breeding plumage the Spotted Sandpiper is one of the most distinctive waders. The spotted underparts are an important clue to identification, and also noticeable are the numerous blackish cross-bars on the olive-brown upperparts. There is a whitish supercilium and the base of the bill and the legs are orange-yellow or pinkish.

Out of breeding plumage the Spotted Sandpiper may be distinguished from similar birds, such as the Solitary Sandpiper, by its smaller size, its relatively pale, unmarked olive- or grey-brown upperparts and its white underparts. A dark patch extends on to the sides of the neck, and between this and the bend of the wing is a very distinctive white shoulder-patch. The bird's legs are yellowish.

Spotted Sandpipers need to be distinguished from vagrant Common Sandpipers in the outer Aleutians, the Pribilofs and St. Lawrence Island. The situation is reversed in western Europe where the Spotted Sandpiper is a rare vagrant. In non-breeding plumage this is no easy task. The Spotted Sandpiper has a slightly shorter tail than the Common Sandpiper and its wingbar is confined to the base of the primaries rather than extending on to the inner wing. Spotted Sandpipers have upperparts that are of a slightly greyer brown than those of the Common Sandpiper. Notably, the mantle is relatively unmarked compared to the wing coverts, which are finely but noticeably barred dark brown and pale buff. The tertials are also plain, with only fine markings near the tip. In

LENGTH: 180-200 mm (7-7¾ in)

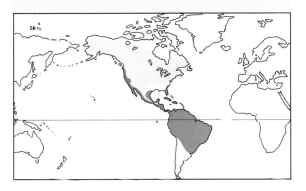

juvenile Common Sandpipers the tertials are finely barred along their entire fringe and the mantle feathers have more prominent notches and cross-bars so that the coverts, though barred brown and dull-buff, contrast less. The Common Sandpiper normally has duller and greyer legs than the Spotted Sandpiper's yellow ones, and usually lacks a contrastingly paler base to the bill.

One of the best ways of distinguishing Spotted and Common Sandpipers is by their voices. The Common Sandpiper's flight call is a descending series of notes, a 'dee-dee-dee-dee . . .', compared with Spotted Sandpiper's shrill 'peet-weet' and 'weet-weet-weet . . . '. A quiet 'pit', quite unlike the Common Sandpiper's call, is also given.

The breeding range of this bird extends across North America from Alaska to Newfoundland, and south to southern California, North Carolina and Maryland. It nests in a variety of habitats, usually near water, (though it will sometimes breed away from it) from sea-level to the timberline, and uses farmland and pasture more than its counterpart in Europe.

Spotted Sandpipers pass through the U.S.A. northwards from early April to June and their eggs are laid from mid-May to June. The female is dominant in courtship. She approaches the male on foot or sometimes flies up and then glides back to the ground to land near him,

◁*A Spotted Sandpiper in summer plumage is easily identified by the distinctive markings on its breast.*

displaying with head held high, tail spread, and wings drooped. All the time she gives a shrill 'tweeting' call. She selects a potential site for the nest, where the male makes several scrapes from which she makes her final choice.

Some females have several mates, and each male will defend a small territory around his nest from her other suitors. The nest is a shallow cup formed in grass, among rocks or other cover. Normally four eggs are laid. These are light buff, heavily spotted and blotched with russet. Incubation takes 20 to 22 days. When a female has a single mate, the hen will share incubation with the male. If there are several mates she will only share incubation with the male of the last clutch to be laid. Fledging takes place after 18 to 21 days.

The post-breeding passage across the U.S.A., is on a broad front and very protracted, with birds present from early July to September. The species winters in very small numbers north to British Columbia and South Carolina, but the bulk move to an area from Mexico and the West Indies south to central South America and the Galapagos. In winter and on passage the species occurs singly or in small groups anywhere where there is water, including the seashore.

Spotted Sandpipers are vagrants to eastern Siberia, Tristan da Cunha and Marshall Island in the central Pacific, as well as to western Europe. In Britain 83 have been recorded, almost all since the late 1960s in winter, spring and fall. In view of the difficulty of distinguishing this bird from the Common Sandpiper, it is not surprising that a relatively high proportion of records involves summer-plumaged adults. Of 51 individuals in the ten years 1977–1986, no less than 19 (37 per cent) were summer adults, whereas the vast majority of American waders reaching the British Isles are autumn juveniles. It seems probable that numbers of immature Spotted Sandpipers are still arriving in Britain undetected.

Nevertheless, records have increased from a mean of between one and two per year between the mid 1950s and the mid 1970s to rather more than five per year in the last decade. Improved identification techniques no doubt account for part of this increase, but it seems likely that a genuine increase is also involved, and the Spotted Sandpiper became the first American wader to nest in Britain when a pair attempted to breed – unfortunately unsuccessfully – in Scotland in 1975. Equally, overwintering has occurred on five occasions, and a further three individuals have remained at least into December. Although more than a third of the occurrences in the past decade have been in south-west England or Ireland, the remainder have been well scattered around the British Isles, with five in Scotland, five in Wales, and several well inland, including three in the west Midlands.

Wandering Tattler

Heteroscelus incanus

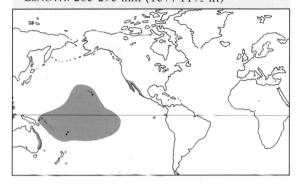

This bird is one of a pair of distinctive waders based around the Pacific basin: the new world Wandering Tattler and the old world Grey-tailed Tattler. The Wandering Tattler is a regular migrant along the Pacific coast of North America, while the Grey-tailed Tattler occurs on passage in Alaska. The two species are best distinguished by voice.

The Wandering Tattler breeds in areas of south coastal, central, and western Alaska, east to the Yukon and British Columbia. It probably also breeds in far eastern Siberia alongside the Grey-tailed Tattler. The bird's breeding habitat is in the alpine zone of the mountains and highlands, where it nests on islands in fast-flowing, gravel-bottomed streams, and feeds in the shallower reaches and quiet pools. Its diet consists mainly of the adults and larvae of the caddis fly.

The birds arrive on their breeding grounds in late May and lay their eggs a week to ten days later. Each territory is centred on a valley containing a suitable stream. The displays include one or sometimes both birds flying at great height – 150 to 300 metres (500 to 1,000 ft) – down the valley, every so often giving a high-

Other Names: American Grey-rumped Sandpiper
Length: 260-290 mm (10¼-11½ in)

pitched, rapid whistle. This performance ceases once the clutch of eggs is laid.

The nest, made of roots and twigs, is located in a depression in the ground. It is sometimes quite substantial, but sometimes barely more than a scrape. Four greenish eggs are laid, spotted and blotched with brown, and are incubated either by both sexes or by the male alone for 23 to 25 days. Both sexes tend the chicks in their first week of life. The fledging period is unknown.

◁ *An adult Wandering Tattler in full breeding plumage.*

The breeding grounds are deserted after August and the species can be seen on migration along the Pacific coast of North America, occurring casually inland in the coastal states, as well as in Japan. The Wandering Tattler winters from southern California south to Ecuador, and also on the Galapagos and Hawaiian islands and on the islands of the central and South Pacific west to Australia's Great Barrier Reef and northern New Zealand. As is the case with so many shorebirds, non-breeding first-year birds may spend the summer in these 'winter' quarters. The species is a vagrant to Manitoba, Peru, and Chatham Island.

On passage and in winter the Wandering Tattler frequents rocky coasts and reefs, feeding singly or in small groups among the breakers, as well as on nearby sand and shingle beaches. On passage it sometimes also occurs on the shores of ponds well away from salt water. It is often tame and approachable. Its winter food comprises mainly items such as crustaceans, worms, and small molluscs.

The tattlers are like stocky, short-legged shanks, and they often bob and teeter in a similar fashion to the shanks when they are feeding. Slightly bigger and bulkier than the Lesser Yellowlegs, the Wandering Tattler is

△ *The Wandering Tattler is often viewed as no more than a silhouette perched on a pinnacle of rock from where it utters its rippling trill as it flies to another vantage point.*

◁ *A Wandering Tattler in non-breeding plumage shares its preferred rocky coastline winter haunt with Black Turnstones seen in the background of this photograph.*

mainly slate-grey in all its plumages. Breeding adults are grey above with a short, narrow, whitish supercilium and, most notably, grey barring over all the underparts, including the undertail-coverts. The bill is black with a variable yellowish base and the legs are yellow. In the winter and juvenile plumage, there is no barring on the underparts, but there is a dark grey wash over the breast and flanks. The juvenile also has very fine pale fringes to the feathers of the upperparts. In flight the upperparts are a uniform grey, with no wingbars or paler markings on the rump or tail, and the underwing is rather dark grey.

On the outer Aleutians, the Pribilofs, and St. Lawrence Island, as well as on the coast of northern Alaska, the Grey-tailed Tattler is a regular migrant, and has to be distinguished from the Wandering Tattler. The birds are very similar in all plumages, but the Wandering Tattler is slightly darker above and, in breeding plumage, more heavily barred below, with only a small un-barred area on the belly. The juvenile is not as heavily spotted as the juvenile Grey-tailed Tattler. At all ages, the Wandering Tattler has longer wings, which extend well beyond the tip of the tail when the bird is at rest. The length of the nasal groove (the shallow depression on the bill within which the nostril is situated) is an important feature for identification. In the Wandering Tattler this groove extends almost three-quarters of the way to the tip of the bill, in the Grey-tailed Tattler it extends only slightly more than half-way; however, this is a feature which can seldom be seen except at close quarters.

The best distinction between the two species at all times is by call. The Wandering Tattler's is a rippling trill, a rapid, accelerating series of hollow whistles, all on the same pitch. This is totally different to the Grey-tailed Tattler's call, which is a 'too-weet', reminiscent of the American Golden Plover.

Willet
Catoptrophorus semipalmatus

At first sight the Willet is a rather uninspiring bird. This is especially true of its drab winter dress, when the bird's appearance might suggest several possible species. It is not unlike one of the shanks, and also similar to a godwit or a tattler. But all confusion as to its identity is removed when its wings are raised, instantly transforming it from an ordinary-looking bird, into an unmistakable Willet, with its startling black and white wings.

At rest the Willet's upperparts, including the nape, mantle, scapulars, and wing coverts, are light to brownish grey, with fine white edging on all the feathers. The expressionless face is finely streaked with grey, with a bold white ring around the eye, joined to the base of the bill by a white loral stripe, giving the effect of a pair of white spectacles when viewed front on. The Willet's breast is plain grey while its belly is white.

Out of the breeding season, the Willet occupies a wide range of habitats in mainly coastal localities, including mud flats, sandy beaches, salt marshes, wet grasslands, and edges of lakes and lagoons. While feeding in these places the bird indulges in endless bouts of aggression with its fellows, squabbling over food and territory, jumping into the air, wings aloft and legs splayed out, landing on its rival's back, then chasing the transgressor out of its space in high-stepping pursuit. This aggression is not confined to the Willet's own kind, for smaller waders are also attacked, relentless jabs of the bill forcing them to relinquish their foraging area. The long grey-blue legs and medium-size stout bill enable the Willet to feed in a number of ways, from wading in deep water, picking prey from the surface, to vigorously probing in the mud. By these means it obtains a variety of food, which includes fish, molluscs, marine worms, and aquatic insects. However, the bird's preferred prey consists of fiddler crabs, which it stalks along the shoreline. Occasionally a rapid chase is needed to secure the quarry if the crab is not surprised in the first instance.

LENGTH: 330-410 mm (14-16¼ in)

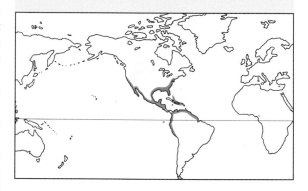

A shy and wary bird, the Willet is easily disturbed. If this happens it takes to noisy flight, shrieking its loud 'kip-kip' alarm notes. On the wing a distinctive pattern is also revealed, comprising black primaries and coverts with a broad white lateral bar. The underwing is more strikingly contrasting, with its black linings, axillaries, and primary tips set against translucent white secondaries. The white rump and finely barred tail and projecting legs further aid the identification of this bird. However, it should be remembered that the Hudsonian Godwit also has a similar pattern on the underwing.

▽ *A Willet in summer plumage along a Florida Coastline.*

There are two separate breeding populations of this bird in the U.S.A., the western (or inland) Willet and the eastern Willet. There are some differences in the breeding plumage, which varies from the eastern Willet's boldly barred and brown-spotted neck, breast, and flanks, to the plain liberally streaked breast of the western Willet. The two, however, have similar upperparts, which are grey-brown, barred with buff and dark brown.

During the breeding season the two races are to be found in totally different areas. The western Willet is the slightly larger of the two forms, and is confined to the prairie lands and central southern Canada, including the states of Oregon, Idaho, Alberta, Colorado, Nebraska, northern California, and North and South Dakota. Here it nests in marshy areas

△On the ground the Willet frequently raises its wings in display, revealing the black and white patterning.

▷A Willet on its north American breeding grounds.

with scattered saline and fresh-water lakes and pools. The eastern Willet is a strictly coastal-nesting species and is to be found in a continuous strip along the Atlantic seaboard, from Nova Scotia southwards to Florida and then westwards along the Gulf coast to Texas, predominantly in a salt-marsh habitat.

Some birds are probably paired when they arrive on the breeding grounds, but communal displays take place close to the nesting area, when a great deal of flying about and calling takes place. On the ground the wings are frequently raised to display the striking pattern.

The nest is a hollow among long grass, lined with dry grass and twigs. Although most of the nests are well concealed, some are sited in the open on sandy soils. The four olive-buff eggs, evenly blotched with brown, are laid at intervals of between one and four days. These are incubated mainly by the female, while the male stands guard on fence posts or nearby trees, occasionally circling the nesting territory uttering his musical 'pill-will-willit' song, from which the bird's name derives. At night the male takes over the incubation. This procedure continues from 21 to 29 days, when the eggs

hatch in a staggered sequence, very often causing the abandonment of the remaining unhatched eggs after the first young have emerged. After two weeks the young become independent, and the adults then vacate the site to gather in large post-breeding flocks. After four or five weeks the young fly to join the adults in the birds' winter territory.

As a breeding species, the Willet is confined mostly to North America with smaller populations in northern Mexico and the Caribbean. The western race is highly migratory with winter dispersals to southern California, Peru, and the Galapagos. The eastern Willet is more sedentary over much of its range, especially in the Gulf coast and the Caribbean regions, although some of the northernmost breeding birds are known to move as far south as northern Brazil.

Though much of the traditional breeding habitat of this bird has been destroyed through drainage and other development, the species' status seems to be reasonably secure. Certainly at migration times along the beaches where Willets gather to feed and rest, several thousand may be seen at any one time.

Turnstone

Arenaria interpres

The Turnstone is one of the most distinctive of the medium-sized waders that haunt the shore-line. The striking plumage, robust gait, short wedge-shaped bill, and orange legs make the species easy to identify. The bird also has distinctive feeding antics, particularly its habit of quickly flipping over a pebble or shell in search of food, hence its common name.

It is the bird's structure which enables it to show such an individual feeding action. Its short legs allow it to crouch easily and look underneath objects, while its stout bill is the ideal shape for levering and overturning stones, seaweed, and other objects. Individuals or groups of these birds methodically roam the shoreline seeking out insects, molluscs, and crustaceans in this way. At times, when the Turnstone is confronted with larger stones that cannot be levered with the bill alone, the bird pushes its breast up against the stone and moves it in this way. At other times Turnstones are just as likely to use a 'probe-and-jab' technique. The species has a wide range of other feeding techniques, which include opening shells, taking animal tissue from carcasses, extracting fly larvae from rotting flesh, and even eating food thrown away by man, which highlight the bird's scavenging tendency. Piles of rotting seaweed heaped up above the tide-line are also an attraction to the species and it frequently shares this resource with Rock Pipits and Starlings.

Outside the breeding season the Turnstone freely associates with many of the other open-shore waders. It remains relatively tame and quite approachable, often feeding on beaches, jetties, and slipways adjacent to footpaths and houses.

In summer plumage, both sexes have a pied head and upper breast, forming a strong facial pattern and black chest band. The male has the whiter crown at this stage. The mantle and wings are predominantly chestnut in colour, with bands of black. The lower breast and belly are pure white. In flight, the bird shows a white stripe down the centre of the back, a pair of

OTHER NAME: Ruddy Turnstone
LENGTH: 210-255 mm (9¼ in)

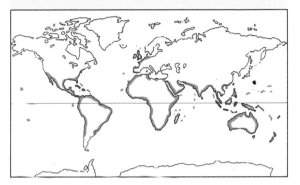

△ A Turnstone's nest containing a full clutch of eggs.

◁*A Turnstone on its nest.*

white shoulder stripes, and a white wing bar. The tail is also white with a broad subterminal black band giving the whole bird an unmistakable pattern in flight. In winter the head, back, and coverts take on a brown colour, but the basic design of the plumage is essentially the same.

The breeding range spans the Arctic from Alaska, east to Siberia; it penetrates as far south as peninsular Sweden. Here the Turnstones choose to nest in a variety of habitats from rocky coastal islands to more elevated tundra. Nesting does not normally begin until June, even though the birds may have reached a suitable habitat in May. Pairing usually takes place before the birds arrive on territory and the courtship chase-displays can sometimes be seen as the birds move northward in the spring. The nest is a shallow cup sited on well vegetated rocky or gravelly ground, not far from the sea. The eggs, usually four in number, are glossy, and brownish or olive-green with some grey mottling and black spots. These are incubated by both parents for about 24 days. The young feed themselves but are tended and brooded by both parents in their early days. After about 24 to 26 days the young can fly, at which time the female leaves the family group. The male remains with the young for a further 10 to 14 days.

During this time food consists mainly of plant material, but may also include some adult and larval insects as well as other invertebrates. By the time the juveniles head south in their adult's wake their plumage is dark brown above with a white throat, dark breast band, and white below; the feathers of the upperparts are finely edged with buff. Their legs are bright orange, like those of the adults.

Winter time finds Turnstones around the coasts of all the warm continents, while a substantial number remain on the Atlantic fringe of western Europe. In Britain and Ireland the total mid-winter population is around

△ *A group of summer-plumaged Turnstones pause briefly to rest as they migrate northwards.*

▽ *A juvenile Turnstone wades in a shoreline pool.*

50,000 birds. The species is not averse to overland migrating and is frequently noted at inland reservoirs and gravel pits in spring and autumn. In winter, the birds prefer the larger estuaries, rocky coastlines, and mixed pebble and sand beaches. At such places they can be seen flying together in tight formations giving a rapid staccato 'trik-tuc-tuc-tuc' call as they move from one feeding location to another. Even when feeding they can be noisy, frequently uttering a low 'tuc' note as individuals flutter to a higher level of seaweed-covered rock. Turnstones usually roost on rocks above the high tideline, or on sand or shingle spits.

The Turnstone is a hardy long-distance traveller to be found on beaches throughout the world. The success of the species is no doubt due to its ability to use many habitat types and to its industrious character. Its attractive plumage and distinctive habits make it widely admired and it is a favourite species for many shorebird enthusiasts.

Black Turnstone

Arenaria melanocephala

A striking black and white shorebird, the Black Turnstone is a close relative of the wide-ranging Turnstone, but, as its name implies, is drabber and less colourful. It is exclusively found on the Pacific coasts of North America, and does not occur inland with any regularity on passage. Fractionally larger than the Turnstone, the Black Turnstone can be distinguished from the Turnstone at all times by the following features: its near-uniform slate-grey upperparts, its dark chin, throat and breast, and its duller, dark reddish-brown legs.

In breeding plumage there are fine white streaks on the head and breast, a whitish super-

LENGTH: 220-250 mm (8¾-9¾ in)

cilium, and a large whitish patch at the base of the bill. The non-breeding adult lacks these markings, having only fine whitish fringes to the wing feathers. The juvenile is a little browner, with a fine pattern of buff fringes to the feathers of the upperparts.

In its winter quarters the Black Turnstone is most likely to be confused with a winter-plumaged Surfbird, which is similarly grey above with a grey head and breast. But the Surfbird is larger, with a yellowish base to its bill and yellowish legs. It also looks rather different in flight, lacking the Black Turnstone's white on its lower back and the base of its wings, and generally looking much less variegated.

When flying, the Black Turnstone shows a pattern of light and dark which is essentially the same as Turnstone: white wingbars, rump, and sides to the tail, and a white patch at the base of each wing and in the centre of the lower back. But the Black Turnstone has a little less white on the rump and its wingbar is broader. It is also much blacker than the Turnstone. Its calls include a trilling 'skirr' and a guttural rattle, higher-pitched than the equivalent call of the Turnstone.

Black Turnstones breed on the coastal plain of western Alaska, on the grass-covered shore-lines of brackish pools and tidal sloughs. They nest close to the water's edge, especially near small inlets or promontories. The birds are present from May to July. The male's display includes a snipe-like drumming, in which he climbs so high that he is invisible, before dive-bombing back to earth, producing a noise from the vibration of certain feathers. Other displays include zig-zag chases, with the male in hot-pursuit of the female.

The nest is placed on grass, but sometimes on virtually bare mud, with little or no lining. The species is occasionally semicolonial, nests being grouped together. The eggs are olive with dark brown spots and darker spots and blotches of brown. They differ from those of the Turnstone in lacking gloss and being less contrasty in patterning. The usual clutch is four

◁ *The Black Turnstone can be found along almost the full length of the western coast of North America on suitable rocky shores during the winter.*

▽ *A Black Turnstone on its nest in the coarse grassy setting of its Alaskan summer home.*

in number and these are usually laid around mid-May. Both sexes incubate the eggs for 21 or 22 days. If disturbed, the adults give a clear, piping, 'weet-weet-too-weet' call. Once fledged, the young birds move from the tundra to feed on the coast.

The species winters on rocky coasts, jetties, barnacle-covered reefs, and islets, only occasionally being seen on sandy beaches or mudflats. It is often found with Surfbirds, Rock Sandpipers and Black Oystercatchers and, like those species, can be difficult to pick out against the dark rocks. The birds feed in a manner similar to Turnstones, turning over sea-

△A Black Turnstone in winter plumage.

weed or picking food from the surface of the sand above the tideline. They feed on invertebrates such as small shrimps, molluscs, barnacles, and sea slugs.

Wintering Black Turnstones reach as far south as the Gulf of California. The species is a vagrant inland in the Pacific coast states and provinces, with a record also from Montana. On spring passage, the species occurs as far west as Wrangel Island in the far-eastern U.S.S.R. Some of the immature birds remain in their 'winter' quarters all year.

Wilson's Phalarope

Phalaropus tricolor

This species, the largest of the three phalaropes, is the least likely to be observed on the open sea and is more frequently found along muddy shorelines or shallow pools. In the latter habitat it is most likely to be seen pirouetting in endless circles, stirring up insects with its partially lobed feet. It can also be observed snatching prey from the surface of the water with rapid strikes of its long delicately thin, needle-shaped bill.

During its migrations, however, Wilson's Phalarope can be encountered in a wide variety of habitats ranging from estuaries, coastal bays, and saline and freshwater lakes and pools to sewage works and flooded fields. When feeding in the muddy areas of such places it loses some of its elegance, for when out of the water its disproportionately large, bulky body mismatches the long slender neck and small rounded head. Additionally the bird's shortish legs, placed well back on its body, give it a top-heavy, almost pot-bellied look. At such times it appears rather awkward and comical as it dashes with short strides from one spot to the next, frantically jabbing away at the mud in search of food.

On occasions it will wade in shallow water, sweeping its bill in a side-to-side motion. When it does this its head is sometimes completely submerged. Occasionally it will crouch in a heron-like posture, stalking with slow deliberate movements, finally ending the manoeuvre with a swift strike of its bill. All these techniques reward this species with a varied diet of spiders, beetles, crustaceans, insects and their larvae, and, to a lesser extent, aquatic plant seeds.

From April to May, Wilson's Phalaropes return from their South American wintering haunts, stopping off at regular staging posts in California and Texas. At certain sites, several hundred or more, often all the same sex, gather together, swimming in tight colourful rafts. At other times equally large numbers seethe over mud flats and fields as they feed up for the journey north.

LENGTH: 220-240 mm (8¾-9½ in)

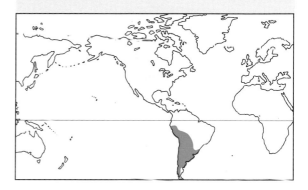

Sometimes small groups or solitary birds will associate with flocks of 'Calidrid' waders. In this company, the bird's clean white underparts and colourful chestnut and grey upperparts, cause it to 'glow' among its duller relatives, especially when on dark muddy terrain.

As in the other two Phalarope species, the female Wilson's Phalarope far outshines the more dowdy male. She is resplendent in her nuptial dress, with a strikingly pronounced thick black patch extending from the base of her bill through her face, then down the side of the neck, separating the bright white throat, chestnut foreneck, and upper breast from the pearl-grey crown, hindneck, and nape. In this plumage the species is unmistakable, even at great distances. A more unusual aspect of its summer transformation is the change of leg colour from the straw yellow of winter to the black of its breeding plumage.

The bird's northward migration is generally inland with a westerly bias, though a few birds are seen east of the Mississippi. The breeding grounds, reached by mid-May, comprise a vast area of the north-west, north central and the middle of the U.S.A., and Canada. This range includes at least sixteen states, from Manitoba, south to central California, stretching to Kansas then north-east to the Great Lakes. In Canada its expanding range now extends from British Columbia to Ontario.

◁*The female Wilson's Phalarope in summer plumage is much more brightly coloured than the male.*

Prairie wetland meadows with their many pools and lakes are the preferred sites for nesting, where the aggressive female chases off rivals and performs the majority of the courtship rituals. Both sexes share in the excavation of a series of scrapes among long grass. The male then removes more of the vegetation from a few of the these scrapes and in one of her choosing the female lays the eggs. These are usually four in number. They are yellowish, heavily spotted with black. Shortly afterwards, the female abandons the male and the nest, taking no further part in breeding duties. The male then incubates the eggs for a period of between 16 and 21 days. There is no reliable information on the fledging period.

In the mostly densely populated nesting areas the females, after leaving the nest, gather into large flocks on nearby pools. Here moulting begins, during which time frenetic feeding takes place for a few weeks, before the females depart southwards in late June. The males and

young leave much later, usually by the middle of August. Movement is prolonged with birds lingering at favourable feeding areas as they take an inland route through the western states of the U.S.A., across the inner part of the Gulf of Mexico and the Isthmus of Tehuantepec, and finally over the Pacific towards Equador and more southerly areas of South America. During this period large flocks form on upland lakes, especially in California, by which time the birds have lost their colourful breeding plumage and look very pale. But the lack of any wing bar or white rump, and the yellow legs, prevent misidentification.

As a breeding bird Wilson's Phalarope is restricted to North America, where it is thriving on the agricultural land of the prairies. Its present status is very healthy and in certain areas the population is actually increasing. Unlike the other two Phalaropes, which prefer a winter existence on the open sea, Wilson's Phalarope winters entirely on inland lakes and pools of the Argentinian and Chilean pampas, and also on high altitude lakes in Peru.

Wilson's Phalarope was not recorded in the British Isles until 1954, when one was seen in Fife. Two more followed in 1958 and 1959 and since 1961 the species has appeared annually, with a peak of 19 in 1979. A total of over 190 individuals had been recorded up to 1980 making this the fifth most numerous of the transatlantic waders reaching Britain and Ireland, a remarkable increase given that its first appearance was little more than thirty years ago. Of 45 recorded during the five year period 1982 to 1986, 19 were in Ireland or south-west England, 16 in eastern or south-east England and five in Scotland. Most appeared in autumn, with 41 between August and October and 18 (40 per cent) in September. However, there were four spring and early summer records of Wilson's Phalarope during the five years, including an individual which wandered between Suffolk, Norfolk, and Humberside during June and July 1983.

△ Not recorded in Britain before 1954, Wilson's Phalarope is now recorded annually. This is a first winter bird photographed in Hampshire in 1987.

▽ Less characteristic out of the water, this juvenile Wilson's Phalarope reveals the yellow legs of an immature or non-breeding bird.

Red-necked Phalarope
Phalaropus lobatus

Like all phalaropes, this is a dainty wader that is also a habitual swimmer. It breeds right across the Holarctic region and, like its relatives, the breeding adults of the species have reversed roles, with the brightly coloured females establishing the pair bond, and the drabber males tending the young. The sexes are similar in appearance in winter, when they take to the open sea and look rather like miniature gulls.

The size of a Dunlin, the Red-necked Phalarope is the smallest phalarope and can be easily overlooked when it is swimming close to the shore. With a slim neck, small oval head, and

OTHER NAME: Northern Phalarope
SIZE: 180-190 mm (7-7½ in)

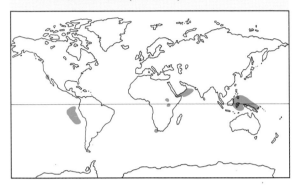

long, needle-fine bill, the bird's overall appearance is slender and elegant. But when it is out of the water, its legs appear disproportionately short. Breeding females have a slate grey head and back, with buff edgings to the scapulars and mantle, brownish wings, a white throat and belly, and a grey breast band. Their most striking and distinctive feature, though, is the orange-red horseshoe on their foreneck. The males are similarly patterned, but much duller and more diffuse, with browner upperparts, a paler orange neck, and a less distinctive breast band. Winter adults are often confused with Grey Phalaropes, but apart from their much finer bill, they are less uniform and a darker grey above, with some white streaking. The face and underparts are white, except for a bold black patch behind each eye. Juveniles can be distinguished by a brownish-black cap and dark brown upperparts, with buff margins to the mantle and scapulars. Their white underparts also have a buffish suffusion. This plumage is replaced during their first winter by one which closely resembles that of the adult bird, except that the crown remains darker and browner and the mantle retains some dark mottling. The species is generally regarded as silent, though individuals can be noisy at times.

The northward migration of the Red-necked Phalarope is late for its breeding latitudes, occurring between April and early June. The pairs nest singly or in loose colonies around coasts and near inland pools, particularly where there is emergent vegetation. Marshy ground with tiny pools and watercourses set amongst a rich, lowland vegetation is the typical habitat. The nest site is often in lush, damp pastures. In Scotland, where up to 50 pairs breed in the Outer Hebrides and the Northern Isles, peat diggings and iris beds are frequently favoured.

Although the males have a dancing display flight, the females initiate pair formation through their bright plumage, advertising display, and song. Much of the courtship ritual occurs on the water. Once a bond has been forged, the female selects one of several shallow scrapes, and the nest is built. Most nests of this species are in open ground or short, tussocky vegetation. The scrape is lined with leaves and stems before the four eggs are laid. Laying is synchronized to coincide with the hatching of Chironomid midges. Incubation, which takes three weeks, is undertaken by the males. Meanwhile, many of the females begin to return south soon after hatching in late June, having spent barely a month on their breeding ground. Where there are surplus males, however, the females may take another mate and lay a second clutch. The young take three weeks to fledge after hatching but the males begin to return south in July, just two weeks or so after the females, leaving the young to follow in August or early September.

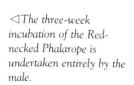

◁The three-week incubation of the Red-necked Phalarope is undertaken entirely by the male.

▷A Red-necked Phalarope in winter plumage.

This staggered departure brings a protracted passage of Red-necked Phalaropes across Europe from mid-July until October. The migration occurs overland, with European birds travelling south-eastwards to winter in the Arabian Sea, and North American birds passing through Alberta, Saskatchewan, British Columbia, and California in large numbers en route for their wintering grounds in the Pacific. During these overland migrations the birds may stop to rest and feed on any lake or pool, no matter how small. The main wintering areas are all in

▽ A female Red-necked Phalarope roosts among *waterside vegetation.*

warm latitudes, principally off Peru, in the Arabian Sea, and amongst the East Indies, where vast flocks of several thousand may assemble.

Red-necked Phalaropes feed mainly on small insects and their larvae, which may be taken while the birds are walking, wading, or swimming. This species sometimes pecks food from vegetation or up-ends in shallow water, but its most characteristic feeding technique is to take food from the water's surface while spinning. Outside the breeding season the Red-necked Phalarope may consort with ducks, grebes, and avocets, particularly when feeding.

Grey Phalarope

Phalaropus fulicarius

This tame wader of the Holarctic region is the most maritime of the phalaropes, approaching land only to breed or when storm-driven. Indeed, the Grey Phalarope is prone to occasional 'wrecks' after severe gales, despite being a buoyant swimmer well able to ride out rough water. In size it is between the Red-necked Phalarope and Wilson's Phalarope and as with its relatives, the sexual roles are reversed, with the larger, brighter females doing the courting, and the drabber males incubating and tending the chicks. However, the plumage differences between breeding males and females are less marked than in the other two species.

Grey Phalaropes are quite unmistakeable during the breeding season. They have prominent white cheeks, rich chestnut underparts, blackish-brown backs with pale buff feather edgings, and black-tipped yellow bills. The females have an unstreaked black-brown chin, crown, and hindneck. The males are similar, but duller and more mottled. They have streaking on the crown, dingier cheeks, and drabber underparts, often with some white on the belly. The legs are proportionately very short. The commonest call is a whistling 'wit'. The short-lived juvenile plumage suggests a washed-out adult, being dark brown above with broad buff fringes to the feathers, suffused with buff on the neck and breast, and white on the cheeks and belly. By the time they migrate, however, most of the juveniles have already moulted the feathers on their heads, necks, and backs, so that they resemble non-breeding adult birds.

The non-breeding birds are harder to identify. They are basically white, except for a blackish-grey crown that extends some way on to the hindneck, a pale grey back, and a blackish mark through and behind the eye. This readily identifies the birds as phalaropes, but distinguishing them from the Red-necked Phalarope can be difficult, especially as they are usually well offshore in adverse viewing conditions. At close quarters the Grey Phala-

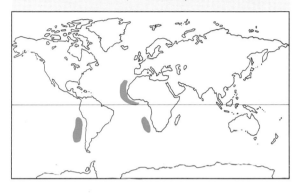

OTHER NAME: Red Phalarope
SIZE: 200-220 mm (7¾-8¾ in)

rope can be seen to have a paler, more uniform grey back, though on juveniles this may be relieved by vestiges of black on the mantle, scapulars, and tertials.

Identification by structural differences and posture is more reliable. The Grey Phalarope is larger, stockier, and more robust than the Red-necked, and has a shorter, thicker, and broader bill. It also has a larger head and thicker neck. On the water it swims with its back horizontal and tail held higher. This combined with its robust appearance and contrasting head markings, recalls the Little Gull. In flight the Grey Phalarope shows longer, broader wings and a slower, stronger wing-beat. Its wing-bars are also less obvious.

The Grey Phalaropes leave their wintering grounds between February and April to head for their breeding territories. These stretch discontinuously around the Arctic Circle. Uniquely for a wader, the migration routes are almost entirely oceanic, though in some years large numbers appear off the coasts of North America. Most of the birds reach the edge of the pack ice in late May or June, and they often have to wait on the sea here for two or three weeks until the ground thaws. They breed semi-colonially in the marshy tundra that surrounds the Arctic coasts and islands, usually where there are pools with muddy shorelines.

Pair formation, initiated by the females courting the males, is rapid and short-lived. Most nests are sited in short vegetation close to water, often on a tussock in swampy ground. The shallow cup is lined with any available material before four olive eggs with dark spots and blotches are laid. As soon as the clutch is complete, the female moves away, leaving the male to incubate the eggs and tend the young. In some cases she will pair with another male, although most females are monogamous and produce a single brood in each year. Incubation lasts for nearly three weeks, but once the chicks have hatched they quickly become

independent, although it takes just over a fort-night for them to fledge.

The return passage of the Grey Phalarope begins with all the populations seemingly moving eastwards then south-eastwards, to cross either the Atlantic or the Pacific and reach their winter quarters. The adult females leave in the first half of July, with the males and juveniles following in late July and August. In western Europe, though, few are seen until September or October, when autumn gales drive them onshore, sometimes in large numbers. Indeed, severe storms across Britain may result in some of these birds appearing inland. Juveniles seem to predominate when this happens. In North America the Grey Phalarope is more numerous along the Pacific seaboard than along the Atlantic coast. Most are seen between September and December, but small numbers occasionally winter off both seaboards and some may appear inland following severe storms. The main wintering grounds are off the coasts of West and South Africa and Chile, where upwellings make the oceans rich in plankton. However a few of the birds may remain as far north as the North Sea.

When ashore, Grey Phalaropes feed by pecking and probing while they wade or walk along the shoreline. On water they frequently spin like a top to stir up larvae, crustaceans, and insects, which they then seize from the surface or just below it. They will also snap at flying insects and sometimes perch on the backs of whales to feed on parasites. Vegetable matter and seeds are also taken. Grey Phalaropes are mostly seen singly or in small parties, but gatherings of 1,000 or more are occasionally recorded, particularly in the wintering areas.

◁ A pair of Grey Phalaropes in summer plumage. The more brightly coloured female is on the left.

△ A Grey Phalarope in its sombre winter plumage.

APPENDIX

The following is a list of species not included in the main text, but which have been recorded either regularly or intermittently in North America or Europe.

Double-striped Thick-knee

Burhinus bistriatus
OTHER NAMES: Double-striped Stone-curlew, Mexican Thick-knee
Breeds in northern South America and parts of Central America. Usually sedentary but odd individuals have reached Curacao and Texas, where one was shot in 1961.

Kittlitz's Plover

Charadrius pecuarius
OTHER NAME: Kittlitz's Sand Plover
Breeds in Africa, where it is almost entirely sedentary. One extraordinary record of a bird collected in Norway in 1913.

Lesser Sand Plover

Charadrius mongolus
OTHER NAMES: Mongolian Plover, Mongolian Sand Plover, Mongolian Dotterel
Breeds in scattered localities from E. Asia to N.E. Siberia and rarely Alaska; winters on coasts from E. Africa to Australia. Strongly migratory with vagrants to Spain, Norway, Poland, Austria, E. Mediterranean, parts of Africa, W. Alaska, Yukon Territory, Ontario, Oregon, California, and Louisiana.

Greater Sand Plover

Charadrius leschenaultii
OTHER NAMES: Large Sand Dotterel, Large Sand Plover, Geoffrey's Plover
Breeds from S. U.S.S.R., east to Mongolia; winters on coasts from E. Africa to Australia. Passage migrant and vagrant to many parts of the world. More prone to westward vagrancy than the Lesser Sand Plover, with records across Europe to France and Scandinavia. 7 records for the British Isles.

Caspian Plover

Charadrius asiaticus
Breeds S.E. U.S.S.R., and W. central Asia; winters in S. and E. Africa. Vagrant south-eastwards to Australia and westwards across Europe to Italy, Malta, France, and Norway. One British record in 1890.

Spur-winged Lapwing

Hoplopterus spinosus
OTHER NAME: Spur-winged Plover
Breeds in Africa (mainly sedentary), and Greece and Turkey (summer visitor only). Occurs on passage in Crete and Cyprus. Vagrants have reached Spain, Belgium, W. Germany, Czechoslovakia, Malta, some Middle Eastern countries, and the Black Sea.

Sociable Plover

Chettusia gregaria
OTHER NAME: Sociable Lapwing
Breeds in S.E. U.S.S.R., and western central Asia; winters farther south in Asia and Africa. Is strongly migratory, with westward vagrancy to most European countries except Scandinavia. 29 records for the British Isles.

White-tailed Lapwing

Chettusia leucura
OTHER NAME: White-tailed Plover
Breeding and wintering ranges similar to Sociable Plover, but also breeds in the Middle East. Less prone to westward vagrancy, but has occurred north to Finland and Sweden, and west to France and the British Isles, with 4 records in the latter country.

Red-necked Stint

Calidris ruficollis

OTHER NAMES: Rufous-necked Stint, Rufous-necked Sandpiper

Breeds in N. and N.E. Siberia and occasionally W. Alaska; winters in S.E. Asia and Australasia. In North America a vagrant to S.E. Alaska, British Columbia, Oregon, California, the Atlantic coast of the U.S.A., and Bermuda. In Europe a vagrant to W. U.S.S.R., and both E. and W. Germany; a 1986 record from Britain is still under consideration.

Long-toed Stint

Calidris subminuta

Breeds in Siberia; winters in S.E. Asia, the Philippines and Australasia. A vagrant to Sweden, British Isles (1 record), W. Aleutians, W. Alaska, and Oregon, plus one or two places in E. Africa and the Indian Ocean.

Sharp-tailed Sandpiper

Calidris acuminata

OTHER NAME: Siberian Pectoral Sandpiper

Breeds in N. Siberia; winters in Australasia. Regular passage migrant to W. Alaska. A vagrant to Canada and the U.S.A., (mostly on Pacific coast), Scandinavia, France, the British Isles (19 records), and parts of Asia.

Cox's Sandpiper

Calidris paramelanotos

First described in 1982 on basis of specimens collected in South Australia. Breeding area unknown, but probably somewhere in U.S.S.R. A juvenile caught, ringed and photographed at Duxbury Beach, Massachusetts, U.S.A. 15 September 1987. This is only the second record of the 'species' away from the Australian wintering grounds, the other reported in Hong Kong, Spring 1987.

Spoon-billed Sandpiper

Eurynorhynchus pygmeus

OTHER NAME: Spoonbill Sandpiper

A rare breeder in E. Siberia; winters in S.E. Asia. A vagrant to W. Aleutians, W. Alaska, and Vancouver.

Little Whimbrel

Numenius minutus

OTHER NAME: Little Curlew

Rare breeder in central and N.E. Siberia; winters in Australasia. Vagrant to British Isles (2 records), Norway, California, and a few other scattered areas outside Europe and North America.

Bristle-thighed Curlew

Numenius tahitiensis

A rare wader that breeds in W. Alaska; winters on Pacific islands. A vagrant to a number of west Pacific localities and in North America to S. Alaska, Vancouver Island, British Columbia, and Washington.

Slender-billed Curlew

Numenius tenuirostris

A very rare breeder from central Siberia; winters in the Mediterranean basin. Records are very few. Vagrants have occurred in Oman, the Canaries and Azores, Netherlands, Germany, Poland, and the Canadian shore of Lake Erie, where one was collected in about 1925.

Far-eastern Curlew

Numenius madagascariensis

OTHER NAMES: Eastern or Australian Curlew

Breeds in E. U.S.S.R.; winters in Australasia and Indonesia. A fairly regular spring vagrant to W. Alaska and the Aleutian Islands; generally records are rather few.

Grey-rumped Sandpiper

Heteroscelus brevipes

OTHER NAMES: Grey-tailed Tattler, Polynesian or Siberian Tattler

Breeds N. and N.E. Siberia; winters in Australasia, Indonesia, and the Philippines. A vagrant to west Alaska and once to S.E. Alaska and California near Los Angeles.

BIBLIOGRAPY

Connors, P.G. (1983), Taxonomy, distribution and evolution of Golden Plovers (*Pluvialis dominica* and *Pluvialis fluva*), *Auk* 100: 607–620.

Cramp, S. and Simmons, K.E.L. (eds.) (1983), *The Birds of the Western Palearctic*, vol. 3, Oxford.

Day, D. (1981), *The doomsday book of animals*, New York: The Viking Press (A Studio Book).

Dement'ev, G.P. & Gladkov, N.A. (eds.) (1969), *Birds of the Soviet Union*, vol. 3, Jerusalem: Israel Program for Scientific Translation.

Godfrey, W.E. (1966), *The Birds of Canada*, Ottawa: National Museums of Canada.

Hayman, P., Marchant, J. and Prater, A. (1986), *Shorebirds: an identification guide to the waders of the world*, Beckenham.

Jolnsgard, P.A. (1981), *The Plovers, Sandpipers and Snipes of the World*, Lincoln and London: University of Nebraska Press.

Jonsson, L. & Grant, P.J. (1984), Identification of stints and peeps, *Brit. Birds* 77: 293–315.

King, W.B. (comp.) (1981), *Endangered Birds of the World. The ICBP Bird Red Data Book*, Washington: Smithsonian Inst. & ICBP.

Knox, A. (1987), Taxonomic status of 'Lesser Golden Plovers', *Brit. Birds* 80: 482–487.

National Geographic Society (1983), *Field guide to the birds of North America*, Nat. Geog. Soc.

Pitelka, F.A. (1950), Geographic variation and the species problem in the shorebird genus *Limnodromus*. *Univ. Calif. Publ. Zool.*, 50: 1–108.

Roberson, D. (1980), *Rare birds of the West Coast of North America*, Pacific Grove, California: Woodcock Publications.

Sharrock, J.T.R.S. and Sharrock, E.M. (1976), *Rare Birds in Britain and Ireland*, Berkhamsted.

Stout, G.D. (ed) (1967), *The Shorebirds of North America*, New York.

Taylor, P.B. (1981), Field characters and habitat preferences of Great Snipe and Snipe, *Dutch Birding* 3: 52–54.

Viet, R.R. & Jonsson, L. (1987), Field identification of smaller sandpipers within the genus *Calidris*, *American Birds* 41: 213–236.

Wallace, D.I.M. (1981), *Birdwatching in the Seventies*, London.

ACKNOWLEDGEMENTS

In writing this book I am greatly indebted to John Belsey, Graham Harrison, Gavin Peplow and Steve Whitehouse who kindly gave me the benefit of their wide experience, which without question has added greatly to the value of the text. I am grateful to Graham Harrison for reading through the finished draft and checking proofs. I must thank Janet Harrison, who spent many hours sorting out rough drafts for me and saw that text, maps and pictures all came together in the right order. I have also to thank the many photographers whose work is represented in this book, for it is the excellence of their illustrations, which I am sure as much as anything will commend the reader to this work. Their names are listed here against the page number where their photographs appear throughout this volume.

The majority of the statistics relating to the occurrences in Britain and Ireland of vagrant shorebirds are derived from the annual reports of the British Birds Rarities Committee, which are published in the monthly magazine *British Birds*. All records of rare birds reported in Britain since 1958 have been adjudicated by the committee (there is a separate committee for Ireland) and the cumulative totals refer to the figures up to and including the publication of their 1986 report, but not including any potential late additions for that year. I am greatly indebted to Alan Dean for gathering this information together for me, which has made the text for the species in question so much more meaningful.

Photographers Acknowledgements

Front Cover W. Lankinen
Half Title Page M. C. Wilkes
Title Page R. T. Mills

Page
9 R. T. Mills
10 C. Smith
11 R. T. Mills
12 G. Huntington
13 R. T. Mills
14 R. T. Mills
15 R. T. Mills
17 top P. T. Castell
17 bottom B. Speake
18 A. J. Bond
19 H. Cruikshank/Vireo
21 top E. T. Jones
21 bottom J. B. & S. Bottomley
22 B. Hawkes
23 D. K. Richards
24 P. T. Castell
25 B. L. Sage
26 B. L. Sage
27 E. Soothill
29 E. Soothill

30 M. J. Thomas
31 Larking and Powell
32 A. J. Bond
33 P. T. Castell
34 M. Lane
35 E. Soothill
36 P. Doherty
38 P. T. Castell
39 R. Maier
40 B. L. Sage
41 T. Leach
42 T. Leach
43 J. B. & S. Bottomley
44 H. Cruikshank/Vireo
46 top E. T. Jones
46 bottom W. Lankinen
47 E. Soothill
49 top E. Soothill
49 bottom B. Lebaron/Vireo
50 J. L. Roberts
51 J. L. Roberts
53 B. McCafferey/Vireo
54 D. M. Cotteridge
55 K. Carlson
56 D. S. Whitaker

57 W. Lankinen
58 T. Leach
59 B. Hawkes
61 top C. Greaves
61 bottom R. P. Tipper
63 top P. T. Castell
63 bottom K. Carlson
64 A. W. M. Airchison
66 top R. Glover
66 bottom R. Glover
67 P. T. Castell
68 B. Speake
69 B. Hawkes
70 D. Robey/K. Brink/Vireo
71 E. D. Mackrill
72 C. Huntington
73 R. Glover
74 M. C. Wilkes
76 top M. C. Wilkes
76 bottom M. C. Wilkes
77 top B. Hawkes
77 bottom W. Lankinen
79 Dr J. Davies
80 A. Morris/Vireo
81 P. Doherty

INDEX
OF VERNACULAR AND SCIENTIFIC NAMES

In this Index, numbers in **bold** type refer to the first page of the main entry for the species; page numbers in *italics* refer to pages on which colour photographs occur.